SEAMUS HEANEY AND MEDI

Seamus Heaney's engagement with medieval literature constitutes a significant body of work by a major poet that extends across four decades, including a landmark translation of *Beowulf*. This book, the first to look exclusively at Heaney's engagement with the poetry of the Middle Ages, examines both Heaney's direct translations and his adaptation of medieval material in his original poems. Each of the four chapters focuses substantially on a single major text: *Sweeney Astray* (1983), *Station Island* (1984), *Beowulf* (1999), and *The Testament of Cresseid* (2004). The discussion examines Heaney's translation practice in relation to source texts from a variety of languages (Irish, Italian, Old English, and Middle Scots) from across the medieval period, and also in relation to Heaney's own broader body of work. It suggests that Heaney's translations and adaptations give a contemporary voice to medieval texts, bringing the past to bear upon contemporary concerns both personal and political.

CONOR MCCARTHY's previous publications include *Love, Sex and Marriage in the Middle Ages: A Sourcebook*, and *Marriage in Medieval England: Law, Literature and Practice*.

SEAMUS HEANEY
AND
MEDIEVAL POETRY

Conor McCarthy

D. S. BREWER

First published 2008
D. S. Brewer, Cambridge

Transferred to digital printing

ISBN 978-1-84384-141-8

D. S. Brewer is an imprint of Boydell & Brewer Ltd
PO Box 9, Woodbridge, Suffolk IP12 3DF, UK
and of Boydell & Brewer Inc.
668 Mt Hope Avenue, Rochester, NY 14620, USA
website: www.boydellandbrewer.com

A CiP catalogue record for this book is available
from the British Library

This publication is printed on acid-free paper

Contents

Acknowledgements

As with previous publications, it is a pleasure to thank family and friends for support and encouragement: I'm particularly grateful to my parents Michael and Nuala McCarthy, my brothers Michael and David McCarthy, Anne van den Dungen, Margot Durcan, Dario and Juliette Brollo, and Darren and Emily Brollo. Thanks most of all to Deidre Brollo, who lived with the writing of this book, supportive throughout.

At Boydell & Brewer, I'm especially grateful to Caroline Palmer for supporting this project, and to Anna Morton, Vanda Andrews, and to Jeffrey Dean at The Stingray Office for seeing it into print. I'm obliged to Ron Moore for comment on parts of the text; I am also grateful to an anonymous reader for Boydell & Brewer for useful guidance. For the practicalities of access to source material, I must thank the Fisher Library, University of Sydney, for use of their resources. It is also once again both appropriate and a pleasure to thank Gerald Morgan, who first encouraged me in reading medieval literature.

Parts of Chapter 3 were previously presented at the Centre for Medieval and Renaissance Studies at Trinity College, Dublin; my thanks to Sarah Alyn Stacey for the opportunity, and audience members for their comments. Parts of this chapter have also appeared in print as 'Language and History in Seamus Heaney's *Beowulf*,' *English* 50 (2001), 149–58.

Extracts from the works of Seamus Heaney are quoted under fair dealing conventions, with thanks to Faber & Faber: quotations are from *Door Into the Dark*, copyright © Seamus Heaney 1969; *Wintering Out*, copyright © Seamus Heaney 1972; *North*, copyright © Seamus Heaney 1975; *Field Work*, copyright © Seamus Heaney 1979; *Preoccupations: Selected Prose, 1968–1978*, copyright © Seamus Heaney 1980; *Sweeney Astray*, copyright © Seamus Heaney 1983; *Station Island*, copyright © Seamus Heaney 1984; *The Government of the Tongue: The 1986 T. S. Eliot Memorial Lectures and Other Critical Writings*, copyright © Seamus Heaney 1988; *Seeing Things*, copyright © Seamus Heaney 1991; *The Cure at Troy*, copyright © Seamus Heaney 1991; *The Redress of Poetry: Oxford Lectures*, copyright © Seamus Heaney 1995; *The Spirit Level*, copyright © Seamus Heaney 1996; *Opened*

Ground: Poems, 1966–1996, copyright © Seamus Heaney 1998; *Beowulf,* copyright © Seamus Heaney 1999, *Electric Light*, copyright © Seamus Heaney 2001; *Finders Keepers: Selected Prose, 1971–2001*, copyright © Seamus Heaney 2002; *The Testament of Cresseid*, copyright © Seamus Heaney 2004; and *District and Circle*, copyright © Seamus Heaney 2006.

Every effort has been made to acknowledge copyright holders; apologies are offered for any omission, and the publishers will be pleased to add any necessary acknowledgement in subsequent editions.

Conor McCarthy
Sydney
June 2007

Abbreviations

DIL	*Dictionary of the Irish Language*
EETS	Early English Text Society
MED	*Middle English Dictionary*
OED	*Oxford English Dictionary*
TLS	*Times Literary Supplement*

Introduction

I⊤'s unlikely to be news to the general reader that Seamus Heaney is a distinguished translator of medieval poetry, for subsequent to its publication in 1999, Heaney's translation of the Old English poem *Beowulf* provoked extensive comment, garnered substantial sales, and won the Whitbread Prize.[1] Important as the *Beowulf* translation is, however, it is not the full extent of Heaney's engagement with medieval poetry. In 1983, Heaney published a translation of the medieval Irish *Buile Suibhne*,[2] and he has held an extensive dialogue with Dante's *Commedia* involving translation, adaptation, and allusion across three books in particular: *Field Work*, *Station Island*, and *Seeing Things*.[3] Further to that, the *Beowulf* translation is not Heaney's most recent translation of a major work of medieval literature, for it has been followed by a modern English translation of Robert Henryson's Middle Scots text, *The Testament of Cresseid*.[4] Heaney's translations and adaptations of medieval poetry, then, form a substantial body of work, drawn from across the medieval period and from a number of languages (Irish, Italian, Old English, Middle Scots), extending through much of his career.

These translations of medieval material are not the full extent of Heaney's translation work, of course, for Heaney's translations now make for a considerable list, and that list covers a number of categories: as well as medieval poetry, he has made translations from classical material, from Eastern European poetry, and from post-medieval poetry in Irish and Scots Gaelic. Reviewing Heaney's *Beowulf* translation in *The Irish Times* in 1999, Bernard O'Donoghue commented that 'from early in his career

---

[1] *Beowulf*, trans. Seamus Heaney (London: Faber, 1999).

[2] Seamus Heaney, *Sweeney Astray* (Derry: Field Day, 1983; London: Faber, 1984).

[3] Seamus Heaney, *Field Work* (London: Faber, 1979); Heaney, *Station Island* (London: Faber, 1984); Heaney, *Seeing Things* (London: Faber, 1991).

[4] Seamus Heaney, *The Testament of Cresseid: A Retelling of Robert Henryson's Poem by Seamus Heaney with Images by Hughie O'Donoghue* (London: Enitharmon Editions, 2004).

Seamus Heaney has been recognised as a major critic as well as poet, in the great English tradition of artist/commentators from Sidney to Coleridge to Eliot. What has dawned on us more slowly is that he is also – to borrow a phrase used to describe Chaucer – a great translator.'[1]

It is my contention here that Heaney's engagement with medieval literature constitutes a significant body of work by a major poet, a body of work worthy of independent consideration, or at least semi-independent, for, as the discussion below argues at length, Heaney's original work and translation practice are mutually informing, and Heaney's engagement with the literature of the Middle Ages extends to adaptation and allusion as well as translation. This discussion looks in two directions in seeking to examine Heaney's use of the literature of the Middle Ages both in relation to the medieval source materials and with reference to Heaney's own broader body of work. Its focus is on four texts: the translation of *Buile Suibhne* and the accompanying adaptation of that work in the 'Sweeney Redivivus' sequence, the adaptation of Dante's *Commedia* in 'Station Island,' the *Beowulf* translation, and the recent translation of Robert Henryson's *Testament of Cresseid*. In discussing these works, I argue here that the version of the medieval that Heaney presents to us is complex and multifaceted, a reality that is taken to be equal in complexity to our own, and hence a resource for understanding of our present circumstances. I further suggest that, because the medieval is brought to bear upon the contemporary in Heaney's work, there is an ongoing dialogue between the translations and the original poetry, a dialogue traced in some detail in the discussion that follows.

Echoes of the Middle Ages: translation, adaptation, allusion

Heaney's translations from medieval poetry begin with his version of the medieval Irish *Buile Suibhne*, published as *Sweeney Astray* in 1983. Both his translation of the story of Ugolino, from cantos XXXII and XXXIII of the *Inferno* (published as 'Ugolino' in *Field Work* in 1979),[2] and a translation of the Middle English short poem 'The Names of the Hare' (1981) actually saw print first, but Heaney had been working on *Sweeney Astray* for many years before its publication, and it's noticeable that in *Opened Ground*, Heaney's most recent gathering of his earlier work, the sequence of selections breaks chronological order just once, to give *Sweeney Astray* precedence

---

[1] Bernard O'Donoghue, 'The Master's Voice-Right,' *Irish Times* (9 Oct. 1999).

[2] Heaney, *Field Work*, 61–64; Seamus Heaney, *Opened Ground: Poems 1966–1996* (London: Faber, 1998), 187–90.

over the Middle English poem.[1] Heaney also translated the opening cantos of Dante's *Inferno* around 1982–83, intending to embark upon a translation of the entire *Inferno*, but then abandoning the project.[2] His version of the first three cantos was published in 1993 as part of a collaborative translation of the *Inferno* edited by Daniel Halpern, fragments having previously appeared in other Heaney poems, and a portion of Canto III having formed the closing section of *Seeing Things* as 'The Crossing.'[3] In 1999, Heaney published an award-winning translation of the Old English poem *Beowulf*: again, this was a project on which he had originally embarked many years earlier, with a portion of the translation appearing in print as early as 1987 as 'The Ship of Death' in *The Haw Lantern*.[4] Since then, there have been translations of Robert Henryson's Middle Scots poems *The Cock and the Jasp* and *The Testament of Cresseid*, with the suggestion that there might be more translations of Henryson's fables to come.[5] Most recently, in April 2006, *Poetry* magazine published an issue on translation that opened with Heaney's version of the ninth-century Irish poem, 'Pangur Bán.'[6]

Heaney's engagement with medieval poetry as a translator, then, is considerable. But a consideration of the translations from medieval poetry on their own is clearly inadequate: the account of Heaney's engagement with Dante just given mentions the translations, but not the long adaptation of the *Commedia* in 'Station Island,' the critical essay on Dante, 'Envies and Identifications,' or the many allusions to Dante elsewhere in Heaney's poetry, particularly in *Field Work* and *Seeing Things*. An account of Heaney's responses to medieval poetry, then, also needs to take heed of the adaptions of medieval material in his original work. This is the case not least because of the extent to which Heaney writes other people's poetry into his own, just as, through his translation practice, he writes his own poetry into that of others. The extent of this intertextual give-and-take is visible across Heaney's work. In an overview of intertextual references in *North*, Neil Corcoran lists *Njal's Saga*, Tacitus' *Germania* and *Agricola*, *Hamlet*,

---

[1] Heaney, *Opened Ground*, 191–211.

[2] Maria Cristina Fumagalli, *The Flight of the Vernacular: Seamus Heaney, Derek Walcott, and the Impress of Dante* (Amsterdam and New York: Rodopi, 2001), 260, cites a letter of Heaney's saying 'after completing three cantos I reneged'; cf. Heaney's comment in 'Envies and Identifications: Dante and the Modern Poet,' *Irish University Review* 15 (1985), 5–19 at 18, repr. in *Dante Readings*, ed. Eric Haywood (Dublin: Irish Academic Press, 1987), 29–46, that he had translated, but not published, the first four cantos.

[3] *Dante's Inferno: Translations by Twenty Contemporary Poets*, ed. Daniel Halpern (New York: Ecco, 1993); Heaney, *Seeing Things*, 111–13.

[4] Seamus Heaney, *The Haw Lantern* (London: Faber, 1987), 22.

[5] Heaney's *Testament* suggests (p. 8) a possible future book of *Four Fables and a Testament*.

[6] 'Pangur Bán,' trans. Seamus Heaney, *Poetry* 188/1 (April 2006), 3–5.

A Portrait of the Artist as a Young Man, *The Playboy of the Western World*, Bede's *History of the English Church and People*, Yeats's poems and *Autobiographies*, writings by Walter Ralegh, John Aubrey, and Edmund Spenser, the Old English *Battle of Maldon*, Conor Cruise O'Brien's *States of Ireland*, Horace's *Odes*, R. H. Barrow's *The Romans*, Wordsworth's *The Prelude*, Patrick Kavanagh, Hopkins's *Journals*, and Osip Mandelstam.[1] Bernard O'Donoghue has a similarly long list for *Station Island*;[2] equivalent lists might be compiled for most of Heaney's books.

While the list of Heaney's translations from medieval poetry is in itself substantial, then, it's a list that would be significantly lengthened if expanded to include all of Heaney's original poems that show the influence of the Middle Ages. That list would at least include the following: 'The Wanderer' from *Stations*, which draws on the Old English poem of the same name;[3] 'Funeral Rites,' which retells a story from *Njal's Saga*, 'North' and 'Viking Dublin: Trial Pieces,' which draw on Viking archaeology, 'Bone Dreams,' which quotes a fragment of Old English and alludes to Bede, and 'Hercules and Antaeus,' which refers to *Lebor Gabála Érenn* and *The Battle of Maldon*, all from *North*;[4] 'The Strand at Lough Beg,' which quotes from Dante (in Dorothy L. Sayers's translation) and alludes to *Buile Suibhne*, 'An Afterwards,' where Heaney imagines himself condemned to Dante's ninth circle of hell, 'Leavings,' which contains another reference to Dante's hell, the translation of the first line of the *Commedia* in 'September Song,' possible allusions to Dante in 'A Dream of Jealousy' and 'The Harvest Bow,' and a line quoted from James Stephens's version of the medieval Irish tale 'The Boyhood of Fionn,' all in *Field Work*;[5] the allusion to the story of Guy de Montfort from the *Commedia* in 'Sandstone Keepsake,' and the direct reference to Dante in 'The Loaning,' the 'Station Island' sequence itself, which draws upon Dante's *Commedia*, and the subsequent 'Sweeney Redivivus' sequence, which draws on *Buile Suibhne*,

---

[1] Neil Corcoran, *The Poetry of Seamus Heaney: A Critical Study* (London: Faber, 1998), 56.

[2] Bernard O'Donoghue, *Seamus Heaney and the Language of Poetry* (Hemel Hempstead: Harvester, 1994), 104.

[3] Heaney, *Opened Ground*, 88.

[4] Seamus Heaney, *North* (London: Faber, 1975), 15–24, 27–30, 52–53; Heaney, *Opened Ground*, 96–111, 129–30.

[5] Heaney, *Field Work*, 17–18, 43, 44, 50, 56, 57, 58; Heaney, *Opened Ground*, 152–53, 173, 177, 181, 182, 183; for those possible allusions to Dante, see Bernard O'Donoghue, 'Dante's Versatility and Seamus Heaney's Modernism,' in *Dante's Modern Afterlife: Reception and Response from Blake to Heaney*, ed. Nick Havely (London: Macmillan, 1998), 242–57 at 244–45; the phrase from James Stephens's *Irish Fairy Stories* is from the words of Fionn when asked what is the finest music: 'The music of what happens,' said great Fionn, 'that is the finest music in the world.'

all in *Station Island*;[1] the figure of Larkin quoting (Heaney's translation of) Dante in 'The Journey Back,' the story of Thor, Hymer, and the world-serpent in 'A Haul,' the allusion to the *Purgatorio* in 'The Biretta,' the quotation from the opening line of the *Commedia* in 'The Schoolbag,' the medieval otherworldly vision in 'Lightenings' viii, the mention of Snorri Sturluson in 'Settings' xxiii, the suggestion of Dante in 'Crossings' xxvi, followed by the allusion in 'Crossings' xxxvi, and the reference back to 'The Names of the Hare' in 'Squarings' xliii, all from *Seeing Things*;[2] the retelling of a story from Gerald of Wales in 'St Kevin and the Blackbird,' the allusion to *Sweeney Astray* and the quotation from Dante in 'The Flight Path,' 'Whitby-sur-Moyola' and its version of the Cædmon story from Bede, and the story of the seventh-century Saint Adamnan from 'The Thimble' in *The Spirit Level*;[3] from *Electric Light*, the allusions to *Beowulf* in 'The Border Campaign' and 'On his Work in the English Tongue,' the echo of Dante in 'The Gaeltacht,' the allusion to Bede in 'The Bookcase,' and the references in 'Ten Glosses' to both Moling (he of *Sweeney Astray*) and Gerald of Wales;[4] and, from *District and Circle*, the references to the Vikings in 'Out of Shot' and to the fifteenth-century English poem 'Smoke Blackened Smiths' in 'Midnight Anvil.'[5]

Medieval resonances: the personal and the political

Heaney himself, commenting on Yeats's poem 'Ego Dominus Tuus' and that poem's representation of Dante, notes that 'when poets turn to the great masters of the past, they turn to an image of their own creation, one which is likely to be a reflection of their own imaginative needs, their own artistic inclinations and procedures.'[6] This is true of Heaney no less than it is of Yeats, and the uses to which Heaney puts medieval literature extend to the personal. There is a sense of identification or empathy to be found between Heaney himself and figures as diverse as Suibhne Geilt, Dante Alighieri, and Cædmon, and notwithstanding the complexities attached to the first-person pronoun in Heaney's use of it, Heaney can be seen to write versions of himself into several of the works discussed below. The figure

---

[1] Heaney, *Station Island*, 20, 61–121; Heaney, *Opened Ground*, 217, 242–88.

[2] Heaney, *Seeing Things*, 7, 12, 26–27, 30, 62, 79, 94, 103; Heaney, *Opened Ground*, 364, 380, 387.

[3] Seamus Heaney, *The Spirit Level* (London: Faber, 1996), 20–21, 22–26, 41, 42–43; Heaney, *Opened Ground*, 410–13, 425.

[4] Seamus Heaney, *Electric Light* (London: Faber, 2001), 18, 44, 51–52, 54–56.

[5] Seamus Heaney, *District and Circle* (London: Faber, 2006), 15, 26–27.

[6] Heaney, 'Envies and Identifications,' 5.

of Sweeney is, among other things, an autobiographical self-projection for Heaney; the 'Station Island' sequence is, in part, a sort of personal purgation; the *Beowulf* translation sees Heaney write his personal foundations, in the form of his home place of Mossbawn, into the foundations of literature in English; and the figure of Cresseid, while not a self-projection along the lines of the Sweeney figure, is, like Sweeney, one of a sequence of outcast figures treated with empathy in Heaney's work.

If Heaney writes himself into his versions of medieval texts, there is also a give-and-take between the translations and the original poetry. Not only does Heaney's original work draw upon the work of translation (as in the 'Sweeney Redivivus' sequence, for example, where the character of Sweeney from Heaney's translation of the medieval Irish text *Buile Suibhne* appears in a sequence of original poems), and sometimes eclipse it (as in Heaney's debts to Dante, where fragments of translation from *Inferno* I–III are incorporated into the wider body of work across several volumes, while the translation itself is published only in retrospect), but the translations themselves echo and resonate with the original work (as with the *Beowulf* translation's clearly signalled debts to Heaney's earlier bog poems).

If Heaney's translations and adaptations use medieval texts to give expression to themes of personal relevance, they also bring medieval texts to bear upon political concerns. In his survey of Irish translation practice, Michael Cronin has argued that the motivation for the turn to translation visible in the work of a number of contemporary Northern Irish poets, including Heaney, has been threefold. First, Irish writing in English has engaged through translation in a dialogue with the Irish language, the other vernacular on the island, a dialogue Cronin sees as an act of self-understanding. Secondly, there is translation as liberation, an escape from Irish politics and history into other worlds of language and expression. Thirdly, there is the use of translation as an indirect means of addressing the Northern Irish conflict.[1] My discussion below approaches Heaney's translation practice in relation to this third motivation for translation as identified by Cronin by focusing on how Heaney has brought medieval literary texts to bear upon contemporary issues, and in particular upon the problems that afflicted Northern Ireland during twenty-five years of conflict from 1969 to 1994. In doing so, the discussion here views Heaney's translation practice as one where the translated texts share the concerns of his original work: as such, the conflict in Northern Ireland between 1969 and 1994 and the subsequent attempts to reach a political settlement are

[1] Michael Cronin, *Translating Ireland: Translation, Languages, Cultures* (Cork: Cork University Press, 1996), 181.

seen a substantial factor in the translations, just as they are in his original poems.

Heaney has been explicit in stating that the original motivation for his translation of *Buile Suibhne* was political. He comments that he began the translation at a time when writers sought 'images and analogies that could ease the strain of the present,' and he asked himself how *Buile Suibhne* could be seen as relating to contemporary Ulster: 'what had all this amalgam in verse and prose to do with me or the moment? How could a text engendered within the Gaelic order of medieval Ireland speak to a modern Ulster audience riven by divisions resulting from the final destruction of that order? [...] What had the translation of the tale of a Celtic wild man to do with the devastations of the new wild men of the Provisional IRA?'[1] That said, however, the essay in which Heaney poses these questions provides more than one answer to the questions posed, and the differing answers express a tension visible through much of Heaney's work, between a desire for a poetry that engages with the demands of the present and a competing desire for a transcendent poetry concerned with an art that can surpass all that. If the questions posed here suggest a desire to bring the literature of the past to bear on present concerns, the essay also expresses a desire for the translation to be a thing in itself, 'a poem from beyond' as Heaney puts it.[2] Heaney's translation of *Buile Suibhne*, then, fits to a certain extent all three of Cronin's categories – a translation into English from Irish literature, it encompasses a tension between a political and a transcendent poetry.

Medieval multiplicities

Heaney's translations of and adaptations from medieval literature represent the Middle Ages not as premodern and monocultural, or as some prelapsarian point of origin, but as a multicultural and complex reality equivalent to our own. Although Heaney's work engages significantly with medieval literature, it's not surprising to find that his critical writing doesn't discuss the medieval *per se*: the medieval literature that Heaney translates and alludes to is seen as being of relevance to contemporary concerns rather than demarcated as separate from them. In his introduction to the *Beowulf* translation, Heaney argues that as a work of art, the poem

[1] Seamus Heaney, 'Earning a Rhyme,' in Heaney, *Finders Keepers: Selected Prose, 1971–2001* (London: Faber, 2002), 59–66 at 60–61, first published in *Poetry Ireland Review* (Spring 1989).
[2] Heaney, 'Earning a Rhyme,' 65.

'lives in its own continuous present, equal to our knowledge of reality in the present time' (p. ix).[1] The implication of this is not that art is timeless and unchanging; rather, it is that the poem is as much a complex response to a complex reality as any piece of contemporary writing could be. Given that the medieval is often thought of as being both premodern and marginal,[2] this is a challenging assertion that a medieval text can be expressive of a complex understanding of a reality of equal value to our own.

The sense of diversity present in Heaney's engagement with medieval poetry is evident in several ways. First, it's noticeable that Heaney's work does not seek to produce a single, stable, fixed reworking of a medieval text, but rather constitutes an ongoing engagement with the source texts. Heaney says in his introduction to *Sweeney's Flight* that 'in the case of translation, it is even truer than usual that a poem is never completed, merely abandoned,'[3] and if that is the case, what is abandoned is also revisited. His translation of *Buile Suibhne* produces not one text, but several – the *Sweeney Astray* translation published in 1983 (itself a second attempt at the translation), an adaptation of the Sweeney story for autobiographical purposes in the 'Sweeney Redivivus' sequence from *Station Island* (autobiographical purposes that are revisited again briefly in section three of 'The Flight Path' from *The Spirit Level*), the inclusion of echoes of Sweeney in the other *Station Island* poems, including the title sequence, a selection of portions of the translation (slightly revised) to accompany Rachel Giese's images in *Sweeney's Flight*, and the revision of the entire translation for that same collaboration. The adaptation and translation of Dante in both 'The Strand at Lough Beg' and 'Ugolino' in *Field Work* is similarly revisited in later poems when 'Station Island' and 'The Flight Path' both react to and rework these poems; aside from these specific instances of reworkings of earlier responses to Dante, Heaney's engagement with Dante in general is both multifaceted and ongoing. More recently, the *Beowulf* translation is striking not just for what the text does in reimagining an Old English poem in a way that bears upon the concerns of Ulster at the end of the second millenium, but for the introduction's opening up of a range of further alternative imaginative spaces, from *bunraku* to animation, where *Beowulf* might be reimagined, further translated, and reworked again (p. xiii). Parts

---

[1] Heaney may have in mind here Mandelstam's comment on Dante: 'Dante is an antimodernist. His contemporaneity is inexhaustible, measureless, and unending'; Osip Mandelstam, 'Conversation about Dante', trans. Clarence Brown and Robert Hughes, in *Osip Mandelstam: Selected Essays*, trans. Sidney Monas (Austin and London: University of Texas Press, 1977), 3–44 at 24.

[2] On which see Lee Patterson, 'On the Margin: Postmodernism, Ironic History, and Medieval Studies,' *Speculum* 65 (1990), 87–108.

[3] Seamus Heaney and Rachel Giese, *Sweeney's Flight* (London: Faber, 1992), p. vii.

of the *Beowulf* translation also appear elsewhere in Heaney's poetry (in 1987's *The Haw Lantern* and 2001's *Electric Light*), as earlier or later drafts, with the text slightly reworked – here, again, the translation is something open to revision, rather than fixed in print. Given also that the *Beowulf* translation revisits the concerns of Heaney's earlier engagement with Germanic literatures in *North*, it's possible to suggest that the 1999 translation is a re-engagement with a set of concerns visible since the 1970s.[1] This circling back and reworking of earlier translations extends even to 'The Names of the Hare,' a brief piece of Middle English linguistic exuberance translated in 1981 and revisited in 'Squarings' xliii from *Seeing Things*.[2]

Further to this ability to produce multiple responses to a given medieval text, Heaney's translation practice embodies a commitment to vernacularity in which linguistic diversity is a prominent feature, a stance that has its debts to Dante among others. This commitment to linguistic diversity has posed challenges: if the medieval is often thought of as premodern and hence marginal, it can also (paradoxically) be thought of as foundational, and so reworkings of medieval texts that challenge what seem from a contemporary persepective to be linear narratives of cultural evolution can impinge upon contemporary notions of identity. This was noticeably the case for Heaney's use of an Irish-inflected vernacular in translating *Beowulf*, a poem thought to be inaccessible to contemporary English speakers but at the same time at least potentially foundational for English cultural identity, and both Heaney himself and the translation's many commentators and reviewers have felt it necessary to discuss the implications of an Irish poet translating an Anglo-Saxon poem into an Irish-inflected English. The question is partly one of the language chosen: another popular translation of a foundational medieval English text by an Irish writer, Nevill Coghill's translation of Chaucer's *Canterbury Tales*, poses no such problems given its choice of 'standard' English, which does not threaten to disrupt a sense of a linear literary tradition.[3] Heaney's rendering of *Beowulf* in an English inflected with an Ulster vernacular raises the question of the claim which speakers of non-standard English might have upon the English literary canon. Rather than adopting an adversarial stance, however,

[1] Chris Jones, *Strange Likeness: The Use of Old English in Twentieth-Century Poetry* (Oxford: Oxford University Press, 2006), 228, makes the case for *Beowulf* as one of Heaney's 'major preoccupations.'

[2] Heaney, *Opened Ground*, 209–11, 387; Heaney, *Seeing Things*, 103.

[3] On Coghill's translation and criticisms of it, see Steve Ellis, *Chaucer at Large: The Poet in the Modern Imagination,* Medieval Cultures 24 (Minneapolis and London: University of Minnesota Press, 2000), 98–120; for Coghill's biography, see John Carey, 'Coghill, Nevill Henry Kendal Aylmer (1899–1980),' *Oxford Dictionary of National Biography* (Oxford: Oxford University Press, 2004).

Heaney's embrace of lingusitic diversity in translating an Old English text
is a gesture towards breaking down the barriers that are perceived to exist
between Irish and English, an attempt to move past the either/or positions
that define English and Irish as adversarial and opposing terms. His commitment to linguistic pluralism is a way of overcoming a binary view of
English and Irish, in favour of what he refers to in the introduction to the
Beowulf translation as an unpartitioned linguistic country, where language
is not a badge of identity but an entry into further language (p. xxv).

Heaney's commitment to lingustic diversity, and his refusal of a separation between literatures in Irish and English, is also something visible
when the translation process moves in the opposite direction, whether in
Sweeney Astray, where the translation includes echoes of Irish but also Ulster dialect words of Old English and Scots origin, or in the recent translation of the short medieval Irish poem 'Pangur Bán,' where a canonical
medieval Irish poem is placed in relation to what Heaney calls the 'big cat
English' of Blake's 'The Tyger' (p. 5).[1] Nor is this advocacy of a dialogue
between poetic cultures something artificially imposed by the translation
on the medieval source text. Heaney (following earlier commentators)
notes that the name of the cat, *Pangur Bán*, 'White Pangur,' comes from an
old spelling of the Welsh word for 'fuller' (p. 5), and this linguistic echo,
along with the location of the poem's composition in Carinthia (modern-
day Austria), emphasises that the poem is multicultural to start with.

Important in this refusal of a separation of cultures is Heaney's advocacy of what he calls the 'through-other,' a strategy discussed specifically
in relation to the *Beowulf* translation, but perhaps visible elsewhere in
Heaney's responses to the medieval, as in his retelling of an Irish story
via Gerald of Wales in 'Saint Kevin and the Blackbird'[2] (Gerald of Wales
being, among other things, the chronicler of the 1169 incursion of the
Anglo-Normans into Irish affairs, which served as a point of origin for
all that followed). This notion of the 'through-other' is also present in
Heaney's self-identification with the Anglo-Saxon cowherd turned poet,
Cædmon, in 'Whitby-sur-Moyola,'[3] although Cædmon may himself be

---

[1] There is a point of connection between these two medieval Irish poems translated
by Heaney: a fragment of a ninth-century version of *Buile Suibhne* is preserved in the
same manuscript as *Pangur Bán*: the fragment is translated into English in *A Golden Treasury of Irish Poetry*, ed. and trans. David Greene and Frank O'Connor (London: Macmillan,
1967), 100–101; the manuscript's contents are discussed in the second chapter of Robin
Flower, *The Irish Tradition* (Oxford: Oxford University Press, 1947), 24–66.

[2] Heaney, *The Spirit Level*, 20–21; Heaney, *Opened Ground*, 410–11; the source of the
story retold by Heaney here is Gerald of Wales, *The History and Topography of Ireland*, trans.
John J. O'Meara (Harmondsworth: Penguin, 1982), 77–79.

[3] Heaney, *The Spirit Level*, 41; Heaney, *Opened Ground*, 425.

an example of the 'through-other,' because, as Chris Jones explains, his name is of British rather than Anglo-Saxon origin, and so it's possible that, for Heaney, the founding text of English literature (Cædmon's 'Hymn') comes 'with its cultural margins already built into its centre.'[1] Heaney's advocacy of the 'through-other' also seems in keeping with an earlier motif where the act of imagination is conceived of as being analogous to boundary-crossing, something visible for instance in the poems 'Terminus' and 'From the Frontier of Writing' from *The Haw Lantern*, and in the similarly titled essay 'Frontiers of Writing' from *The Redress of Poetry*.[2] The crossing of boundaries is something particularly evident in the act of translation, etymologically a carrying across, and at the end of 'Frontiers of Writing,' Heaney brings this motif of boundary crossing to bear upon a retelling of a narrative of crossing between this world and the next, itself a translation from a medieval Irish text.[3]

The complexity of Heaney's response to the medieval, however, extends not only to his ability to produce multiple responses over time to individual source texts, or to his ability to give a view of medieval texts as being multicultural rather than monocultural in their affinities and resonances. It also extends to the complex layerings visible within the poetry, as medieval texts are given a contemporary voice and brought to bear upon contemporary concerns. An example might be the opening of 'Station Island.' The poem is an account of a pilgrimage to Lough Derg, set in the present, and concerned at least in part with contemporary social and political issues, in particular Irish Catholicism and the conflict in Northern Ireland. It is also, however, an adaptation in an Irish context of Dante's *Commedia*: the narrative of 'Station Island' describes the poet's encounters with multiple revenants, and there are allusions to and quotations from Dante in the text. The poem opens with the figure of Simon Sweeney, a woodcutter, a character reminiscent of the medieval Ulster king from *Sweeney Astray*, of the similar figure invoked in the poem 'The King of the Ditchbacks,' of Dante as described by Osip Mandelstam, and

[1] Jones, *Strange Likeness*, 184–86; note Jones's caveat (184 n.) regarding this possibility.
[2] Heaney, *The Haw Lantern*, 4–7, Heaney, *Opened Ground*, 295–98; Seamus Heaney, 'Frontiers of Writing,' in Heaney, *The Redress of Poetry: Oxford Lectures* (London: Faber, 1995), 186–203.
[3] 'Lightenings' viii, which Heaney quotes at the end of his essay, is a loose translation from an Old Irish anecdote found in *Anecdota from Irish Manuscripts*, iii, ed. O. J. Bergin, R. I. Best, Kuno Meyer, J. G. O'Keeffe (Halle: Max Niemeyer; Dublin: Hodges Figgis, 1910), 8–9: see the archives of the Old Irish discussion list at https://listserv.heanet.ie/old-irish-l.html for June 2000 (Dennis King's posting on 20 June to the thread 'Minks [*mistake for* Monks] at Clonmacnoise'), which identifies this text as the source for Heaney's poem.

others. Sweeney is elsewhere reminiscent of the figure of the Wanderer from the Anglo-Saxon poem of that name, of Ulysses, of Icarus, and of Heaney himself. This procedure of creating compound allusions extends to characterisation and to intertextual allusion, and like Heaney's practice of revisiting and reworking the same material in different ways, produces complex layers of comparison. This process of layering, of producing multiple echoes, is something visible in many of the texts discussed below, not least where Heaney writes echoes of his original poetry into his translations and adaptations from the medieval.

Heaney's engagement with medieval literature is not merely significant and enduring, but also coherent, in that the complexity of his response to medieval literature is something in evidence from the very outset. Heaney's use of medieval texts to address contemporary concerns, both personal and political, his establishment of a dialogue between his original work and his translation practice, his representation of medieval texts as multicultural rather than monocultural in their affinities, and his willingness to produce multiple and diverse responses to a given medieval source text: all of this is present right at the beginning, with Heaney's self-projection as the exiled Sweeney in *Sweeney Astray*.

1

Sweeney Astray

From 'Buile Suibhne' to 'Sweeney Astray'

SWEENEY *Astray* is Seamus Heaney's translation of the medieval Irish text *Buile Suibhne*, 'The Madness of Suibhne,' a tale in verse and prose that describes how Suibhne (Sweeney), an Ulster king, clashes with a local cleric, Rónán, and having been cursed by the cleric, goes mad during the battle of Magh Rath (modernised to Moira in Heaney's version) in the year 637. Believing himself to have been transformed into a bird, Suibhne retreats into the wilderness where he lives a life of hardship, wandering from place to place, and reciting poetry that describes his suffering. Attempts by those close to him to help Suibhne recover his senses meet only temporary success, and he remains an outcast until his reconciliation with the Church through another cleric, Moling, which takes place as Suibhne lies dying.[1]

Heaney's translation, published in 1983, is based upon J. G. O'Keeffe's edition and translation, published in 1913 by the Irish Texts Society. O'Keeffe's edition is based on a manuscript written in the 1670s, and there are no surviving manuscripts from before the seventeenth century.[2] Heaney nonetheless cites O'Keeffe as believing on linguistic evidence that 'the text might have been composed at any time between the years 1200 and 1500,' notes external evidence to suggest that 'the thing was already taking shape in the ninth century,' and suggests that the work derives from earlier

---

[1] Reference to *Sweeney Astray* is to Seamus Heaney, *Sweeney Astray* (Derry: Field Day, 1983; London: Faber, 1984). Reference to *Buile Suibhne* is to *Buile Suibhne (The Frenzy of Suibhne), being the Adventures of Suibhne Geilt: A Middle-Irish Romance*, ed. and trans. J. G. O'Keeffe (London: Irish Texts Society, 1913).

[2] The surviving manuscripts are Royal Irish Academy B IV 1, pp. 82a–95b, from the 1670s, Royal Irish Academy 23 K 44, pp. 131–80, from the 1720s, and Royal Library Brussels 3410, fo. 59a–61b from 1629.

traditions yet, leading back towards the historical seventh-century battle described early in the narrative (p. v).[1]

Buile Suibhne has exercised a considerable influence on twentieth-century Irish writing, as Heaney acknowledges in the introduction to his translation. The best-known treatment of the story occurs in the novel by Brian O'Nolan (Flann O'Brien), *At Swim-Two-Birds*, which takes its title from *Buile Suibhne*, and contains a translation of the medieval work as a tale-within-a-tale-within-another-tale inside the novel's complex structure.[2] O'Nolan had previously undertaken a translation of portions of the work as part of a thesis on Irish nature poetry. As well as appearing within the novel as a medieval tale told by Finn MacCool to some of the other characters, Anne Clune argues that *Buile Suibhne* also appears a second time, metamorphosed in 'a free adaptation by Orlic Trellis, a character in the novel, which changes Sweeny into Dermot Trellis and has St Moling and the Pooka Fergus McPhellimy sharing the role of Ronan.'[3]

While Flann O'Brien's incorporation of *Buile Suibhne* into *At Swim-Two-Birds* is the best-known twentieth-century adaptation of the medieval work, it is by no means the only one. As Heaney observes in introducing his own version, 'a number of other poets and scholars have continued to make translations of different sections of the verse' (p. v), and there have been adaptations in both English and Irish. This process goes on both before and after Heaney's translation, and there are translations, adaptations, and moments of parody by Gerard Murphy, Frank O'Connor, Austin Clarke, John Montague, Derek Mahon, Tom MacIntyre, Nuala Ní Dhomhnaill, Thomas Kinsella, Cathal O'Searcaigh, and Paul Muldoon.[4] Ian Duhig's

---

[1] On the historical battle, see Dáibhí Ó Cróinín, 'Ireland, 400–800,' in *A New History of Ireland*, i: *Prehistoric and Early Ireland*, ed. Ó Cróinín (Oxford: Oxford University Press, 2005), 182–234 at 217–18. On the second Ulster cycle, the literary sequence that deals with the battle (of which *Buile Suibhne* is part), see James Carney, 'Language and Literature to 1169,' in *A New History of Ireland*, i, ed. Ó Cróinín, 451–510 at 478–79, and the entries for *Cath Maige Rath*, *Fled Dúin na nGéd*, and *Buile Suibhne* in *The Concise Oxford Companion to Irish Literature*, ed. Robert Welch (Oxford: Oxford University Press, 2000).

[2] Flann O'Brien, *At Swim-Two-Birds* (London: Longmans Green, 1939; repr. Harmondsworth: Penguin, 1967), 64–91.

[3] Anne Clune, 'Mythologising Sweeney,' *Irish University Review* 26 (1996), 48–60 at 52.

[4] *Early Irish Lyrics: Eighth to Twelfth Century*, ed. Gerard Murphy (Oxford: Oxford University Press, 1956), 118–41; *Golden Treasury of Irish Poetry*, ed. and trans. Greene and O'Connor, 179–80; Austin Clarke, 'The Frenzy of Suibhne' and 'The Trees of the Forest,' in Clarke, *Collected Poems*, ed. Liam Miller (Dublin: Dolmen, 1974), 131–34, 507–09; John Montague, *A Chosen Light* (London: MacGibbon and Kee, 1967); Derek Mahon, 'Epitaph for Flann O'Brien,' in *The Snow Party* (London: Oxford University Press, 1975), 28; Tom MacIntyre, 'Sweeney Among the Branches,' in *The Harper's Turn* (Oldcastle: Gallery, 1982); MacIntyre, 'Rise Up, Lovely Sweeney,' in *The Word for Yes* (Oldcastle:

'Margin Prayer from an Ancient Psalter' narrates a preface to the Sweeney story (closer in tone to Flann O'Brien than Heaney), while in prose fiction Dermot Bolger draws upon the Sweeney myth in his novel *A Second Life*.[1] While all of these versions of the Sweeney story are an indication of the influence of the work upon the imaginations of a range of twentieth-century writers, they do not mean that Heaney's translation is in any way redundant, for his is the first full-length English version since O'Keeffe's. Furthermore, since O'Keeffe's version, with the full apparatus of original text, notes, and glossary, was aimed at scholars of medieval Irish literature rather than a broader public, Heaney's translation might be seen as serving a need in making an influential text more widely available to a more general audience. As Ciaran Carson commented in reviewing Heaney's version, 'until *Sweeney Astray*, *Buile Suibhne* has lain nearly moribund in the shelves of libraries.'[2]

Heaney's motivation in translating *Buile Suibhne* was not that of anti-quarianism. In his short introduction to the published work, and in a more detailed fashion in the later essay 'Earning a Rhyme,' he offers a number of justifications for the work's interest – aesthetic, political, and autobiographical. The translation process itself, he tells us, occurred in two parts. The initial effort, begun in 1972, the year of Heaney's move south from Belfast to Wicklow, followed the example of Robert Lowell in producing a fairly free translation with an autobiographical slant:

> I began to inflate myself and my situation into Sweeney's, to make analogies between the early medieval Ulsterman who rocketed out of the North, as a result of vehement squabbles there among the petty dynasties, and this poet from County Derry who had only

Gallery, 1991); Nuala Ní Dhomhnaill, 'Muirghil castigates Sweeny,' in Ní Dhomhnaill, *Selected Poems: Rogha Dánta* (Dublin: Raven Arts Press, 1991); *The New Oxford Book of Irish Verse*, ed. Thomas Kinsella (Oxford: Oxford University Press, 1986), 72–78; Cathal O'Searcaigh, *Súile Shuibhne* (1983); O'Searcaigh, *Suibhne* (1987); Paul Muldoon, 'The More a Man Has, The More a Man Wants,' in Muldoon, *Poems, 1968–1998* (London: Faber, 2001), 127–47. The list presented here draws on references in Clune, 'Mythologizing Sweeney,' 48, Neil Corcoran, *After Yeats and Joyce: Reading Modern Irish Literature* (Oxford: Oxford University Press, 1997), 20, *The Concise Oxford Companion to Irish Literature*, ed. Welch.

[1] Ian Duhig, 'Margin Prayer from an Ancient Psalter,' in Duhig, *The Bradford Count* (Newcastle-upon-Tyne: Bloodaxe, 1991), repr. in *Emergency Kit: Poems for Strange Times*, ed. Jo Shapcott and Matthew Sweeney (London: Faber, 1996), 265–67; Dermot Bolger, *A Second Life* (Harmondsworth: Penguin, 1994).

[2] Ciaran Carson, '*Sweeney Astray*: Escaping from Limbo,' in *The Art of Seamus Heaney*, ed. Tony Curtis, 4th edn (Bridgend: Seren, 2001), 141–48 at 148.

recently come south to County Wicklow for purposes of retreat and composure.[1]

Although this initial effort produced a complete version of the text, Heaney felt that the whole was less than the sum of its parts, and laid it aside, returning to the task in 1979 to produce a more restrained and literal version of the original.[2] There was less emphasis on the autobiographical in this revised translation, although comparisons still stand up: as Bernard O'Donoghue writes, 'the Ulster poet who has run foul of clerisy and the Irish high-king in combination, and has been transformed into a bird to flee the length and breadth of Ireland, is clearly a useful self-projection for Heaney post-1972.'[3] But if the translation itself was less autobiographical in this second version, it was now accompanied by a sequence of original poems where Heaney drew on the Sweeney persona for his own purposes: the 'Sweeney Redivivus' poems collected in *Station Island*.

Translation practice

One of the best examples of Heaney's practice in translating *Buile Suibhne* may be his translation of the work's title. *Sweeney Astray* is not quite a literal translation of *Buile Suibhne*, which O'Keeffe translated as 'The Frenzy of Suibhne' and others have given as 'The Madness of Sweeney.'[4] Rendering *Suibhne* as 'Sweeney' is an unproblematic anglicization, and there is the precedent of Flann O'Brien's 'Sweeny'. 'Astray,' however, expands the sense of the original somewhat, for as well as describing Sweeney's state of mind, it also describes his physical state – Sweeney is astray in his wanderings around Ireland, as well as being astray in his wits after the battle of Moira.[5] Further to that, the phrase has a Hiberno-English flavour in that it recalls the Irish *ar strae*,[6] and is more colloquial and intimate in tone than a literal translation. Heaney's translation of the work's title, then, may not be strictly literal, but is subtly suggestive in more than one way.

Heaney's primary interest in the translation, then, is not a strict, lit-

---

[1] Heaney, 'Earning a Rhyme,' 63.

[2] Heaney, 'Earning a Rhyme,' 62–65.

[3] O'Donoghue, *Seamus Heaney and the Language of Poetry*, 88.

[4] Hence Denis Donoghue's criticism of 'astray' as inexact in 'Heaney's Sweeney,' in Donoghue, *We Irish: Essays on Irish Literature and Society* (New York: Knopf, 1986), 267–71 at 270, first published in *The New Republic* (30 April 1984).

[5] Clune, 'Mythologizing Sweeney,' 54.

[6] See *Foclóir Gaeilge–Béarla*, ed. Niall Ó Dónaill (Dublin/Baile Átha Cliath: Oifig an tSoláthair, 1977), s.v. *strae*.

eral adherence to the Irish-language text: after all, O'Keeffe's translation already broadly fulfils the purpose of providing an English text that attempts a word-for-word paraphrase of the Irish. Heaney's brief notes preceding the text acknowledge a number of omissions from the original (p. ix),[1] and he acknowledges that his verse does not attempt to parallel the source-text's variety of Irish metrical forms (p. vii). His emphasis is on the English translation as a coherent work in itself, rather than fidelity to the source-text. In a 1988 interview, he offers a discussion of two motives for translation:

> I believe that there are two good motives for translation and they both sponsor slightly different procedures. One motive, which is the absolutely pure one, is to so love the work in the first language that you're hurt that it isn't shared in the next language. You will do everything that is possible to bring across the unique and beloved features of the original, and this will involve an attempt at all kinds of precisions, equivalents, and honesties. And you keep saying: 'Oh no, it's not like that.' You hurt until it gets nearly right and then you end up unsatisfied because it can never be the same in the other language. That kind of absolute command which is there if you love the thing in the original and know it deeply, that produces the highest motive and the highest kind of translation and the highest failure. So there are two motives, one of which is that pure one, and another of which is impure. But the impure motive has its own *verité*. You are listening through the wall of the original language as to a conversation in another room in a motel. Dully, you can hear something that is really interesting. And you say: 'God, I wish I was in this room.' So you forage; you blunder through the wall. You go needily after something. This is what happened in English with the sonnet form when in the sixteenth century the courtly makers heard through the wall of English the Italian melody and the Petrarchan thing. One of the greatest sonnets in English is an abusive translation of Petrarch: Wyatt's 'Whoso list to hunt I know where is an hind.' Wyatt indulges in a kind of Lowellesque bullying of the Petrarchan original and yet his poem is a great gift to the second language. I think that is the Lowell pattern, and it's the Chaucerian, the notion of translation as taking it over: taking it over in two senses – in the slightly imperial

---

[1] H. A. Kelly, 'Heaney's Sweeney: The Poet as Version-Maker,' *Philological Quarterly* 65 (1986), 293–310 at 298, also notes an unacknowledged cut from section 45, as does Carson, '*Sweeney Astray*: Escaping from Limbo,' 142–43, who offers a close reading of some of the omitted lines.

sense and in the original etymological sense of carrying a thing across.[1]

Heaney now goes on to say that the second motive was his own in his translation of the Ugolino passage from the *Commedia*, and that this was partly true of *Sweeney Astray* also:

> To some extent that was also true of *Sweeney Astray*. Even though I can read Irish, the *Buile Suibhne* wasn't singing in me as a great structure that I previously knew and loved in Irish. In fact, it was in order to get to know it that I wanted to pull it out of Irish. And of course I felt I had the right to it. It wasn't that original linguistic love-right, but was a cultural, political, historical in-placeness, a 'we are all in there together' feeling.[2]

Heaney's methods and purpose, then, are quite unlike those of O'Keeffe, whose English translation is focused on the original text, and really functions as a gloss to the Irish rather than a stand-alone text. In focusing on the result of the translation process rather than the source, Heaney seeks to provide not a modern English gloss to the medieval Irish text, but a twentieth-century reworking in English that can be read separately from the original, as a literary work in itself.

If Heaney's project is focused on the English-language version being produced rather than the Irish-language source, this is not to say that it is entirely focused on the norms of the target language. In a discussion of his translation, he cites John Millington Synge's creation of an Hiberno-English literary dialect indebted to the Irish language that unsettles a sense of linear continuity and identity between the English language and English literature.[3] The language of Heaney's translation is not identical with that of Synge's plays, but it does leaven the standard with a sprinkling of the local. As we shall see, the translation contains some untranslated place names and some Ulster dialect terms of Scottish and Old English derivation. There is also the occasional problematic piece of Irish-language archaism – 'erenach' (p. 28), for instance, is glossed in O'Keeffe, but left unexplained in Heaney.[4]

What has attracted questions from critics, however, is less the antique

---

[1] Randy Brandes, 'Seamus Heaney: An Interview,' *Salmagundi* 80 (1988), 4–21 at 11–12.

[2] Brandes, 'Seamus Heaney: An Interview,' 12.

[3] Heaney, 'Earning a Rhyme,' 59–60.

[4] O'Keeffe, *Buile Suibhne*, 164–65, n. to p. 29, cites a 17th-century explanation of the office of erenach (*airchinnech*) as the hereditary caretaker of a church; cf. *DIL* s.v. *airchinnech*, which offers 'name of a monastic office, anglicised *erenagh*.'

than the modern. Both H. A. Kelly and Denis Donoghue, for example, object to Heaney's use of the word 'mesmerized' (p. 9) as recalling the historical but very much post-medieval figure of Dr Mesmer.[1] Both also question Eorann's words to Sweeney, where she says 'I wish we could fly away together, / be rolling stones, birds of a feather' (p. 28). For Kelly, the implied proverbs conflict: rolling stones that gather no moss, and birds of a feather that flock together.[2] It's likely that the proverbial references are intended, and, in context, the proverbs complement one another. Eorann is saying that she and Sweeney belong together ('birds of a feather'), and that they could both live the untethered life that is now Sweeney's ('rolling stones'). This works thematically, but it is true to say that this is language with a contemporary echo that necessarily creates resonances for a contemporary audiences not present in the medieval Irish original. Kelly comments that it is anachronistic for Sweeney to quote Shakespeare;[3] if so, it is even more inappropriate for him to quote Heaney (as he does in several places). It would indeed be odd to find these things in a medieval text, and jarring for a reader of a translation that purported to offer an exact equivalent of its medieval source, but Heaney, focused upon the result rather than the source, has inserted new resonances into the translation to bring the work to life for a contemporary audience.

Commentators on the work have also drawn comparisons between the voice of *Sweeney Astray* and that of Heaney.[4] The person quoting both Shakespeare and Heaney, then, is not so much Sweeney as Heaney himself, and the language of Heaney's translation is the mixed diction of a 'middle voice' between local and standard usage that Bernard O'Donoghue shows to be recurrent in Heaney.[5] If the language of the translation is that of a 'middle voice' between the standard and the local, the same is true of the verse. Although Heaney does not attempt to reproduce the verse-forms of the original, O'Donoghue observes that the translation does include a feature of the Irish *deibidhe* rhyme that, he says, Heaney uses so often that it is 'by now almost a recognisable tune of Heaney's own'[6] This is a rhyme

---

[1] Kelly, 'Heaney's Sweeney,' 301; Donoghue, 'Heaney's Sweeney,' 270.

[2] Kelly, 'Heaney's Sweeney,' 302; cf. Donoghue, 'Heaney's Sweeney,' 271, for whom the lines are beautiful, but 'it's hard to think of rolling stones now without striking against the other Rolling Stones.'

[3] Kelly, 'Heaney's Sweeney,' 301.

[4] Kelly, 'Heaney's Sweeney,' 301, 303, 308 and n. 20; Carson, '*Sweeney Astray*: Escaping from Limbo,' 148; Donoghue, 'Heaney's Sweeney,' 270. While agreeing that the voice is a contemporary one, I differ from Kelly's view that the translation's tone is 'expressive of a modern-day quirky whimsicality.'

[5] O'Donoghue, *Seamus Heaney and the Language of Poetry*, 91–92.

[6] O'Donoghue, *Seamus Heaney and the Language of Poetry*, 90.

also found in other Irish poetry in English, from Austin Clarke to Paul Muldoon, and elsewhere in Heaney, although (there as here) in conjunction with an English octosyllabic line, rather than the seven-syllable Irish *deibidhe* line.[1] That *deibidhe* rhyme is the rhyming of a monosyllable with a disyllable, where the two-syllable word is stressed on the non-rhyming syllable. Examples of the rhyme from section 6 of *Sweeney Astray* might be 'bear'/'prayer,' 'hand'/'command,' 'decree'/'be' (pp. 5, 6), and so on. Again, Heaney's practice here echoes Irish usage in a departure from standard English practice, and it also contains an echo of the original, for *Buile Suibhne* also employs *deibidhe* in this section, rhyming *lais/hégmais, n-anba/ionnarba, lesg/thormesg*, and so on (p. 6).

Suibhne Geilt and the artist as outcast

In part, the reason for identifying Heaney with Sweeney is that Sweeney is a poet; in part, it is that Sweeney is an uprooted figure, an outcast, an exile, an 'inner emigré.' Heaney combines both of these elements by suggesting that Sweeney can be read as 'a figure of the artist, displaced, guilty, assuaging himself by his utterance' (p. vi). The reason for Heaney's description of Sweeney in these terms may be deeply embedded in the original text: the description of Suibhne as *geilt*.[2] The word is present in Rónán's curse on Sweeney, and repeated throughout the text:

> Ro-ionnsaigh an cath go cían
> dar chláon a chonn is a chíall,
> sirfidh Éirinn 'na gheilt ghlas
> agus bidh do rinn raghas. (p. 6)

Heaney translates:

> From far off he approached the field
> that drove his mind and senses wild.
> He shall roam Ireland, mad and bare.
> He shall find death on the point of a spear. (p. 5)

Later in the text, we find Sweeney describing himself as *gealtán gealtach* (p. 30), a crazy madman,[3] as *gealtán Ghlinne Bolcáin* (p. 30), which Heaney

---

[1] O'Donoghue, *Seamus Heaney and the Language of Poetry*, 31–39, 90.
[2] *DIL* defines *geilt* as 'one who goes mad from terror; a panic-stricken fugitive from battle; a crazy person living in the woods and supposed to be endowed with the power of levitation; a lunatic.'
[3] Heaney omits the phrase here.

gives as 'the madman of Glen Bolcain' (p. 17), and as *Suibhne Geilt* (p. 34), 'Mad Sweeney' in Heaney's version (p. 19).

As Henry Hart notes, Heaney elsewhere praises P. L. Henry's book on *The Early English and Celtic Lyric*, a book that may be influential for Heaney's view of Sweeney as *geilt*.[1] One of the arguments of Henry's book is that Old English *gylt, gelt* (modern English *guilt*) is very close in meaning to Irish and Scots Gaelic *geilt* and may derive from it. Henry's description of the *geilt* uses language quite close to that of Heaney's description of Sweeney:

> The Christian *geilt*, subsisting on the diet of birds and animals, is like Suibhne an outcast, culpable, living in fear and expiating sin. This new meaning is imprinted on the associated abstractum which comes to connote what we understand by *guilt*: OE *gelt, gylt* is born.[2]

Heaney's description above of Suibhne as 'displaced, guilty, assuaging himself by his utterance' seems to echo this description of the *geilt* as 'an outcast, culpable, living in fear and expiating sin,' and Heaney may be following Henry's argument in using the English word 'guilty' to echo the Irish word *geilt*.

But if Heaney's characterization of the artist as guilty has deep roots in the language of the original text, it may also have an autobiographical tinge. This is a suggestion that has been made about Heaney's work by others – Terence Brown writes that 'from the start Seamus Heaney has seemed oddly guilty about being a poet at all,' going on to explain that for Heaney, 'the aesthetic impulse must reckon with the ethical and social demands of a grievous historical crisis.' While Heaney's poetry of the 1970s struggled with the predicament of poetry's place in a time of suffering, as well as that suffering itself, Brown suggests that 'in Heaney's poetry of that difficult decade there are suggestions of guilty fear that has betrayed his art to the gross conditions of a squalid conflict, and, conversely, that he has stood idly by as others have suffered, his only contribution the telling of a species of poetic rosary beads.' These feelings of guilt, Brown writes, are the subject matter of *Station Island*, published by Faber in the same year

---

[1] Henry Hart, *Seamus Heaney: Poet of Contrary Progressions* (Syracuse, NY: Syracuse University Press, 1992), 146; P. L. Henry, *The Early English and Celtic Lyric* (London: Allen & Unwin, 1966), cited in Seamus Heaney, 'The God in the Tree: Early Irish Nature Poetry,' in Heaney, *Preoccupations: Selected Prose, 1968–1978* (London: Faber, 1980), 181–89 at 183.

[2] Henry, *The Early English and Celtic Lyric*, 202. *Geilt* appears in its Irish sense only rarely in English: *OED* s.v. *gelt* cites Spenser's *Faerie Queene* iv. vii. 21: 'Like a ghastly Gelt whose wits are reaved.'

as *Sweeney Astray*. Brown quotes a review of *Station Island* by Aidan Carl
Mathews, in which Mathews summarizes Heaney's feelings of guilt:

> He pleads guilty to having left home; he pleads guilty to having exer-
> cised his gifts with something not unlike single-mindedness at a time
> when murder and mayhem have blocked the sewers of his home and
> hinterland; he pleads guilty to not having felt deeply enough about
> it all, as if deep feelings weren't, in every sense, a bloody liability
> in such a situation; he pleads guilty to having devoted a great part
> of his life to, well himself and his loved ones [...] he pleads guilty
> to having become a laureate and luminary by writing poems about
> events which have walked filth, misery, and strickenness into the
> living-room carpets of a legion of families affected by louts with ka-
> lashnikovs; and in a strange and sad way he pleads guilty to the very
> fact that he exists.

This is a long list, but, Brown suggests, it is not a comprehensive one.
Brown argues that not only does Heaney feel guilt about having written
poetry while people suffered (in all the ways that Mathews suggests here),
but he also feels that in trying to take account of that suffering in his poetry, he might have betrayed his art 'to the ethical demands of a decent but
inadequate humanism and concern for his people.'[1]

Ciaran Carson, noting Heaney's suggestion of artistic guilt in *Sweeney
Astray*, suggests that guilt about the relationship of art and suffering is not
the sort of guilt found here – 'that kind of guilt belongs to *Station Island*'
– and that what's found in the *Sweeney Astray* translation may be linguistic
guilt, a guilt that comes from being caught between languages, between
Irish and English, in 'the limbo of lost words.'[2] Perhaps; *Buile Suibhne* is
explicitly about loss and the desire to remedy that sense of loss, whether
that be the loss of home, of family, of society, or of sanity, and it may be
possible to read into *Sweeney Astray* a further sense of loss of language,
something not uncommon in Irish writers, including both Heaney and
Carson himself.[3] That said, Heaney is quite explicit in his introduction of

---

[1] Terence Brown, 'The Witnessing Eye and the Speaking Tongue,' in *Seamus Heaney:
A Collection of Critical Essays*, ed. Elmer Andrews (New York: St Martin's Press, 1992),
182–92 at 182, 184, 185, 186.

[2] Carson, '*Sweeney Astray*: Escaping from Limbo,' 147.

[3] Heaney comments in the introduction to the *Beowulf* translation on living 'within
a cultural and ideological frame that regarded it [Irish] as the language that I should by
rights have been speaking but I had been robbed of' (pp. xxiii–xxiv); Carson comments
in the introduction to his translation of Brian Merriman's *Cúirt an Mheán Oíche*: 'I hesi-
tate to call myself a native speaker: true, Irish is, or was, my first language, but I learned it
from parents for whom it was a second language; and it has been a long time since it was

the theme of art and obligation here, commenting that the work may be read as 'an aspect of the quarrel between free creative imagination and the constraints of religion, political, and domestic obligation' (p. vi), an enduring theme in Heaney's work. Furthermore, Carson's distinction between *Sweeney Astray* and *Station Island* is difficult to uphold, for the two books are not easily disentangled: the figure of Sweeney is visible throughout the *Station Island* collection, (not just in the 'Sweeney Redivivus' section).[1] The Sweeney figure in 'The First Flight' describes how 'they began to pronounce me / a feeder off battlefields,'[2] which sounds like the sort of guilt just described.

Either way, Heaney's sense of the guilt that comes with poetry cannot be seen as identical with the guilt of Sweeney, whose guilt, and consequent madness and exile, results from sacrilege and murder. Sweeney attacks Ronan at the outset of the narrative, and throws his psalter into a nearby lake; he is in the process of dragging Ronan out of the church when he is interrupted by a cry of alarm, summoning him to battle. Flann O'Brien's version of the story goes further than either the original or Heaney's version in suggesting Sweeney's interrupted intention to murder Ronan: 'after that he took the hard grip of the cleric's hand and ran with a wind-swift stride to the lake without a halting or a letting go of the hand because he had a mind to place the cleric by the side of his psalter in the lake, on the bottom, to speak precisely.'[3] Ronan recovers his psalter, but curses Sweeney, and Sweeney subsequently thwarts all of Ronan's attempts to make peace during the battle of Moira. As Heaney's version puts it: 'Sweeney, however, would continually violate every peace and truce which the cleric had ratified, slaying a man each day before the sides were engaged and slaying another each evening when the combat was finished' (p. 6). Sweeney then murders one of Ronan's psalmists, and makes an attempt on the life of Ronan himself: Ronan responds by repeating his curse on Sweeney, which is shortly fulfilled. As Henry Hart says, then, 'Heaney shares with a difference his persona's obsession with sin, guilt, penance, and poetry.'[4] The theme of the outcast and penitent poet is a useful one for Heaney, but there can be no literal equivalence between Heaney's sense of guilt and Sweeney's.

---

the first language in which I think, or express myself, though I sometimes dream in it'; Ciaran Carson, *The Midnight Court* (Oldcastle: Gallery, 2005), 14.

[1] Corcoran, *Poetry of Seamus Heaney*, 110, states of *Station Island* that 'the book has a formal unity, signalled by the presence, in all three parts, of the Sweeney figure.'

[2] Heaney, *Station Island*, 102, Heaney, *Opened Ground*, 274.

[3] O'Brien, *At Swim-Two-Birds*, 64.

[4] Hart, *Seamus Heaney: Poet of Contrary Progressions*, 143.

For P. L. Henry, commenting on the original text, the themes of exile and penance are closely bound up in *Buile Suibhne*,[1] and there are elements in Heaney's translation to suggest the same: 'I have endured purgatories since the feathers grew on me,' says Sweeney (p. 66).[2] This link between madness, exile, and penance may also be present more generally in medieval literary representations of madness. In her book on representations of madness in Middle English literature, Penelope Doob distinguishes between three literary conventions of madness: the 'Mad Sinner' suffers madness as punishment, the 'Unholy Wild Man' endures madness as purgation, while the 'Holy Wild Man' takes to the wilderness as a form of test.[3] In some ways, Sweeney shows characteristics of all three types described by Doob. He is certainly the 'Mad Sinner' whose attack on the servants of God is punished by madness and bestiality: it is Sweeney's attacks on Ronan and his servants that lead to the curse of madness and exile inflicted on Sweeney. He is also a figure of the 'Unholy Wild Man,' for one of the texts that Doob discusses under this heading is a tale of Merlin analogous to that of Sweeney.[4] But late in the text, Sweeney is also explicitly a 'Holy Wild Man,' for Moling's lament on Sweeney's death describes him as a *náoimhgheilt*, a holy madman.[5]

As Doob argues, all of these different types of literary madman in the Middle Ages are in any case indebted to the biblical figure of Nebuchadnezzar, who is transformed into a bestial figure, with some specifically birdlike qualities. This is the curse and description of Nebuchadnezzar from Daniel 4: 29–30:

> 29. Et ab hominibus ejicient te, et cum bestiis et feris erit habitatio tua: foenum quasi bos comedes, et septem tempora mutabuntur super te, donec scias quod dominetur Excelsus in regno hominum, et cuicumque voluerit, det illud.
>
> 30. Eadem hora sermo completus est super Nabuchodonosor, et ex hominibus abjectus est, et foenum ut bos comedit, et rore caeli corpus ejus infectum est, donec capilli ejus in similitudinem aquilarum crescerent, et ungues ejus quasi avium.

---

[1] Henry, *The Early English and Celtic Lyric*, 25.

[2] The original reads 'as mor do dhocruibh rofhuilinges-sa, o rofhás mo chluimh gus anocht,' translated by O'Keeffe, *Buile Suibhne*, 118, 119, as 'great is the suffering I have endured from the time my feathers have grown until tonight.'

[3] Penelope B. R. Doob, *Nebuchadnezzar's Children: Conventions of Madness in Middle English Literature* (New Haven and London: Yale University Press, 1974), 54–55.

[4] Doob, *Nebuchadnezzar's Children*, 153–58.

[5] O'Keeffe, *Buile Suibhne*, 156; Heaney's translation omits the phrase.

29. And they shall cast thee out from among men: and thy dwelling shall be with cattle and wild beasts: thou shalt eat grass like an ox, and seven times shall pass over thee, till thou know that the most High ruleth in the kingdom of men and giveth it to whomsoever he will.

30. The same hour the word was fulfilled upon Nabuchodonosor, and he was driven away from among men and did eat grass like an ox, and his body was wet with the dew of heaven; till his hairs grew like the feathers of eagles and his nails like birds' claws.[1]

Chaucer's description of Nebuchadnezzar in 'The Monk's Tale' describes the mad king as 'lyk a beest,' retaining the avian features of the biblical description:

> And lik an egles fetheres wax his heres;
> His nayles lyk a briddes clawes weere; (*Canterbury Tales*, vii. 2175–76)[2]

The parallels with Sweeney have not gone unnoticed: P. L. Henry suggests that the Nebuchadnezzar story provides 'a most significant precedent' to *Buile Suibhne*, and Corinne Saunders notes that the Suibhne story, and its analogues featuring Lailoken and Myrddin, are 'particularly close to that of Nebuchadnezzar.'[3]

If *Buile Suibhne* does contain this element of Christian moralization and penitential exile, however, it does so in tension with other elements present in the tale. As Heaney comments of Sweeney, 'the literary imagination which fastened upon him as an image was clearly in the grip of a tension between the newly dominant Christian ethos and the older, recalcitrant Celtic temperament' (pp. v–vi). Heaney had earlier described Sweeney as 'at once the enemy and the captive of the monastic tradition,'[4] and it's possible to read the tale as we have it as a progress from one state to the other. Sweeney clashes with Ronan at the outset, but it is another saint, Moling, who appears at the end of the tale to act as Sweeney's amanuensis and to record, and so in a sense capture, his story.

It has been argued that the Christian elements of the tale describing Sweeney's sundering from and reconciliation to the Church, concentrated

---

[1] Biblical references throughout are to the Douai–Rheims translation of the Vulgate.

[2] References to Chaucer throughout are to *The Riverside Chaucer*, ed. Larry D. Benson (Boston: Houghton Mifflin, 1987).

[3] Henry, *The Early English and Celtic Lyric*, 235; Corinne J. Saunders, *The Forest of Medieval Romance: Avernus, Broceliande, Arden* (Cambridge: Brewer, 1993), 115; see also John Carey, 'Suibhne Geilt and Tuán Mac Cairill,' *Éigse* 20 (1984), 93–105 at 101 n. 47.

[4] Heaney, 'The God in the Tree,' 187.

at the beginning and the end of the narrative, may be a later addition.[1] James Carney suggested, pointing to British analogues of the Sweeney story, that 'in the tale of Suibhne as originally told the din of battle, the carnage, and a vision in the sky were alone the causes of his madness, and not the curse of a saint.'[2] There may be some evidence for this in the existing text, because the occasion of Sweeney's madness is indeed a moment in battle, when he looks up at the sky in response to the echoing sounds of the battle cries. In Heaney's translation:

> When Sweeney heard these howls and echoes assumed into the travelling clouds and amplified through the vaults of space, he looked up and he was possessed by a dark rending energy. (p. 9)

It is at this point that Sweeney loses his mind, flees the battlefield 'ar gealtacht agus ar geinidecht' (p. 14) – 'in madness and imbecility' as O'Keeffe puts it (p. 15) – and Ronan's curse is fulfilled.

As well as evidence within the text for the sound of battle as a possible cause of Sweeney's affliction, there is also evidence elsewhere for the possibility of terror in battle as a cause of *geltacht*. P. L. Henry quotes the following passage from the Norse account of Irish mirabilia in the *Speculum Regale*, which suggests that the madness of the *geilt* is caused by fear in battle:

> There is also one thing, which will seem very wonderful, about men who are called *gelt*. It happens that when two hosts meet and are arranged in battle-array, and when the battle-cry is raised loudly on both sides, that cowardly men run wild, and lose their wits from the dread and fear which seize them. And then they run into a wood away from other men, and live there like beasts, and shun the meeting of men like wild beasts. And it is said of these men that when they have lived in the woods in that condition for twenty years, then feathers grow on their bodies as on birds, whereby their bodies are protected against frost or cold; but the feathers are not so large that they may fly like birds. Yet their swiftness is said to be so great that other men cannot approach them. [...] For these people run along the trees almost as swiftly as monkeys or squirrels.[3]

Pádraig Ó Riain argues, however, that the battle-terror and priestly curse

---

[1] O'Keeffe, *Buile Suibhne*, p. xxxiv; James Carney, '"Suibhne Geilt" and "The Children of Lir",' *Éigse* 6 (1950), 83–110 at 90–94.

[2] Carney, '"Suibhne Geilt" and "The Children of Lir",' 90.

[3] Henry, *The Early English and Celtic Lyric*, 200–201; Hart, *Seamus Heaney: Poet of Contrary Progressions*, 146, also quotes this passage.

are not mutually exclusive options as causes of the madness of the *geilt*. He suggests that terrifying roars or visions in the sky during battle debilitating to the opposition can be associated with a priestly figure, and cites as an example the following story from *Foras Droma Damgaire*, which links these things, albeit in a pagan context:

> 'I came,' said he [Gadra the druid], 'to cause terror and fear to the hosts and to produce the strength of a woman in labour in each man at the hour of battle and combat.' And he proceeded in that guise to Druim Damgaire, and made a circuit of the hill three times, emitting three deafening roars, and he showed himself to them in that manner so that terror and fear gripped all of them, and he relieved each of them of half of his vigour and all of his activeness.[1]

The priestly curse and terror in battle, then, are not necessarily separate motifs: they may be related.

The tension that Heaney describes, however, 'between the newly domi-nant Christian ethos and the older, recalcitrant Celtic temperament,' is present in the text insofar as Sweeney, as *geilt*, is a figure with similar sacral powers to the saintly Christian figures of Ronan and Moling: the text sug-gests a shamanic aspect to his madness. As J. F. Nagy argues, after going mad Sweeney becomes a poet, a figure who possesses special supernatural knowledge and inspiration.[2] The Irish word *fili*, 'poet,' etymologically means 'seer,' as does the alternative term *éices*; the *bard* was a less honoured type of poet.[3] There is, then, a productive side to Sweeney's *geltacht*, and it may be in this sense that Sweeney is a holy madman, a *náoimhgheilt*. The su-pernatural knowledge possessed by Sweeney is clearest at the point in the narrative where he first meets Moling, and the two recognize each other's abilities.[4] In the original text, this exchange goes:

> *Moling:*   Mochthráth sin, a ghealtagáin,
>   re ceileabhradh cóir.

---

[1] Pádraig Ó Riain, 'A Study of the Irish Legend of the Wild Man,' *Éigse* 14 (1972), 179–206 at 190.

[2] J. F. Nagy, 'The Wisdom of the Geilt,' *Éigse* 19 (1982), 44–60 at 45; cf. Kathleen McCracken, 'Madness or Inspiration? The Poet and Poetry in Seamus Heaney's *Sweeney Astray*,' *Notes on Modern Irish Literature* 2 (1990), 42–51.

[3] Gerard Murphy, *Early Irish Metrics* (Dublin: Royal Irish Academy, 1961), 26; cf. *DIL* s.v. *fili*, which defines the word as 'orig. *seer, diviner* [...] and in earlier documents gener-ally implies occult powers or knowledge' as well as '*Poet (historian, panegyrist, satirist), man of learning*'; likewise s.v. *éices*, where 'the original meaning is probably *seer*,' but 'it is com-monest in the general sense of *scholar, learned man, sage, poet*'; in constrast, s.v. *bard*, '*poet or rhymester* inferior in qualifications and status to the "fili".'

[4] Nagy, 'The Wisdom of the Geilt,' 45.

> *Suibhne:* Gidh moch leat-sa, a chlérecháin,
> tanic tert ag Róimh.
>
> *Moling:* Ga fios duit-si, a ghealtagáin,
> cuin tig tert ag Róimh?
> *Suibhne:* Fios tig dhamh om Thigerna
> gach madain 's gach nóin.
>
> *Moling:* Innis tre rún ráitsighe
> sgela Fíadhat finn.
> *Suibhne:* Agut-sa ata an fháitsine
> masa thú Moling. (pp. 136, 138)

Heaney translates:

> *Moling:* So, you would steal a march on us,
> up and breakfasting so early!
> *Sweeney:* Not so very early, priest.
> Terce has come in Rome already.
>
> *Moling:* And what knowledge has a fool
> about the hour of terce in Rome?
> *Sweeney:* The Lord makes me His oracle
> from sunrise till sun's going down.
>
> *Moling:* Then speak to us of hidden things,
> give us tidings of the Lord.
> *Sweeney:* Not I. But if you are Moling,
> you are gifted with the Word. (pp. 76–77)

The conversation concludes with each of the pair revealing that they are aware of Sweeney's eventual fate. The original reads:

> *Moling:* Cáit i ttig do shaogal-sa,
> in a ccill no i loch?
> *Suibhne:* Aeghaire dot aeghairibh
> nommharbhann go moch.' Muchthrath.
> 'As mochen éimh do thecht sonn, a Shuibhne,' ar Moling, 'ar atá
> a ndán duit bheith annso agus do sháogal do thecht ann [...].' (pp.
> 140, 142)

Heaney translates,

> *Moling:* When your end comes, will it be
> death by water, in holy ground?
> *Sweeney:* It will be early when I die.
> One of your herds will make the wound.

— You are more than welcome here, Sweeney, said Moling, for you are fated to live and die here. (p. 79)

This exchange parallels the incident earlier in the narrative where Sweeney and the madman that he meets in Britain each predict their own fates (p. 58), and echoes Sweeney's earlier foreshadowing of his death at Teach Moling (p. 45). Sweeney's inspiration to poetry includes supernatural knowledge as well as versecraft.

Again, this is something deeply rooted in the language of the original text. Ciaran Carson notes the occurrence of the word *beann* and related forms a total of 43 times through the 65 quatrains of section 40.[1] Citing Dinneen's dictionary definition of *beann* as (among other things) 'a point, a peak; a crest, a spire; a wing, a branch; a prong; a horn,'[2] Carson points out that the text plays on all of these meanings, highlighting Sweeney's obsession with mountain-tops, antlers, the tops of trees, spear-points. The text plays on *da mbeinn*, 'if I were' (from the verb *bí*, 'to be') and *beann*, 'point,' and at one point Sweeney describes himself as *fer benn*, 'man of the points' or 'man of the peaks,' and by implication, as Carson puts it, 'man of being.' His very existence is tied up in the two spear-points that mark the tale's origin and conclusion: as Sweeney's original transgression is caused by a spear, so too he will die by a spear.[3] The original reads:

> As mé Suibhni sirtheachán,
> luath reithim tar glenn,
> nocha n-é mh'ainm dlightheachán,
> mó is ainm damh fer benn. (p. 80)

O'Keeffe translates as follows, leaving *fer benn* untranslated, and glossing the phrase as 'man of the peaks':

> I am Suibhne, a poor suppliant,
> swiftly do I race across the glen;
> that is not my lawful name,
> rather it is Fer benn. (p. 81)

Although not a literal rendering of the lines, the emphasis on *beann* endures

---

[1] Carson, '*Sweeney Astray*: Escaping from Limbo,' 143. O'Keeffe, *Buile Suibhne*, 169 n., comments: 'Note the constant use of *benn* in most of the stanzas that follow; there is evidently a play intended on the word. I find it difficult to grasp the significance of many of the stanzas between p. 74 and p. 80; no doubt some curious folk-lore is embedded in them.'

[2] *Foclóir Gaedhilge agus Béarla: An Irish–English Dictionary*, ed Patrick S. Dinneen (Dublin: Irish Texts Society, 1927), s.v. *beann*.

[3] Carson, '*Sweeney Astray*: Escaping from Limbo,' 143.

in Heaney's version, which picks up on the mountain-peak and stag-head imagery from the surrounding stanzas:

> I am Sweeney, the whinger,
> the scuttler in the valley.
> But call me, instead,
> Peak-pate, Stag-head (p. 45).

If all of these pointed references in Sweeney's verse are a foretelling of Sweeney's end, they constitute an example of his supernatural foreknowledge woven into the poetry. Further to that, it's perhaps worth noting that one of the divination rituals mentioned in the early Irish *Sanas Cormac* is called *díchetal di chennaib*, 'incantation from the tips.'[1]

The figure of the *geilt*, then, is both outcast and inspired, displaced from both his reason and his home, but inspired to poetic knowledge. The English word 'guilt' may itself derive from the possible penitential implications of the Irish notion of *geilt*, present in the parallels with the Nebuchadnezzar story. In Heaney's description of Suibhne, then, as 'displaced, guilty, assuaging himself by his utterance,' all of these terms relate to the *geilt* — outcast and culpable, but inspired to (and perhaps consoled by) poetry. As Henry Hart puts it, '*geilt* encapsulates most of *Buile Suibhne* in one syllable.'[2]

Dinnseanchas

As Ciaran Carson says, *Sweeney Astray* is 'at times, a catalogue of place names recited with loving care, all the more so because Sweeney is homeless,'[3] and in his introduction to the translation, Heaney identifies his fundamental relation with Sweeney as topographical:

> His kingdom lay in what is now south County Antrim and north County Down, and for over thirty years I lived on the verges of that territory, in sight of some of Sweeney's places and in earshot of others — Slemish, Rasharkin, Benevenagh, Dunseverick, the Bann, the Roe, the Mournes. (p. vii).

Following Heaney's move to Wicklow, where he began work on the translation, he was living not far from Sweeney's eventual resting place (p. viii). It is not surprising, then, to find that some of the place names in *Sweeney*

---

[1] McCracken, 'Madness or Inspiration?' 43.
[2] Hart, *Seamus Heaney: Poet of Contrary Progressions*, 146.
[3] Carson, '*Sweeney Astray*: Escaping from Limbo,' 142.

Astray appear elsewhere in Heaney's work, several in 'The Sense of Place,' an essay on the relationship of poetry and place. As Heaney says at the beginning of that essay,

> In Irish poetry there is a whole genre of writing called *dinnseanchas*, poems and tales which relate the original meanings of place names and constitute a form of mythological etymology. An early epic like the *Tain Bo Cuailgne* is full of incidental *dinnseanchas*, insofar as it connects various incidents on the journey of the Connacht armies from Cruachan to Carlingford with the names of places as we now know them, or at least as they were known in the Gaelic past.[1]

Cuailgne – Cooley in Co. Louth – is itself mentioned three times in *Buile Suibhne*, and twice in Heaney's translation, as in this example:

> Ata crioth ar mo lámha
> tar gach mbioth fatha mbúaidre,
> do Shlíabh Mis ar Sliabh Cuillenn,
> do Shléibh Cuillenn co Cuailgne. (p. 30)

In Heaney's version, this is

> and the pain of frostbite
> has put me astray,
> from Slemish to Slieve Gullion,
> from Slieve Gullion to Cooley. (p. 18)

As Heaney makes clear in 'The Sense of Place,' some of the Irish landscape continues to have cultural associations, both ancient and modern: Slemish, mentioned here, which on a clear day was visible in the distance as part of Heaney's childhood landscape, continues to have cultural associations as the mountain on which the young Saint Patrick tended sheep.[2] Another mountain mentioned in the text, Ben Bulben (p. 40), has associations with the poetry of Yeats.[3]

Much, however, has been lost, for contemporary Irish culture is at some remove from a culture that connected the landscape and mythology through naming: Heaney cites John Montague as saying that 'the whole of the Irish landscape [...] is a manuscript which we have lost the skill to

---

[1] Seamus Heaney, 'The Sense of Place,' in Heaney, *Preoccupations: Selected Prose, 1968–1978* (London: Faber, 1980), 131–49 at 131.

[2] Heaney, 'The Sense of Place,' 133.

[3] Heaney, 'The Sense of Place,' 132; Heaney cites the late-medieval 'Oisin's praise of Ben Bulben' in 'The God in the Tree,' 184–85; for Yeats's 'Under Ben Bulben,' see W. B. Yeats, *The Poems*, ed. Daniel Albright (London: Dent, 1994), 373–76.

read.'[1] The loss of that sense of a landscape embodying cultural memory is
the focus of Brian Friel's play, *Translations*, where the nineteenth-century
mapping of the Irish landscape, and the translation of place names into anglicized equivalents, involves an emptying out of the memories embodied
in the names being translated.[2] Slemish is a useful example, for in addition
to its enduring association with Saint Patrick, in its Gaelic form it is *Sliabh
Mis*, the mountain of Mis, a mythological figure who resembles Sweeney.
In the surviving version of her story, Mis goes mad when she sees her father's death at the Battle of Ventry, drinking his blood and fleeing to the
mountains, where she grows hairy and lives like an animal. She is found
on Sliabh Mis by Dub Ruis, the harper to king Feidlimid mac Criuthainn,
who tames her by evoking memories of her father's court and then with
her first experience of sex. This is followed by music, cooked food, and
a bath; the now tamed figure of Mis loses her fur, and returns to civilisa-
tion with Dub Ruis, whom she then marries.[3] Austin Clarke's poem 'The
Healing of Mis,' from the 1970 collection *Orphide and other Poems*, describes
her as a *geilt*, and emphasises the comparison with Sweeney by juxtaposing 'The Healing of Mis' with his version of Sweeney's praise of the trees
in 'The Trees of the Forest.'[4] But although the story survives, Slemish no
longer carries an automatic association in the popular imagination with the
myth of Mis, as it might have for the original audience of *Buile Suibhne*.

In translating *Sweeney Astray*, Heaney translates some (but not all) place
names into their contemporary equivalents. In some cases, then, the lists
of place names can be familiar. Where the original reads:

> Robáoi-siomh i Ros Chomáin an oidhche sin, luid aissein arnamhá-
> rach co Slíabh n-uráoibhinn nEachtghe, aissein co Slíabh mínaluinn
> Mis, aissein co Slíabh bennard Bladhma, aissein co hInis Muread-
> haigh; [...]. (p. 90)

Heaney translates:

> He stayed in Roscommon that night and the next day he went on to
> Slieve Aughty, from there to the pleasant slopes of Slemish, then on

---

[1] Heaney, 'The Sense of Place,' 132; Montague's lines are in John Montague, *The
Rough Field, 1961–1971*, 5th edition (Newcastle-upon-Tyne: Bloodaxe, 1990), 35; cf. Mon-
tague, 'A Primal Gaeltacht,' in Montague, *The Figure in the Cave and Other Essays*, ed.
Antoinette Quinn (Syracuse, NY: Syracuse University Press, 1989), 42–45.

[2] Brian Friel, *Translations*, in Friel, *Plays: One* (London: Faber, 1996), 377–451.

[3] The summary here draws on that of Lisa M. Bitel, *Land of Women: Tales of Sex and
Gender from Early Ireland* (Ithaca and London: Cornell University Press, 1996), 211; the
Irish text is edited by Brian Ó Cúiv, 'The Romance of Mis and Dubh Ruis,' *Celtica* 2/2
(1954), 325–33.

[4] Clarke, *Collected Poems*, 507–16.

to the high peaks of Slieve Bloom, and from there to Inishmurray.
(p. 50)

The effect is to give the contemporary reader a foothold in the landscape of
the narrative, a sense of direction for Sweeney's peregrinations. Occasionally, directions are a little more thorough than in the original – 'St Der-
ville's Church, west of Erris' (p. 20) adds into the text some topographical
information ('west of Erris') not in the original but contained in a footnote
provided by O'Keeffe (p. 166, n. to p. 35). Not all of the places listed in the
original are identifiable, however, and while Heaney coins anglicizations
for some (a process he alerts us to in the notes preceding the text), he leaves
others broadly unchanged. 'Cill Ríagan i tTir Chonuill' (p. 16), then, is
standardized somewhat to read 'Kilreagan in Tyrconnell' (p. 10), but is not
modernized to read 'Kilrean in Donegal,' as O'Keeffe notes it might be,
while doubting the distance involved (p. 162, n. to p. 17). In one case, we
have 'Ros Beraigh i nGlenn Earcáin' (p. 14) translated as 'Ros Bearaigh in
Glen Arkin' (p. 9) – the second name is anglicized and modernized, but the
first is not. The effect is to render the landscape of the text one that is half
familiar and half mysterious, a reminder of the connections between the
there-and-then and the here-and-now.[1]

If much of the landscape of the text is home turf for Heaney, then,
the translation finds him in a similar situation to Sweeney – the exiled
poet reciting the names of familiar places. As well as having an obvious
autobiographical appeal to Heaney, recently exiled to the south when he
begins the translation in 1972, the relationship between place and identity
is a broad theme in Heaney's work.[2] Many Heaney poems are concerned
with his childhood home, his place of origin – as he puts it in the essay
'Mossbawn,' the *omphalos*, 'meaning the navel, and hence the stone that
marked the centre of the world.'[3] Heaney's sense of home, though, is always problematic. Writing of his childhood home, he says, 'if this was the
country of community, it was also the realm of division,'[4] and if there is
a desire for home in his work, it derives in part from a feeling of alienation.

---

[1] Cf. Robert Brazeau, 'Thomas Kinsella and Seamus Heaney: Translation and Representation,' *New Hibernia Review / Iris Éireannach Nua* 5/2 (Summer/Samhraidh 2001),
82–98, who argues that Heaney's translations of place and character names see the translation escape 'into a realm of aesthetic transcendence from one of historical specificity
and cultural difference' (p. 92). Brazeau does not mention that some place names are
untranslated.

[2] For a survey of critical positions on these themes, see the chapter on 'Place, Identity,
Language', in *The Poetry of Seamus Heaney*, ed. Elmer Andrews (Cambridge: Icon, 1998),
40–79.

[3] Seamus Heaney, 'Mossbawn,' in *Preoccupations*, 17–27 at 17.

[4] Heaney, 'Mossbawn,' 20.

Henry Hart cites a 1987 interview in *The Boston Phoenix* where Heaney says he feels exiled wherever he goes, whether it is Belfast, Wicklow, or Boston. His second-class status as a Catholic in Ulster only intensified his awareness of exile on friendlier turf later on. Hart quotes Heaney as saying 'I never had a feeling of comfortable consonance between myself and a place. The travel reinforces a condition that would be there anyway.'[1] While this emphasises Heaney's situation as a member of the North's nationalist minority, Heaney sees this tension between notions of being simultaneously in place and displaced as common to both communities in Ulster:

> Each person in Ulster lives first in the Ulster of the actual present, and then in one or other Ulster of the mind. [...] The fountainhead of the unionist's myth springs in the Crown of England, but he must stand his ground on the island of Ireland. The fountainhead of the nationalist's myth lies in the idea of an integral Ireland, but he too lives in exile from his ideal place.[2]

This sense of place and displacement, then, is common to everyone in Ulster, irrespective of political or cultural alignment. When Heaney writes, in the famous lines at the end of 'The Tollund Man':

> Out there in Jutland
> In the old man-killing parishes
> I will feel lost,
> Unhappy, and at home.[3]

there is the suggestion that the feeling of being at home and the feeling of being lost are unhappily similar. Richard Kearney suggests that in this respect Heaney's work can be aligned with the thinking of Heidegger and Freud, in that his poetry sets up a dialectic of home and homelessness.[4] In reading Heaney this way, Kearney argued that he hoped to 'scotch the stereotype of Heaney as some latter-day piers ploughman from county Derry staving off the plague of modernity and guiding us back to a prelapsarian pastureland.'[5] Such readings persist: a decade later, Antony

---

[1] Hart, *Seamus Heaney: Poet of Contrary Progressions*, 141.

[2] Seamus Heaney, 'Place and Displacement: Recent Poetry from Northern Ireland,' in *Finders Keepers*, 112–33 at 115–16.

[3] Heaney, *Wintering Out*, 48; Heaney, *Opened Ground*, 65.

[4] Richard Kearney, *Transitions: Narratives in Modern Irish Culture* (Dublin: Wolfhound, 1988), 113–22; for a critique of Kearney's reading of Heaney here, cf. Edna Longley, *The Living Stream: Literature and Revisionism in Ireland* (Newcastle upon Tyne: Bloodaxe, 1994), 237.

[5] Kearney, *Transitions*, 113.

Easthope is criticizing Heaney by suggesting that 'again and again his political gestures, calling up ancient wrong, unconscious tradition and the living past, have invoked that old fantasy about premodernity, the organic community.'[1] In fact, Heaney's work, while expressing a desire for home, holds that desire in tension with a recognition that 'at-homeness' is already pre-problematized. In this, the figure of Sweeney, the homesick exile, expresses something far deeper than circumstance for a Northern poet gone south.

The *dinnseanchas* tradition also has a political dimension – as Ciaran Carson says, 'it existed to give historical legitimacy to territorial claims,'[2] and Heaney indicates in his essay 'Earning a Rhyme' that part of his purpose in translating *Buile Suibhne* was to indicate a cultural claim upon the territory of Ulster:

> My hope was that the book might render a unionist audience more pervious to the notion that Ulster was Irish, without coercing them out of their cherished conviction that it was British. Also, because it reached back into a pre-colonial Ulster of monastic Christianity and Celtic kingship, I hoped the book might complicate that sense of entitlement to the land of Ulster which had developed so overbearingly in the Protestant majority as a result of various victories and acts of settlement over the centuries. By extending the span of their historical memory into pre-British time, we might stimulate some sympathy in the unionists for the nationalist minority who located their lost title to sovereignty in that Gaelic dream-place.[3]

Heaney's staking of a cultural claim isn't an exclusive one – what he seeks to do here is to complicate an existing sense of entitlement, to unsettle the exclusivity of British claims to Ulster, rather than to pose another, opposing but equally blinkered view – he makes clear in 'Earning a Rhyme' that he was in search of a means of discussing the issues that lay behind the Troubles without 'yet another repetition of the aggressions and resentments which had been responsible for the quarrel in the first place.'[4] John Kerrigan's suggestion that Heaney's translation of *Buile Suibhne* is 'a national epic to follow his bucolics and poems of digging and ploughing, from *Death of a Naturalist* to *Wintering Out*, rather as the *Aeneid* was

[1] Antony Easthope, 'How Good is Seamus Heaney?' *English* 46 (1997), 21–36 at 30.
[2] Carson, '*Sweeney Astray*: Escaping from Limbo,' 142.
[3] Heaney, 'Earning a Rhyme,' 61.
[4] Heaney, 'Earning a Rhyme,' 60.

preceded by the *Eclogues* and *Georgics*'[1] creates a brilliant analogy between Heaney's career and Virgil's, but it is difficult to accept *Sweeney Astray* as being in any straightforward sense a 'national epic.' Heaney is in no position to produce a 'national' epic at a time when competing nationalisms in Ulster had resulted in a seemingly unresolvable political crisis.[2] Furthermore, his choice of a text to translate is deliberately unheroic. Thomas Kinsella described the *Táin*, which he translated in the late 1960s, as 'the nearest approach to a great epic that Ireland has produced,'[3] but *Buile Suibhne* is not the *Táin*. In the end, it would be Marie Heaney, not Seamus, who would produce versions of the heroic tales of medieval Irish literature.[4]

The *dinnseanchas* tradition is visible elsewhere in Heaney's poetry, not least in the etymological place-name poems such as 'Anahorish,' 'Toome,' and 'Broagh' from *Wintering Out*, and again, what Heaney seems to be doing in these poems is seeking to draw attention to the origins of these place-names in a pre-British Ulster. As he says in the essay 'Belfast,' Broagh and Anahorish are 'forgotten Gaelic music in the throat, *bruach* and *anach fhíor uisce*, the riverbank and the place of clear water,' reminders of a Gaelic culture whose downfall came with plantation.[5] These poems, too, make a claim for possession – 'Anahorish' opens with the narrator's claim for 'My "place of clear water."'[6] In 'The Toome Road' from *Field Work*, which follows on from the place-name poem 'Toome' in *Wintering Out*, the narrator asks of the soldiers on the road: 'How long were they approaching down my roads / As if they owned them?'[7] Again, though, the claims made are not exclusive. In 'Belfast,' Heaney etymologizes the name of the farm he grew up on, 'Mossbawn,' as meaning the planters' house on the bog, from Scots *moss* and *bawn*, the name that English colonists gave to their fortified farmhouses. 'In the syllables of my home,' he writes, 'I see a metaphor of the split culture of Ulster.'[8] The essay ends by suggesting Irish as vowels and English as consonants, but implicit in this is an awareness that both

---

[1] John Kerrigan, 'Ulster Ovids,' in *The Chosen Ground: Essays on the Contemporary Poetry of Northern Ireland*, ed. Neil Corcoran (Bridgend: Seren, 1992), 237–69 at 243.

[2] On the Ulster conflict as the result of competing nationalisms, Irish and British, see Richard Kearney, *Postnationalist Ireland: Politics, Culture, Philosophy* (London and New York: Routledge, 1997), 9–11.

[3] *The Tain, translated from the Irish epic Tain Bo Cuailgne*, trans. Thomas Kinsella (Dublin: Dolmen, 1969; repr. Oxford: Oxford University Press, 1970), p. vii.

[4] Marie Heaney, *Over Nine Waves* (London: Faber, 1994).

[5] Seamus Heaney, 'Belfast,' in *Preoccupations*, 28–37 at 36.

[6] Heaney, *Wintering Out*, 16; Heaney, *Opened Ground*, 46.

[7] Heaney, *Field Work*, 15; Heaney, *Opened Ground*, 150.

[8] Heaney, 'Belfast,' 35; cf. Seamus Heaney, 'Belderg,' in *North*, 14. In the introduction to his *Beowulf* translation, Heaney again discusses the word *bawn*, which he now

will be required for articulation, and the essay's last line expresses a hope that the poems will be 'vocables adequate to my whole experience' – with an emphasis here on 'whole,' that is, encompassing both the Irish and British sides of Ulster's cultural inheritance.[1] If 'Broagh,' one of the *dinnseanchas* poems of *Wintering Out*, ends with a mention of 'that last / *gh* the strangers found / difficult to manage,'[2] strangers here are people who are not local, for people in South Derry, whether Protestant or Catholic, find saying 'Broagh' straightforward.[3] And if 'Broagh' is a poem that points to the Gaelic underpinning of an Ulster place name, it also incorporates English and Scots dialect terms. As Neil Corcoran points out, the words *rigs*, *docken*, and *pad*, used in the poem, are English or Scottish dialect terms (for 'furrows,' 'dock-leaves,' and 'path'). Another word used in the poem, *boor-trees*, is the old Scots plural for the elderberry, which, as Corcoran again observes, reappears in the fifth of the 'Glanmore sonnets' in *Field Work*, where Heaney constructs the poem from the tree's two names.[4] If these *dinnseanchas* poems stake a cultural claim on Ulster place names, then, they do so in a way that nonetheless acknowledges the blending of cultures in contemporary Ulster.

British influences

The same might be said of *Sweeney Astray*. If Heaney's translation of *Buile Suibhne* is a reminder of the existence of a pre-British Ulster, it is nonetheless a translation that includes points of comparison and influence from England, Scotland, and Wales. There are three explicit ways in which this occurs, highlighted in Heaney's introduction to the translation. First, the introduction points to the fact that *Buile Suibhne*'s topography includes both western Scotland and southern Ireland, suggesting that this 'easy sense of cultural affinity' with both places is 'exemplary for all men and women in contemporary Ulster' (p. vi). Secondly, it points to sections of the work that deal with a British madman, Alan, as possible evidence that the medieval Irish narrative may have derived from a British original. Thirdly, it draws comparisons between *Buile Suibhne* and two canonical

---

notes to be an Elizabethan English word derived from the Irish *bó-dhún*, 'a fort for cattle' (p. xxx).

[1] Heaney, 'Belfast,' 37.

[2] Heaney, *Wintering Out*, 27; Heaney, *Opened Ground*, 54.

[3] O'Donoghue, *Seamus Heaney and the Language of Poetry*, 65, cites Heaney as making this specific point, as does Corcoran, *Poetry of Seamus Heaney*, 47.

[4] Heaney, *Field Work*, 37; Heaney, *Opened Ground*, 167; Corcoran, *Poetry of Seamus Heaney*, 46–47.

works of English literature: *King Lear* and the Anglo-Saxon poem *The Seafarer* (p. vi). In addition to these three explicitly highlighted British influences on either the original Irish text or Heaney's translation of it, there are two others potentially at work here. First, while the language of Heaney's translation contains echoes of Irish in its language and verse, it also deviates from standard English in its use of Scots dialect terms, and, in a prominent example, a dialect term indebted to Old English. And secondly, there are possible influences from Heaney's English contemporaries such as Ted Hughes and Geoffrey Hill on Heaney's decision to translate a medieval Irish work.

Heaney's observation that *Sweeney Astray*'s topography covers both southern Ireland and western Scotland, and the suggestion that this is exemplary for everyone in contemporary Ulster, acknowledges the validity of the affinities proclaimed by each community in contemporary Ulster. In particular, although Heaney has himself moved south and holds a passport from the Republic of Ireland,[1] he can nonetheless point out that here relations exist between the north of Ireland and the west of Scotland that long predate the seventeenth-century plantation of Ulster. Western Scotland was from around 500 the kingdom of Dalriada, whose people migrated from Antrim.[2] Nor did the movement of people between Ireland and Scotland end with the large-scale plantation of Ulster from Scotland in the seventeenth century: in the nineteenth century, Scotland saw large-scale immigration from both Protestant and Catholic communities in Ireland. The Census of Glasgow in 1831 found that of a total population of 202,426 in the city, there were 35,554 Irish, of which 19,333 were Catholic.[3] One of the prominent Scottish place names in *Sweeney Astray* is that of Ailsa Craig in the Firth of Clyde (*Carraic Alustair* in the original text), where Sweeney spends six weeks (p. 50) before completing his journey over the sea to Britain (p. 55). From the late nineteenth century, Ailsa Craig was colloquially known as 'Paddy's milestone,' given its position as a conspicuous landmark for Irish immigrants sailing to Scotland.[4]

The argument that the basic story of *Buile Suibhne* may be British in origin is a long-standing one. James Carney argued in 1950 that Suibhne was identical to his British equivalent, the figure of Myrddin, Lailoken, or Merlin, and that the Suibhne story passed to Ireland from the British king-

---

[1] As he tells us in 'An Open Letter,' published as a pamphlet in 1983, the same year as *Sweeney Astray,* and reprinted as Seamus Heaney, 'An Open Letter,' in *Ireland's Field Day* (London: Hutchinson, 1985), 23–30 at 25.

[2] Michael Lynch, *Scotland: A New History* (London: Century, 1991), 17–19.

[3] Lynch, *Scotland: A New History*, 395.

[4] *The Concise Scots Dictionary*, ed. Mairi Robinson (Aberdeen: Aberdeen University Press, 1985), s.v. *Paddy*.

dom of Strathclyde around the eighth century.[1] As part of his argument, Carney makes the point that Heaney repeats in his introduction: that there is an episode in the later part of the text where Suibhne, having travelled to Britain, comes across a British madman called *Fear Caille*, 'Man of the Wood,' or *Alladhán* (pp. 100, 102), which Heaney anglicizes as 'Alan' (p. 57), and that this British equivalent of Sweeney in the tale may be a reminder of the tale's origins.[2] Carney's argument for the story's British origins has been questioned,[3] but there is general agreement about the resemblance between Sweeney and Merlin, if not the direction of influence.

In addition to these gestures towards topographical and philological links with Britain in the medieval Irish text, the third element in Heaney's introduction that explicitly draws attention to British affinities in the medieval Irish text is the citation of both *King Lear* and the Anglo-Saxon poem *The Seafarer* as points of comparison for *Buile Suibhne*'s poetry of exposure to the natural world. There is much in the text of *Buile Suibhne* about the hardness of winter weather, and the sparseness of Heaney's translation (set against the lushness of Flann O'Brien's) seems to reflect this: in 'Earning a Rhyme,' Heaney says that in his second attempt at the translation, he decided that the stanzas should have 'the definition of hedges in a winter sunset,'[4] and Sweeney himself resembles something similar, as he is 'wind-scourged, stripped / like a winter tree / clad in black frost / and frozen snow' (p. 17). Indeed, this is a noticeably wintry translation, which echoes Heaney's other poetry in its description of Sweeney as 'wintering out among wolf-packs' (p. 23), recalling the phrase in 'Servant Boy' that gives *Wintering Out* its title: 'He is wintering out / the back-end of a bad year,'[5] which is itself in part an echo of the reference in the opening line of Shakespeare's *Richard III* to the 'winter of our discontent.'[6]

Like *Buile Suibhne*, both *Lear* and *The Seafarer* feature exposure to hard weather. Commenting on the first 33-line segment of *The Seafarer*, Peter Orton comments that 'the speaker was hungry, lonely, exhausted, but above all cold; the word *cald* (*ceald*) is used five times in simple or compound forms in these early lines, and there are repeated references to frost, ice and hail, with snow and icicles each putting in a single appearance.'[7]

---

[1] Carney, '"Suibhne Geilt" and "The Children of Lir",' 83.

[2] Carney, '"Suibhne Geilt" and "The Children of Lir",' 101.

[3] Kenneth Jackson, 'A Further Note on Suibhne Geilt and Merlin,' *Éigse* 7 (1953), 112–16.

[4] Heaney, 'Earning a Rhyme,' 63.

[5] Heaney, *Wintering Out*, 17; Heaney, *Opened Ground*, 47.

[6] Corcoran, *Poetry of Seamus Heaney*, 28.

[7] Peter Orton, 'The Form and Structure of *The Seafarer*,' in *Old English Literature: Critical Essays*, ed. R. M. Liuzza (New Haven and London: Yale University Press, 2002),

Buile Suibhne, likewise, is filled with descriptions of hard weather, contrasted with the comforts of life lived indoors. There is no suggestion of influence between the two works, although interpretations of *The Seafarer* as an account of exile with a spiritual purpose have argued that the Irish Church was responsible for transmitting the notion of exile for spiritual benefit to the Anglo-Saxons.[1] In inviting us to draw parallels based on the similar circumstances of hardship faced by Sweeney and the anonymous narrator of *The Seafarer*, Heaney invites sympathy for each, and resists a hard-and-fast division between Irish and English literatures.

Heaney likewise suggests that Poor Tom in *King Lear* provides an interesting parallel to Sweeney's condition. Shakespeare's play provides foul weather in the shape of the storm to which the characters are exposed in Act III, and when Poor Tom appears, his refrain is 'Tom's a-cold.' Lear himself is a king outcast and exposed, and when he sees Tom, he immediately identifies with him, asking 'Didst thou give all to thy two daughters? And art thou come to this?' (III. iv. 47).[2] If Edgar, in disguise as Poor Tom, is a possible parallel for Sweeney, then so too is Lear, and arguments have previously been made for Shakespeare's indebtedness to the 'wild man' theme for his portrayal of the king's madness: a 1946 article compares passages from *Lear* with *Buile Suibhne* and Geoffrey of Monmouth's *Vita Merlini*.[3]

If Heaney is explicit in outlining British influences or parallels with *Sweeney Astray* by noting the work's topographical reach and the possibility of a British original underlying the medieval Irish text, and by drawing parallels with both *The Seafarer* and *King Lear*, there are two other ways in which his translation points away from an exclusivity of emphasis upon medieval Ireland. The first is through the language of the translation. The Scots dialect term *pads*, 'paths,' which as we saw earlier is included in the place-name poem 'Broagh' as a gesture towards the multiple sources of the contemporary language of Ulster, reappears here (p. 17). Likewise, the word *thole*, derived from the Old English *þolian*, 'endure, suffer, hold out,' makes an appearance in the translation (p. 68); it reappears later in

353–380 at 356, first published in *Studia Neophilologica* 33 (1991), 37–55; for text and translation of *The Seafarer*, see *A Choice of Anglo-Saxon Verse*, ed. and trans. Richard Hamer (London: Faber, 1970), 186–95.

[1] Peter Orton, 'To be a Pilgrim: The Old English *Seafarer* and its Irish Affinities,' in *Lexis and Texts in Early English: Studies presented to Jane Roberts*, ed. Christian J. Kay and Louise M. Sylvester (Amsterdam and Atlanta: Rodopi, 2001), 213–23.

[2] Reference is to the Arden edition: *King Lear*, ed. R. A. Foakes (Surrey: Nelson, 1997).

[3] Roland M. Smith, 'King Lear and the Merlin Tradition,' *Modern Language Quarterly* 7 (1946), 153–74; Merlin gets a single mention in *Lear* at III. ii. 95.

Heaney's translation of a portion of Brian Merriman's eighteenth-century Irish poem *Cúirt an Mheán Oíche*.[1] Heaney will discuss the word at length in the introduction to his later translation of *Beowulf*, where he indicates that the word was a point of contact between Ulster vocabulary and Old English poetry that gave him a point of access to the language of the Old English poem (pp. xxv–xxvi). Here, many years earlier, the presence of a dialect word from Old English in a translation of a medieval Irish text stands as a sign that Heaney's commitment to linguistic pluralism began long before his insertion of Irish dialect terms into his translation from Old English.

A final British influence upon the translation may be the works of two English poets, Ted Hughes and Geoffrey Hill, each of whom produced collections influenced by medieval literature that precede Heaney's and might be seen as precedents for *Sweeney Astray* (the same might be said of Thomas Kinsella's translation of the medieval Irish epic the *Táin*).[2] It's particularly possible that Heaney has Hughes's *Wodwo* in mind, since aside from Heaney's general debt to Hughes, it's notable that Sweeney *is* a *wodwo*, a wild man of the woods. In his essay 'Englands of the Mind,' Heaney links Hughes to the Middle English alliterative tradition, indebted to Anglo-Saxon, and suggests the closeness of Hughes's work to that of the poet of the fourteenth-century English poem *Sir Gawain and the Green Knight*.[3] If Heaney has Hughes's *Wodwo* in mind, he may also recollect, at one remove, the *Gawain*-poet's description of Gawain's struggles against various opponents (including *wodwos*) in the winter wilderness:

> Sumwhyle wyth wormes he werres, and with wolves als,
> Sumwhyle wyth wodwos that woned in the knarres (l. 720–21)[4]

Like Sweeney, though, much of Gawain's suffering is caused by the harshness of winter:

> For werre wrathed hym not so much that wynter was wors (l. 726)

If Hughes's *Wodwo* offers something of a precedent for a contemporary poem about a medieval wild man, the *Gawain*-poet's allusions to the *wodwos* to be found in the winter wilderness may be recalled here indirectly.

The possibility of the influence on Heaney of Geoffrey Hill's sequence

[1] Seamus Heaney, *The Midnight Verdict* (Oldcastle: Gallery, 1993; repr. 2000), 28.

[2] Ted Hughes, *Wodwo* (London: Faber, 1967), Geoffrey Hill, *Mercian Hymns* (London: Deutsch, 1971).

[3] Seamus Heaney, 'Englands of the Mind,' in *Preoccupations*, 150–69 at 153, 156.

[4] *Sir Gawain and the Green Knight; Pearl; Cleanness; Patience*, ed. J. J. Anderson (London: Dent, 1996).

of prose poems *Mercian Hymns* is suggested by Henry Hart, who argues that Heaney temporarily abandoned his sequence of autobiographical prose poems *Stations* because of the publication of *Mercian Hymns* in 1971, completing *Stations* only after writing the first draft of *Sweeney Astray*. Hart suggests that *Mercian Hymns* was both an obstacle and an enabling force for Heaney, who responds to Hill's accomplishment in different ways across *Stations*, *Sweeney Astray*, the 'Sweeney Redivivus' sequence of *Station Island*, and in 'Station Island' itself, all of which have partial resemblances to Hill's collection. Hart argues that 'Heaney's strategy may have been designed to avoid a head-on collision with Hill's *Hymns* by confronting them on several flanks at different times.'[1] Hill is also discussed by Heaney in 'Englands of the Mind,' where he suggests that Hill 'does what Joyce did in *Ulysses*, confounding modern autobiographical material with literary and historical matter drawn from the past. Offa's story makes contemporary landscape and experience live in the rich shadows of a tradition.'[2] That last sentence might just as easily read 'Sweeney' for 'Offa.'

What Heaney is doing in translating *Buile Suibhne*, then, is complex: he produces a translation of a medieval Irish narrative in a dialect-inflected contemporary English that may be read as a sympathetic reflection of the poet's own exile in the context of conflict in Ulster, and perhaps as both a sympathetic reflection of the position of the nationalist community in Northern Ireland and a staking of a historical and cultural claim to the landscape of Ulster (albeit not an exclusive one). But if much of this might align the work with an Irish nationalist position, the English translation also uses references to canonical works of English literature to bind the translation into the tradition of literature in English, fully aware that the work will have multiple readerships, emphasising that the original Irish text had British analogues (and perhaps sources) while remaining aware that the translation's political implications are at potentially at odds with the conservatism traditionally associated with that English literary canon.[3] John Kerrigan's passing reference to Sweeney as being of 'unmixed Irishness,'[4] then, also seems to be not quite right: Heaney's Sweeney seems deliberately and unmistakeably hybrid.

---

[1] Hart, *Seamus Heaney: Poet of Contrary Progressions*, 155; Heaney comments in an interview with John Haffenden that his hesitation in completing *Stations* was a response to *Mercian Hymns*: John Haffenden, 'Meeting Seamus Heaney,' *London Magazine* 19/3 (1979), 5–28 at 20.

[2] Heaney, 'Englands of the Mind,' 160.

[3] For the potential tensions between the translation and the canon, see Heaney, 'Earning a Rhyme,' 59; for awareness of multiple audiences, Heaney, 'Earning a Rhyme,' 61.

[4] Kerrigan, 'Ulster Ovids,' 249.

Sweeney and Heaney: echoes between poems

That *Sweeney Astray* is not to be seen as a stand-alone exercise separate from the body of Heaney's work is implicit in Heaney's indications of autobiographical identification with the work. It's also suggested by the way in which he uses fragments of the translation elsewhere in his work, and fragments of his other work in the translation, to bind *Sweeney Astray* into a relationship with his original poetry. Given Heaney's observation of the primacy of topography in forging his relationship with *Buile Suibhne*, it's unsurprising to find place names from the translation appearing elsewhere in his poetry, and the landscape of *Sweeney Astray* is explicitly invoked at the opening of 'The Strand at Lough Beg.'[1] In the translation itself, as already observed, *Wintering Out* gets a mention in the line 'wintering out among wolf-packs'; some of the dialect terms (*pads*) are reused from other poems, others (*thole*) will be reused later.

As Neil Corcoran notes, *Sweeney Astray* also reworks a sentence from Heaney's earlier prose poem 'The Wanderer,' from the sequence *Stations*. 'The Wanderer,' as its title suggests, is indebted to the Old English poem of the same name.[2] The first half of the poem sees Heaney recall his departure from his first school, his schoolmaster's praise, and a gift of money. The second portion evokes the Northern Ireland conflict and Heaney's own exile from the North in language reminiscent of Old English poetry: references to a 'ring-giver,' halls, benches, companions, all evoke the heroic ethos of Old English poetry, and the poem as a whole seems to evoke the general atmosphere of lines 29b–50a of the Old English *Wanderer*, where the narrator contrasts previous patronage and companionship with present exile and loneliness.[3]

The final line of 'The Wanderer,' with its description of 'flittings, night-vigils, let-downs, women's cried-out eyes,'[4] is incorporated into *Sweeney Astray*, where Sweeney says:

> I have deserved all this:
> night-vigils, terror,
> flittings across water,
> women's cried-out eyes. (p. 73)

Some of this has a general approximation to the original, which reads:

---

[1] Heaney, *Field Work*, 17; Heaney, *Opened Ground*, 152.
[2] Corcoran, *Poetry of Seamus Heaney*, 126.
[3] *Choice of Anglo-Saxon Verse*, ed. and trans. Hamer, 176–77.
[4] Heaney, *Opened Ground*, 88.

> Cóir cía rogheibhinn-si olc
> mor n-oidhchi rolinges loch,
> mór do rosgaibh ban mbáidhe
> doradus fo eccaoine. (p. 130)

As translated by O'Keeffe, this is:

> 'Tis right that I should get harm;
> many a night have I leaped a lake,
> many eyes of fond women
> have I made weep. (p. 131)

The general themes of exile and sorrow allow Heaney to bring the same material to bear twice, emphasising the autobiographical element in *Sweeney Astray*, and offering a reminder, at one remove, of the similar themes in the Old English poem. But the clearest links between Sweeney and Heaney, and the most transparent entwining of the poet's autobiography and the medieval narrative, are to be found not in *Sweeney Astray*, but in *Station Island*.

'Sweeney Redivivus'

Station Island, published by Faber in 1984 at the same time as their publication of *Sweeney Astray*, contains in its third and final section a sequence of twenty original poems, entitled 'Sweeney Redivivus,' where Heaney brings the persona of Sweeney to bear upon other material, in a similar manner to his use of Dante's *Commedia* for the sequence of poems that make up the collection's middle section, the 'Station Island' sequence. Although the Sweeney character is most visible in this last third of *Station Island*, his presence is to be felt throughout.[1] John Kerrigan notes that allusions to Ovid's *Metamorphoses* in 'The Underground,' the opening poem of *Station Island,* should alert the reader to the role of Sweeney, a man transformed into a bird, in the collection.[2] The concluding poem of part one, 'The King of the Ditchbacks,' sees the narrator dressed in shamanic costume, transformed into the outcast he had previously feared, and initiated into knowledge through exile;[3] the poem alludes to the Sweeney family, travellers who camped in the ditchbacks of Heaney's childhood, who are mentioned in the introduction to *Sweeney Astray* (p. viii), and perhaps also

---

[1] Corcoran, *Poetry of Seamus Heaney*, 110.
[2] Kerrigan, 'Ulster Ovids,' 242.
[3] Seamus Heaney, *Station Island*, 56–58; Heaney, *Opened Ground*, 238–41.

to P. L. Henry's suggestion that Suibhne's feather dress is reminiscent of the costume worn by *fili*, by shamanic figures, and by early Irish hermits.[1] The 'Station Island' sequence itself opens with the figure of Simon Sweeney, who reveals himself as the 'mystery man' of the narrator's childhood who appeared in the preceding poem.[2] In a note to the text that covers the third part of the collection, Heaney comments that the 'Sweeney Redivivus' poems are 'voiced for Sweeney.'[3] If commentators on *Sweeney Astray* observed that the voice of the translation resembled Heaney's, here the use of Sweeney's voice allows Heaney to adopt a different tone in revisiting portions of his earlier work, and considering the possibilities beyond it. Although not entirely remote from the story of Sweeney, Heaney comments in his notes to the sequence that many of the poems 'are imagined in contexts far removed from early medieval Ireland.'[4]

What the 'Sweeney Redivivus' sequence demonstrates is Heaney's ability to bring a reimagined version of a medieval text to bear upon autobiographical material: in this, the sequence has much in common with the 'Station Island' sequence it accompanies. What 'Sweeney Redivivus' also shows is that Heaney is capable of constructing several very different imaginative responses to a single text: responses that can sit alongside one another, for these poems supplement rather than supplant the translation in *Sweeney Astray*. Rather than displaying a desire for a single authoritative retelling of the past, together the translation and the sequence of lyrics suggest that the past is open to multiple reimaginings and reconfigurations. This is something that also proves true of Heaney's own work, for, in reimagining *Sweeney Astray* in the 'Sweeney Redivivus' sequence, he revisits and reinterprets not just his medieval source, but his own past and its representation in his earlier poetry.

The opening poem of the 'Sweeney Redivivus' sequence, 'The First Gloss,' indicates a move from the centre of the page, where we would normally find the text, into the margin, an opening move that positions these poems as gloss rather than text.[5] The move is a paradoxical one, for the text glossed by the poems is absent: the 'Sweeney Redivivus' sequence is published separately from *Sweeney Astray*, and rather than occupying a literally marginal position, the poems appropriate the position of text rather than gloss. These 'glosses' may respond to *Sweeney Astray* (itself a response to *Buile Suibhne*), but they stand apart from it, and Heaney comments in

[1] Henry, *The Early English and Celtic Lyric*, 26.
[2] Heaney, *Station Island*, 61; Heaney, *Opened Ground*, 242–43.
[3] Heaney, *Station Island*, 123.
[4] Heaney, *Station Island*, 123.
[5] Heaney, *Station Island*, 97; Heaney, *Opened Ground*, 269.

a note to the text that he trusts 'these glosses can survive without the support system of the original story.'[1]

The gloss, as H. J. Jackson tells us in her book on modern marginalia, 'in its primary sense, translates or explains foreign or obscure words; its expanded forms are the translation and the paraphrase.'[2] Michael Camille quotes Hugh of St Victor's *Didascalion* on interlinear glossing to this effect: 'The word "gloss" is Greek, and it means tongue (*lingua*), because, in a way, it bespeaks (*loquitur*) the meaning of the word under it.'[3] By calling this opening poem 'The First Gloss,' then, Heaney is from the outset constructing the poems of *Sweeney Redivivus* as a sort of translation. If Heaney comments elsewhere on the etymological meaning of translation as carrying something across,[4] here the translation process extends beyond the carrying of a medieval Irish text into contemporary English; the medieval Irish character is himself translated into the contemporary world.[5]

This opening move into the margin is also a reminder that Sweeney himself is a marginal figure. Although the margins of medieval texts often contained learned gloss and commentary, they also contained irreverence and subversion. As Camille writes,

> The word margin – from the Latin *margo[/-]inis*, meaning edge, border, frontier – only became current with the wider availability of writing. Once the manuscript page becomes a matrix of visual signs and is no longer one of flowing linear speech, the stage is set not only for supplementation and annotation but also for disagreement and juxtaposition – what the scholastics called *disputatio*.[6]

Adopting the persona of Sweeney, the outcast, allows Heaney to revisit his life from the sidelines, and to make disputatious comments. As Bernard O'Donoghue argues, 'The First Gloss' is a gloss not just on *Buile Suibhne*, but also on a foundational early poem of Heaney's, 'Digging,' where the shaft of the pen here recalls the earlier poem's equation of pen and spade,

---

[1] Heaney, *Station Island*, 123; cf. the sequence 'Ten Glosses,' in Heaney, *Electric Light*, 54–56, the eighth of which is 'Moling's Gloss.'

[2] H. J. Jackson, *Marginalia: Readers Writing in Books* (New Haven and London: Yale University Press, 2001), 45.

[3] Michael Camille, *Image on the Edge: The Margins of Medieval Art* (London: Reaktion, 1992; repr. 2000), 20; Hugh of St Victor, *The Didascalion of Hugh of St Victor: A Medieval Guide to the Arts*, trans. Jerome Taylor (New York: Columbia University Press, 1961), 119.

[4] Brandes, 'Seamus Heaney: An Interview,' 12.

[5] A similar resurrection occurs for the character of the Tollund Man in 'The Tollund Man in Springtime,' in Heaney, *District and Circle*, 55–57.

[6] Camille, *Image on the Edge*, 21.

and the verb 'subscribe' sustains the link between digging and writing.[1]
This is the metaphor of poet as archaeologist, familiar in Heaney since the
bog poems of *Wintering Out* and *North*, and used here in bringing to life
a contemporary version of the medieval Sweeney.[2]

The title poem of the sequence, 'Sweeney Redivivus,' describes a literal resurrection of Sweeney suggestive of autobiography on Heaney's
part. The Sweeney character, brought back to life, notices changes. He
describes the bitter smell from the river, with the use of the word 'scutch'
in the description here recalling both the comparison in *Sweeney Astray*
between the battering that Sweeney's army receives and the scutching
of flax (p. 19), and, through the use of the dialect term, the Ulster linen
industry. Sweeney further describes the disappearance of the earlier landscape beneath contemporary housing. This revitalised Sweeney arrives to
find himself an outcast in a landscape that's home to him, but which has
been overwritten and made unfriendly by historical change: a situation
not unlike Heaney's. Neil Corcoran argues that the twinning of Sweeney
and Heaney is suggested in the description of a head like a ball of wet
twine – twine is made by entwining separate strands, here Sweeney and
Heaney.[3] Corcoran sees descriptions of unwinding, in both the 'Sweeney
Redivivus' sequence and in the poem of that name, as Heaney's attempt to
dry out the soakage of the heritage in which he has been immersed.[4] The
concluding lines of 'Sweeney Redivivus' could also apply either to the
fictional figure of the revitalised Sweeney, or to Heaney himself, by now
an eminent poet:

> And there I was, incredible to myself,
> among people far too eager to believe me
> and my story, even if it happened to be true.[5]

These lines set a sceptical tone that is to be found across much of the sequence.

Another of the early 'Sweeney Redivivus' poems, 'In the Beech,' revisits Heaney's childhood: we find the figure of Sweeney hiding in a tree,

---

[1] O'Donoghue, *Seamus Heaney and the Language of Poetry*, 106.

[2] On the poet as archaeologist in Heaney, see Jon Stallworthy, 'The Poet as Archaeologist: W. B. Yeats and Seamus Heaney,' *Review of English Studies* 33 (1982), 158–74, and
Christine Finn, *Past Poetic: Archaeology in the Poetry of W. B. Yeats and Seamus Heaney* (London: Duckworth, 2004).

[3] There may be an echo here of the woven figure that cannot be undone in Louis
MacNeice's 'Valediction': *The Collected Poems of Louis MacNeice*, ed. E. R. Dodds (London:
Faber, 1966), 53.

[4] Heaney, *Station Island*, 99; Corcoran, *Poetry of Seamus Heaney*, 130.

[5] Heaney, *Station Island*, 98; Heaney, *Opened Ground*, 270.

watching the landscape, as Heaney tells us he himself used to hide 'in the throat of an old willow tree at the end of the farmyard.'[1] Just as Sweeney spends his time in *Buile Suibhne* with an ear out for the army, seeking to stay one step ahead, here too he's watching the RAF aerodrome near Heaney's childhood home.[2] As in Heaney's medieval source, Sweeney is once more an outcast, an abandoned lookout, whose vantage point affords him a sort of wisdom, for the tree he is hidden in is a tree of knowledge.[3] In this poem and the poem following, Heaney revisits the world of his childhood to offer balance to earlier accounts. 'In the Beech' acknowledges that the natural world described in Heaney's early poetry sat side by side with a world of military industrialism that that poetry omitted, and 'The First Kingdom' gives a sharply unromantic account of rural Irish life.[4] As Helen Vendler comments (quoting Heaney's 'Terminus' in support), Heaney is a writer especially given to second thoughts,[5] and the Sweeney persona allows him the opportunity to post a sceptical marginal gloss to some thoughts previously expressed.

'The First Flight' gives form to the initial autobiographical analogy between Heaney and Sweeney: Heaney's move south as a version of Sweeney's flight. Here again, the poem's narrator is a marginal figure, formerly held back through attachment before necessary distrust teaches him to observe from out of reach.[6] 'The Cleric' opens by recalling the conflict between Ronan and Sweeney at the outset of *Sweeney Astray*, and here again we have a doubling of Heaney and Sweeney, where the narrator is ousted 'to the marches / Of skulking and whingeing.'[7] The arrival of Christianity in Ireland is what sees Sweeney exiled, but history's planting of standards on church gables and spires might also describe the conflict that sees Heaney himself uprooted. As suggested by the words 'skulking' and 'whingeing' here, though, the poem's narrator here isn't about to indulge in self-pity, and the next line provides a second thought: was he really driven out, or did he desert? The poem ends by echoing the sense,

---

[1] Heaney, 'Mossbawn,' 4; O'Donoghue, *Seamus Heaney and the Language of Poetry*, 100, notes echoes of Yeats in the link between bird, poet, and tree.

[2] Heaney, 'Mossbawn,' 3, describes the aerodrome at Toomebridge, revisited in 'The Aerodrome,' in Heaney, *District and Circle*, 11–12.

[3] Heaney, *Station Island*, 100; Heaney, *Opened Ground*, 271.

[4] Heaney, *Station Island*, 100, 101; Heaney, *Opened Ground*, 271, 272; Corcoran, *Poetry of Seamus Heaney*, 130–31; Helen Vendler, *Seamus Heaney* (Cambridge, MA: Harvard University Press, 1998; repr. 2000), 35–37.

[5] Vendler, *Seamus Heaney*, 10.

[6] Heaney, *Station Island*, 102–3; Heaney, *Opened Ground*, 274.

[7] Heaney, *Station Island*, 107; Heaney, *Opened Ground*, 277–78. For the word 'march,' see the discussion in Chap. 3 below on the word's use in the *Beowulf* translation.

implicit in *Buile Suibhne*, that Sweeney's poetic gift is a benefit that accompanies the pain of being a *geilt*.[1]

In 'The Scribes,' that poetic gift is contrasted with the writing practised by others who themselves scratch and claw in the margins of texts of praise.[2] The practice of these scribes in rendering the holly tree for ink is itself counterpointed in the subsequent poem, 'Holly,' where the narrator reaches for ink and hopes to feel holly. 'Holly' may owe something to Louis MacNeice's 'Snow,' an influential poem much reworked by contemporary Ulster writers, including Derek Mahon, Paul Muldoon, and Ciaran Carson.[3] Where MacNeice's poem juxtaposes snow and roses, one inside, the other outside a window, here the holly plays the part of both: the artificiality of the indoor holly with its red berries and waxy leaves recalling the unseasonal dried roses of the MacNeice poem, and standing in contrast to the real thing, found out in the rain, green and jagged. The two sorts of holly stand at a temporal remove from one another: the artificiality of an indoor present contrasted with the reality of youth, where things are not as they 'should' be in some stereotypical sense of what a winter scene should be (with snow rather than rain and with berries on the holly), but where everything seems more tangible than in a present where the narrator almost forgets what it's like to be soaked with rain or waiting for snow. The doubting narrator seeks (like the biblical Thomas) evidence he can touch: reaching for a book, he hopes for it to come alive in his hand as 'a black-letter bush, a glittering shield-wall / cutting as holly and ice.'[4]

'In the Chestnut Tree' and 'Sweeney's Returns' recall Sweeney's returns to his wife Eorann in *Sweeney Astray*, but in a manner that avoids the dialogues found in the medieval text. In *Buile Suibhne*, Sweeney twice returns to talk to Eorann (in sections 32 and 55), but in these poems, Sweeney never gets as far as talking to her. Instead, 'In the Chestnut Tree' places Sweeney once again in the pose of a viewer from the margins, secretly watching his wife, a queen in her fifties, bathing. The poem compares her to Susannah, implicitly drawing a parallel between Sweeney and the elderly voyeurs of the biblical story.[5] Its companion piece, 'Sweeney's Returns,' is subversive of the archetypal epic return of Ulysses: here Sweeney returns from afar,

---

[1] Heaney, *Station Island*, 107–8; Heaney, *Opened Ground*, 277–78.

[2] Heaney, *Station Island*, 111; Heaney, *Opened Ground*, 281.

[3] On which see Edna Longley, 'The Room where MacNeice wrote "Snow",' in Longley, *The Living Stream*, 252–70, first published in *The Crows Behind the Plough: History and Violence in Anglo-Irish Poetry and Drama*, ed. Geert Lernout (Amsterdam: Rodopi, 1991). For MacNeice's poem, see *The Collected Poems of Louis MacNeice*, 30.

[4] Heaney, *Station Island*, 115; Heaney, *Opened Ground*, 282.

[5] Heaney, *Station Island*, 113.

not to domesticity and the affirmation of his identity by a waiting wife, but to his wife's absence, and a reflection that startles him.[1]

Some poems are at a further remove from the story of Sweeney than others: Neil Corcoran suggests that three poems towards the end of the sequence, 'An Artist' (on Cézanne), 'The Old Icons' (on Irish nationalism), and 'In Illo Tempore' (on religious faith) are closer to Heaney than to Sweeney, although they have some of the scepticism associated with Sweeney.[2] 'In Illo Tempore' seems to move from a religious belief conveyed through Latinate language at the poem's outset to the possibility, tempting but difficult to accept, of artistic belief at the poem's end. The famous strand is Sandymount, famous from *Ulysses*, but the seabirds cry like 'incredible souls,' and here again, as in 'Holly,' the narrator seeks something tangible to support belief, as he presses down on the wall of the promenade to help himself 'credit it.' These Latinate terms for belief and the lack of it, *credit, incredible*, recall the Latinate language of Catholic religious belief described in the poem's opening, and show the narrator to remain incredible to himself, as he was in 'Sweeney Redivivus.' But this language also looks forward to Heaney's later statements of artistic belief, of crediting marvels (in 'Fosterling')[3] and crediting poetry (in his Nobel lecture).[4] This poem and others in *Station Island* seem to stand at a point of transition between a religious belief not yet fully abandoned (a theme of the 'Station Island' sequence) and an artistic belief not yet fully embraced.

The 'Sweeney Redivivus' sequence, and the *Station Island* collection itself, closes with the long poem 'On the Road.' The poet as driver, familiar from other Heaney poems, sees all roads become one: the poem ties together references to Dante (echoing the preceding sequence) and the rich young man of Matthew's gospel (echoing 'The King of the Ditchbacks' at the end of part one as well as the earlier *Stations* sequence[5]), before describing the transformation, Sweeney-like, of poet into bird, which flies up and away, into exile and migration, before coming to rest in contemplation before a prehistoric cave-painting at Lascaux, an image of a deer come to drink at what's described as a dried-up source.[6] There are echoes of

[1]　Heaney, *Station Island*, 114.

[2]　Heaney, *Station Island*, 116–18; Heaney, *Opened Ground*, 283–85; Corcoran, *Poetry of Seamus Heaney*, 130.

[3]　Heaney, *Seeing Things,* 50; Heaney, *Opened Ground*, 357.

[4]　Seamus Heaney, 'Crediting Poetry: The Nobel Lecture, 1995,' in Heaney, *Opened Ground*, 445–67.

[5]　Corcoran, *Poetry of Seamus Heaney*, 126.

[6]　Heaney, *Station Island*, 119–21; Heaney, *Opened Ground*, 286–88.

Yeats here, of 'The Circus Animals' Desertion,'[1] but also a contrast with other Heaney poems, where the discovery of water is a symbol of poetic inspiration: for now, all that is found at the end of this journey is dust and exhaustion, and there is a particular contrast with the water imagery that floods through the final sections of the 'Station Island' sequence that precedes 'Sweeney Redivivus.'[2]

Writing of the poem's contemplative finish, John Kerrigan observes 'an aesthetic of patience' in Heaney's work, noting also that Sweeney has imagined himself transformed into a deer in *Sweeney Astray*, and so 'knows the rock's life from inside.'[3] Sweeney (and so Heaney) can be identified with the deer who has come to drink from a 'dried-up source,' and must now be prepared to wait for signs of life to re-emerge. *Buile Suibhne*, and consequently *Sweeney Astray,* ends with a reconciliation to heal the sundering that occurs at the outset: the narrative comes full circle. No such closure is possible here. The 'Sweeney Redivivus' sequence has allowed Heaney, in the guise of the Sweeney persona, to ask questions from the margins, a process of drawing old certainties into question, rather than a process of seeking after new ones. 'On the Road,' then, marks the end of the sequence with a pause, rather than a firm conclusion.

As Elmer Andrews comments, 'in the poetry after *Field Work* the characteristic imagery changes spectacularly, from the archaeological and excavatory to the aerial and ornithological, from earth to air, darkness to light, expressive of the poet's desire for transcendence.'[4] Flight, though, is not without its risks, and the poetry displays an awareness of this. Robert Tracy compares Sweeney with Stephen Dedalus, protagonist of Joyce's *Portrait of the Artist as a Young Man*, a figure specifically invoked at the end of the 'Station Island' sequence that precedes these poems.[5] Stephen is a figure not just of Daedalus, whose name he shares, but also of his son, Icarus: the birdman who flies too high and falls to earth, a reminder of

---

[1] Yeats, *The Poems*, 394–95.

[2] Corcoran, *Poetry of Seamus Heaney*, 133–34 on Yeats, 202–3, on the imagery of water, wells, and pumps in the poems; it's noticeable that the subsequent collection, *The Haw Lantern*, opens by picking up this motif of drought and water from the end of *Station Island*.

[3] Kerrigan, 'Ulster Ovids,' 254.

[4] *Poetry of Seamus Heaney*, ed. Andrews, 145; if that is true for this stage of Heaney's work, Corcoran, *Poetry of Seamus Heaney*, 192, notes that in 1996 *The Spirit Level* returns from 'lightening' to a renewed self-burdening.

[5] Robert Tracy, 'Into an Irish Free State: Heaney, Sweeney and Clearing Away,' in *Poetry in Contemporary Irish Literature*, ed. Michael Kenneally (Gerrards Cross: Colin Smythe, 1995), 238–62 at 239; Heaney, *Station Island*, 93; the specific reference to Stephen is omitted in the version of 'Station Island' in *Opened Ground*.

the dangers of flight.[1] A tension remains in the poetry between the desire for rootedness and the desire for transcendence, between archaeology and flight, and 'On the Road' contains elements of both: the poet-narrator flies free, transformed into a bird, only to come to rest in contemplation before a prehistoric cave painting at the poem's end. The Sweeney story as a whole embodies this tension between rootedness and release: in the original narrative, Sweeney continually makes attempts at a return home from his peregrinations, never satisfied to remain in exile. Similarly, notwithstanding the very political reading of *Sweeney Astray* that has been offered above, emphasising Heaney's engagement in his poetry with the problems of his home place and the translation's political implications, this is also a work that, as Andrews says, 'speaks of the longing for a depoliticised poetry that draws instead from nature.' What Heaney seeks, Andrews suggests, is 'a Dantean aesthetic that would reconcile the claims of both the earthly and the spiritual, the political and the transcendent.'[2] For now, the poetry holds these pairs in tension without reaching a resolution.

[1] Richard Ellmann, *Ulysses on the Liffey* (London: Faber, 1972), 4.
[2] *Poetry of Seamus Heaney*, ed. Andrews, 145, 146.

2

Station Island

T HE 'Station Island' sequence that forms the heart of the collection
that bears its name is Seamus Heaney's most extensive adaptation
of Dante, a reworking of the *Commedia* in a contemporary Irish
context, where a pilgrimage by the poet to Lough Derg, the Station Island
of the title, leads to encounters with a number of ghostly interlocutors,
some of whom are literary predecessors, others figures from Heaney's life.
While this sequence forms the heart of the discussion here, it is none the
less necessary to note that Heaney's engagement with Dante extends well
beyond this single, albeit substantial, work, and that Dante is a regular
presence in Heaney's work from *Field Work* onwards. This is particularly
the case for both *Field Work* and *Seeing Things*: the former containing several elegies, the latter in part an extended elegy for Heaney's father. Like
Station Island, each of these books makes use of Dante primarily in the
context of a dialogue with the dead, and each closes with a translation
from the *Inferno*.

Heaney and Dante (1): 'Field Work'

Dante's first appearance in Heaney's poetry is in 1979's *Field Work*. Dante
is present most substantially in the closing poem, 'Ugolino,' a translation
from cantos XXXII and XXXIII of the *Inferno*, but his presence is implicit
throughout. Six of the forty-one poems in the collection are elegies.
Three of these are for fellow workers in the field of art: 'Elegy' for Robert Lowell, 'In Memoriam Sean O'Riada' for the composer named in the
poem's title, and 'In Memoriam Francis Ledwidge' for the Meath poet
killed in the First World War while serving in the British army.[1] The remaining three, grouped together near the beginning of the volume, are
for murder victims: 'The Strand at Lough Beg' for Colum MacCartney,

---

[1] Heaney, *Field Work*, 29–32, 59–60; Heaney, *Opened Ground*, 185–86.

'A Postcard from North Antrim' for Sean Armstrong, and 'Casualty' for Louis O'Neill.[1] There are several echoes from Dante in these poems for the dead. At the end of 'Casualty,' having described Louis O'Neill's murder in a bomb attack by his own side, and having asked how culpable he was in breaking the complicity of the tribe, Heaney asks O'Neill's revenant self to question him again: a desire to speak with the dead that echoes Dante and anticipates what is to come in 'Station Island.'[2] In the elegy for Francis Ledwidge, although Ledwidge's divided allegiances separate him from those he serves with, the poem closes with the observation that 'all of you consort now underground,' an address to the dead that provides a lead-in to the *Inferno* translation, which follows this poem and concludes the volume.[3]

Dante is most explicitly present in these elegies in 'The Strand at Lough Beg,' a poem for Heaney's second cousin, Colum MacCartney.[4] The poem opens with a quotation from Dorothy L. Sayers's translation of *Purgatorio* I. 100–103, where Virgil washes the grime of hell from Dante, preparing him for his ascent towards paradise. The quotation here, the first appearance of Dante in Heaney's work, anticipates the poem's conclusion, where Heaney enacts a similar anointing for his murdered cousin. As well as the invocation of Dante, the poem also alludes to *Buile Suibhne*, for the area where Colum MacCartney is murdered in the uplands of the Fews is the same area where Sweeney is pursued by disembodied heads in sections 64 and 65 of the medieval Irish text (pp. 69–70). The juxtaposition of *Buile Suibhne* and the *Commedia* is something that endures into *Station Island*: here, the effect of the reference to Sweeney is to emphasise the nightmarish nature of the murder, while the Dantesque conclusion offers emergence from the infernal scene of the killing to balm, consolation, and ritual. Heaney revisits this poem in section VIII of 'Station Island,' where the revenant figure of his cousin accuses him of writing something other than the fact of the murder. This rewriting of the murder scene in 'Station Island' directly states that the conclusion of the earlier poem, with its invocation of Dante, softened the reality of Colum MacCartney's death. Further to that, the invocation of *Buile Suibhne* to create the nightmarish landscape of the death-scene in 'The Strand at Lough Beg' is stripped away in 'Station

---

[1] Heaney, *Field Work*, 17–24; Heaney, *Opened Ground*, 152–57.
[2] Heaney, *Field Work*, 21–24; Heaney, *Opened Ground*, 154–57; O'Donoghue, 'Dante's Versatility,' 244.
[3] Heaney, *Field Work*, 59–60; Heaney, *Opened Ground*, 185–86.
[4] Heaney, *Field Work*, 17–18; Heaney, *Opened Ground*, 152–53.

Island' and replaced by baldly factual statement, with MacCartney directly accusing 'The Protestant who shot me through the head.'[1]

Not all the references to Dante in *Field Work* are so grim. 'An Afterwards' uses Dante, unusually, for humour: the poet's wife condemns all poets to the ninth circle of hell, where they attempt to gnaw each other's brains out.[2] The effect is comic, and makes a link between the collection's use of Dante and the marriage poems that form one of the collection's other significant subjects, but there is a dark foreshadowing here of what's yet to come. The fate of these poets in hell is directly compared here to that of Ugolino and Archbishop Roger, condemned in Dante to dwell with the treacherous in the ninth circle: their story concludes *Field Work*. Further to that, 'An Afterwards' makes a serious point about the sacrifices an individual and their family are asked to bear for the sake of literary effort, and Heaney concludes by suggesting that attempts to be balanced and even-handed may not be successful in either the public realm of poetry or in domestic life; here, as elsewhere, there is a sense of the guilt that comes with poetry. Heaney's work is capable of blending *gravitas* and humour – notwithstanding the seriousness of much in the *Beowulf* translation, for instance, there must be a gentle humour in the writing of a phrase from the Irish national anthem into the translation of a foundational Anglo-Saxon text.[3] 'An Afterwards' blends humour with serious questions about public and domestic responsibility.

There are brief allusions to Dante elsewhere in the collection. 'Leavings' imagines Thomas Cromwell in hell, walking on scalding cobblestones made from the heads of the statues he destroyed.[4] The opening line of 'September Song' is, as Neil Corcoran suggests, a version of the opening line of the *Commedia*.[5] There are possible echoes elsewhere: Bernard O'Donoghue suggests that 'A Dream of Jealousy' recalls Dante via the Pre-Raphaelites, and that the quotation from Coventry Patmore (via Yeats) in the final verse of 'The Harvest Bow,' 'The end of art is peace,' contains an echo of *Paradiso* III. 85, 'E'n la sua volontade è nostra pace,' 'And in His will is our peace.'[6] This procedure of composite allusion, where a single line

---

[1] Heaney, *Station Island*, 83; Heaney, *Opened Ground*, 261.

[2] Heaney, *Field Work*, 44; Heaney, *Opened Ground*, 173.

[3] The phrase is 'the gap of danger' (p. 45); Heaney draws attention to it in an essay on the translation (Seamus Heaney, 'The Drag of the Golden Chain,' *TLS* (12 Nov. 1999)) without indicating its provenance. O'Donoghue, 'The Master's Voice-Right,' notes its source in the line 'Tonight we man the gap of danger' from the English language version of *A Soldier's Song / Amhrán na bhFiann*.

[4] Heaney, *Field Work*, 57; Heaney, *Opened Ground*, 182.

[5] Heaney, *Field Work*, 43; Corcoran, *Poetry of Seamus Heaney*, 85.

[6] Heaney, *Field Work*, 50, 58; Heaney, *Opened Ground*, 177, 184; O'Donoghue, 'Dante's

can evoke multiple intertextual echoes (here Patmore, Yeats, Dante), is, as we shall see, visible throughout *Station Island*.

All of these earlier references to Dante build to a climax at the book's conclusion, where 'Ugolino' translates a long section from *Inferno* XXXII and XXXIII, describing Count Ugolino's revenge in hell on Archbishop Roger, who had caused Ugolino and his children to starve to death in prison.[1] The Ugolino story has been much translated in English since Chaucer's version in *The Monk's Tale*:[2] Heaney's rendering makes it applicable to Northern Ireland. As he says in a later interview:

> It was a very famous purple passage, but it also happened to have an oblique applicability (in its ferocity of emotion and in its narrative about a divided city) to the Northern Irish situation.[3]

The context of the poem's composition is made clearer in the fourth section of 'The Flight Path,' from the 1996 collection *The Spirit Level*, which revisits the translation of the 'Ugolino' material from *Inferno*, and describes the context of its composition: Heaney had in mind the 'dirty' protest of Ciaran Nugent, a Republican prisoner, whose red eyes are 'like something out of Dante's scurfy hell.'[4] Nugent was the first prisoner convicted following a decision by the British government to treat IRA prisoners as criminals rather than political prisoners: on arriving in prison in 1976, he refused to wear prison uniform, and consequently served his three year sentence wearing only a blanket. Hundreds of other prisoners joined the blanket protest, and in 1978, IRA prisoners also refused to leave their cells to wash and empty their chamber pots, daubing their excreta on the cell

---

Versatility,' 244–45. The passage from Yeats's 'Samhain: 1905' containing the quotation from Patmore appears as the epigraph for Heaney's first prose book, *Preoccupations*. All references to the *Commedia* are to Dante Alighieri, *The Divine Comedy of Dante Alighieri*, ed. and trans. John D. Sinclair, rev. edn, 3 vols. (1948; repr. Oxford: Oxford University Press, 1971).

[1] Heaney, *Field Work*, 61–64; Heaney, *Opened Ground*, 187–90. There are also several ambiguous suggestions of something worse than starvation: Ugolino's children invite him to ease his hunger by eating them, and his position in hell involves an eternal cannibalism. The ambiguity is heightened by the line describing Ugolino's death. See Jorge Luis Borges, 'The False Problem of Ugolino,' in Borges, *The Total Library: Non-Fiction, 1922–1986*, ed. Eliot Weinberger, trans. Esther Allen, Suzanne Jill Levine, and Weinberger (London: Penguin, 2001), 277–79.

[2] *Dante in English*, ed. Eric Griffiths and Matthew Reynolds (London: Penguin, 2005), includes versions by Chaucer, Jonathan Richardson, Thomas Gray, Frederick Howard, and Thomas Medwin with Percy Bysse Shelley as well as Heaney (1–3, 41–44, 50–53, 63–65, 137–40, 439–43).

[3] Brandes, 'Seamus Heaney: An Interview,' 12.

[4] Heaney, *The Spirit Level*, 25; Heaney, *Opened Ground*, 413.

walls instead. This was the dirty protest to which Heaney refers in 'The Flight Path.'[1]

As commentators have noted, the 'Ugolino' translation from 1979 has an awful predictive quality to it, for, in 1980–81, some of those same prisoners would begin to die on hunger strike. The hunger strikes are a subject that Heaney treats directly in section IX of 'Station Island,' and the subject is implicitly present elsewhere.[2] None of this makes 'Ugolino' an exercise in propaganda: the same passage in 'The Flight Path' that provides this context for the translation features an argument between Heaney and an unnamed Provisional IRA member, where Heaney insists on writing for himself in the face of pressure to write something for the Provisionals' purposes. As well as explaining the political circumstances that made the translation of 'Ugolino' seem necessary, section 4 of 'The Flight Path' may also contain a gesture to a literary progenitor of Heaney's translation, in the description of Dante's hell as 'scurfy' – Robert Lowell's translation of the Brunetto Latini section of *Inferno* XV uses the word 'scurf' in Brunetto's description of Andrea de' Mozzi.[3]

Heaney's Ugolino translation contains some deliberate modifications of the original: the description of Ugolino gnawing at Roger's head 'like a famine victim at a loaf of bread' brings the Irish famine of 1845–47 to mind.[4] Heaney's 'famine' picks up on *per fame* in the Italian text (at *Inferno* XXXII. 127), and perhaps the use of the word 'famine' twice in the Medwin and Shelley translation of the Ugolino episode, but also adds a resonance with Irish history to the translation. There are similar aural recollections of the Italian original elsewhere in the translation, where 'blushed' is an echo of *uscio* and 'sizzling' and 'grassy' echo the *si* of the original.[5] Heaney also adds two descriptions of Roger's brain as 'sweet fruit' and like 'some spattered carnal melon.' This, not in the Italian, has been criticised by Eric Griffiths as the climax of 'the long series of vampings-up to which the Ugolino episode was subjected,'[6] but Heaney's use of food imagery, while not faithful to the original, has another purpose. The narrative of one man eating another in the world below in revenge for crimes committed in the world above counterpoints the opening poem of the book, 'Oysters,'

---

[1] Michael Parker, *Seamus Heaney: The Making of the Poet* (Basingstoke: Macmillan, 1993), 178–79.

[2] Parker, *Seamus Heaney*, 180, notes numerous allusions throughout *Station Island* to subjects such as prisons, policemen, informers, punishments, betrayals, and victims of violence.

[3] *Dante in English*, ed. Griffiths and Reynolds, 377; Dante, *The Divine Comedy*, trans. Sinclair, i, 199, uses the same word.

[4] Heaney, *Field Work*, 61; Heaney, *Opened Ground*, 187.

[5] *Dante in English*, ed. Griffiths and Reynolds, 443, n. to line 96.

[6] Eric Griffiths, Introduction to *Dante in English*, ed. Griffiths and Reynolds, p. lvii.

with its explicit reminder that the oysters being eaten are alive. The fruit imagery in 'Ugolino,' then, points up the link to the opening poem of *Field Work*, emphasising the ties that the translation has to the rest of the collection.[1]

Maria Cristina Fumagalli argues that Heaney's version is more sympathetic to Ugolino than Dante's original,[2] and Heaney's version closes with an emphasis on the suffering of innocents caught up in the cycle of revenge. The original reads:

> Chè se 'l conte Ugolino aveva voce
> d'aver tradita te delle castella,
> non dovei tu i figliuoi porre a tal croce.
>
> Innocenti facea l'età novella,
> novella Tebe, Uguiccione e l'Brigata
> e li altri due che 'l canto suso appella. (*Inferno* XXXIII. 85–90)[3]

Heaney translates:

> For the sins
> Of Ugolino, who betrayed your forts,
> Should never have been visited on his sons.
>
> Your atrocity was Theban. They were young
> And innocent: Hugh and Brigata
> And the other two whose names are in my song.[4]

In Heaney's rendering here, as Fumagalli notes, the word 'atrocity,' not in the original, has a resonance with the vocabulary of the Northern Ireland conflict, and the biblical imagery of the original is altered to include the notion that sons should not pay for the sins of the fathers.[5] 'Ugolino' closes *Field Work*, then, with a sympathy for the suffering of innocent victims that ties this translation from Dante back to the elegies for Colum MacCartney, Sean Armstrong, and Louis O'Neill earlier in the collection. It also looks forward to 1984's *Station Island*, in that the symbol adequate to the predicament of Northern Ireland now seems to be a Dantesque descent into hell.

---

[1] As noted by Christopher Ricks, 'The Mouth, the Meal, and the Book: Review of *Field Work*,' in *Seamus Heaney*, ed. Michael Allen (London: Macmillan, 1997), 95–101 at 95–97, first published in the *London Review of Books* (8 Nov. 1979); Corcoran, *Poetry of Seamus Heaney*, 87.

[2] Fumagalli, *Flight of the Vernacular*, 101–4.

[3] Dante, *Divine Comedy*, ed. and trans. Sinclair, i, 408.

[4] Heaney, *Field Work*, 63–64; Heaney, *Opened Ground*, 190.

[5] Fumagalli, *Flight of the Vernacular*, 101–2.

If *Field Work* begins an engagement with Dante that continues into *Station Island*, the following volume, *The Haw Lantern*, contains little reference to Dante aside from the *terza rima* of 'From the Frontier of Writing.'[1] This makes it an exception in a sequence of books showing Dante as a substantial influence, for Dante is once again a prominent figure in Heaney's subsequent collection, *Seeing Things*. If *The Haw Lantern* is an exception in this sequence of books strongly influenced by Dante, there are other ways in which it signals what is to come in the subsequent volume: if *Field Work* and *Station Island* contain elegies that have political as well as personal implications, both *The Haw Lantern* and *Seeing Things* contain elegies for Heaney's parents that are purely personal. *The Haw Lantern* is also a reorientation of Heaney's work towards what Helen Vendler calls 'the virtual,' a reorientation that endures into the following collection.[2]

Heaney and Dante (2): 'Seeing Things'

The motif of the journey to the underworld is a recurrent one in Heaney, to a number of different ends. *Station Island* opens with a poem literally called 'The Underground,' where the newlyweds in the London Underground station are Orpheus and Eurydice, but with a grim reversal – here the return journey is not one upwards into the light, but down under the ground, a preparation in this opening poem for what is to come, as *Station Island* takes the reader down into the depths.[3] Later in Heaney's work, the crossing of boundaries becomes a figure for the possibilities of poetry, and crossing the frontier between this world and the next becomes one representation of such possibilities. The figures of Orpheus, Hermes, Dante, and Virgil, all archetypal of the journey from this world to the next, recur in the poems, and the motif of the underworld journey is perhaps related to other recurring elements – archaeology, funerals, the many elegies.

Seeing Things is particularly concerned with this motif of the journey to the underworld: it opens with one version of the journey, a translation from *Aeneid* VI, and closes with another, from *Inferno* III. The translation from the *Aeneid* recounts Aeneas' visit to the Sibyl of Cumae, to seek her help in entering the underworld. What he seeks is 'one look, one face-to-face meeting with my dear father,' beseeching the Sibyl to 'take pity / On a son and a father.'[4] This sets out one of the themes for a book whose poems

---

[1] Heaney, *The Haw Lantern*, 6–7; Heaney, *Opened Ground*, 297–98.
[2] Vendler, *Seamus Heaney*, 113.
[3] Heaney, *Station Island*, 13; Heaney, *Opened Ground*, 213.
[4] Heaney, *Seeing Things*, 1, 2.

are dominated by the death of Patrick Heaney, the poet's father, in 1986. The motif of the journey into the underworld via Charon's boat is recalled in the repetition of the boat motif across the collection. A boat trip in the first section of 'Seeing Things' is counterpointed by Heaney's encounter with his father in the third;[1] the ash plant that is a symbol of Heaney's father in 'The Ash Plant' and '1. 1. 87' recurs in conjunction with a boat and the soul's journey to the otherworld in *Crossings* xxvii.[2] 'The Biretta' contains four boats: the first made from paper, a second from the *Purgatorio*, a third the bronze-age Broighter boat, and the last from a painted scene.[3] In the following poem, 'The Settle Bed,' the bed is another sort of boat, an ark or a funeral ship:[4] Heaney will later use a quotation from this poem as an epigraph for the *Beowulf* translation, whose dramatic opening scene describing a ship burial appeared in the preceding collection, *The Haw Lantern*, as 'The Ship of Death.'[5] 'The Schoolbag,' which quotes Dante in its *nel mezzo del cammin*, refers to shipping lanes and the blue North Channel; 'A Royal Prospect' contains a pleasure boat.[6]

   The whole second half of the book, the *Squarings* sequence of forty-eight short lyrics, is written in tercets reminiscent of *terza rima*, and contains repeated references to the possibilities of traversing boundaries (one section of the sequence is called *Crossings*).[7] This extended sequence has two debts to the preceding collection, *The Haw Lantern*. First, the sequence recalls the 'Clearances' sequence written in memory of the poet's mother in the previous volume;[8] secondly, it is both formally and thematically reminiscent of 'From the Frontier of Writing,' where the transition through a literal army checkpoint is followed by a repeat experience at the 'frontier of writing,' all rendered in *terza rima*, with the consequent suggestion of Dante's boundary-crossing journey.[9] One of the poems in the 'Squarings' sequence, 'Lightenings' viii, contains a crossing between the next world and this in a ship that floats in the air (a similar ship earlier floated through the first section of the book's title poem); another, *Crossings* xxxvi, refers to Charon's boat in preparation for 'The Crossing,' the translation from *Inferno* iii that closes the book.[10]

---

[1] Heaney, *Seeing Things*, 16, 18; Heaney, *Opened Ground*, 339–41.
[2] Heaney, *Seeing Things*, 19, 20, 85.
[3] Heaney, *Seeing Things*, 26–27.
[4] Heaney, *Seeing Things*, 28–29; Heaney, *Opened Ground*, 345–46.
[5] Heaney, *The Haw Lantern*, 22.
[6] Heaney, *Seeing Things*, 30, 40–41.
[7] Heaney, *Seeing Things*, 53–108; Heaney, *Opened Ground*, 358–92.
[8] Heaney, *The Haw Lantern*, 26–34; Heaney, *Opened Ground*, 306–14.
[9] Heaney, *The Haw Lantern*, 6–7; Heaney, *Opened Ground*, 297–98.
[10] Heaney, *Seeing Things*, 62, 94; Heaney, *Opened Ground*, 364, 380.

The opening translation from Virgil presents Aeneas protesting his fitness to undertake the journey to the underworld – there is no need, he claims, to speak of Orpheus, Pollux, Theseus or Hercules, for he is himself a descendant of Jove.[1] After Dante, however, these lines now come freighted with the contrasting protest of unworthiness found in canto II of the *Inferno*, 'I am not Aeneas and I am not Paul' (*Inferno* II. 32), and the translation from the *Inferno* that concludes *Seeing Things* is from the scene where Charon protests that Dante, still a living soul, cannot cross the river Acheron in his boat. Dante's entry to hell is permitted not through any virtues of his own (as Aeneas might claim for himself), but because, as the Virgil of the *Inferno* puts it, 'There where all can be done that has been willed / This has been willed; so there can be no question' (the original, *Inferno* III. 95–96, reads: 'vuolsi così colà dove si puote / ciò che si vuole, e più non dimandare').[2] As Heaney puts it in his notes to his translation of the first three cantos, in these lines 'Virgil reveals that God in heaven has permitted this suspension of the usual laws of entry into hell.'[3] But there remains Charon's objection, that the mortal and living may not cross, and we know that the usual laws endure outside of this unusual case. Heaney's translation closes with Virgil's lines to Dante: 'if Charon objects to you, / You should understand well what his words imply' ('se Caron di te si lagna, / ben puoi sapere omai che 'l suo dir sona,' *Inferno* III. 128–29).[4] In the context of the *Inferno*, Charon's words imply that Dante is not destined to go to hell after his death (as Heaney's notes to *Inferno* III indicate). In the context of *Seeing Things*, though, they may indicate something different: something much more everyday, and much more poignant. After the confident opening and all these subsequent versions of poetic boundary-crossing, they suggest that the desire to make a physical crossing, the desire of the living to speak with the departed, must still at the end face a strong rebuke at the crossing-point.

If Heaney's work shows the strong influence of Dante in three of the four collections of original poems that appear over the dozen years from 1979 to 1991, there is less of Dante in the subsequent, post-ceasefire collections. In 1993, Heaney's translations of the first three cantos of the *Inferno* appeared in full as part of a collective translation of the *Inferno* by twenty contemporary poets.[5] We know from Heaney's own account that these

---

[1] Heaney, *Seeing Things*, 2.
[2] Heaney, *Seeing Things*, 111; Dante, *Divine Comedy*, ed. and trans. Sinclair, i, 50.
[3] *Dante's Inferno*, ed. Halpern, 172.
[4] Heaney, *Seeing Things*, 113; Dante, *Divine Comedy*, ed. and trans. Sinclair, i, 52.
[5] *Dante's Inferno*, ed. Halpern, 3–15.

translations were completed some ten years previously,[1] and portions had appeared in both *Station Island* and *Seeing Things*: when they appear in print, then, these translations have to a certain extent been overshadowed by the use Heaney has made of them as part of his original work during the intervening decade. Section four of 'The Flight Path' from *The Spirit Level* includes some Dante, but only in retrospect, contextualising and quoting from the Ugolino translation in *Field Work*. 2001's *Electric Light* contains a sonnet that is self-referential in imitation of a sonnet of Dante's.[2] *District and Circle*, however, sees Heaney revisit the underworld motif in the title poem in a way that ties together many of his previous poems on the subject. Here the London Underground is a version of the underworld in a way that recollects the earlier poem 'The Underground' from *Station Island*: a coin that might be offered to a busker is also the coin that might be offered to Charon to gain passage. Like 'Station Island,' the poem alludes to political violence, here the 2005 London bombings: 'blasted weeping rock-walls' are visible through the train window. And here, as in *Seeing Things*, Heaney once again descends into the underworld to come face to face with his father – this time in his own reflection.[3]

Versions of Dante: Eliot and Mandelstam

Dante provides more than simply subject matter for Heaney. In a 1985 essay, 'Envies and Identifications,' he quotes T. S. Eliot, in a 1929 essay, emphasising the universality of Dante's language, steeped as it is in Latin:

> Dante's universality is not solely a personal matter. The Italian language, and especially the Italian language in Dante's age, gains much by being the product of universal Latin. There is something much more *local* about the languages in which Shakespeare and Racine had to express themselves.[4]

Heaney sees Eliot's response to Dante here (and he acknowledges that this is not Eliot's only response to Dante) as part of a desire to achieve a transcendent literature, and argues that 'such a dream of perfection is best served by a language which gives the illusion of absolute authority, of a purity beyond dialect and tribe, an imperial lexicon, in fact, a Roman

---

[1] Fumagalli, *Flight of the Vernacular*, 260; Heaney, 'Envies and Identifications,' 18.

[2] Heaney, *Electric Light*, 44.

[3] Heaney, *District and Circle*, 17–19.

[4] T. S. Eliot, *Dante* (London: Faber, 1965), 9, quoted in Heaney, 'Envies and Identifications,' 8.

vocabulary which is socially and historically patrician.'[1] But Heaney also sees in Dante something else. He agrees that Dante's language is 'confident and classically ratified,' but nonetheless asserts that 'to listen to Eliot, one would almost be led to forget that Dante's great literary contribution was to write in the vernacular and thereby to give the usual language its head.'[2] Heaney's use of the 'middle voice,' his steering between the standard and the local, is a linguistic route taken in the knowledge that standard English, if devoid of dialect, is, like Virgil's Latin, an imperial lexicon, another vocabulary that is socially and historically patrician.

Heaney contrasts Eliot's reading of Dante with that of another poet of the 1930s, Osip Mandelstam, and his essay 'Conversation about Dante.'[3] Mandelstam's essay is an important one for Heaney: he quotes from it extensively in 'Envies and Identifications,' draws on it again in 'The Government of the Tongue,' and alludes to it at the beginning of the introduction to the *Beowulf* translation.[4] As Heaney reads him in the light of Mandelstam, Dante resembles Eliot's Shakespeare, 'an exemplar of the purely creative, intimate and experimental act of writing itself.'[5] In contrast to Eliot's emphasis on the authoritative and universalist aspects of Dante, Mandelstam's Dante ('Heaney's Dante' as Bernard O'Donoghue suggests),[6] is a figure of artistic freedom:

> Mandelstam found a guide and authority for himself also, but a guide who wears no official badge, enforces no party line, does not write paraphrases of Aquinas or commentaries on the classical authors. His Dante is a voluble Shakespearean figure, a woodcutter singing at his work in the dark wood of the larynx.[7]

This version of Dante as a poet of the local and vernacular is an important

---

[1] Heaney, 'Envies and Identifications,' 9.

[2] Heaney, 'Envies and Identifications,' 12.

[3] The version available to me is that previously cited above: Osip Mandelstam, 'Conversation about Dante,' trans. Clarence Brown and Robert Hughes in *Osip Mandelstam: Selected Essays*, trans. Sidney Morris (Austin and London: University of Texas Press, 1977), 3–44. Heaney uses the edition of Mandelstam's complete prose published by Ardis Press in 1979; some details of the translation differ.

[4] Heaney, 'Envies and Identifications,' 14–18; Seamus Heaney, 'The Government of the Tongue,' in *The Government of the Tongue: The 1986 T. S. Eliot Memorial Lectures and Other Critical Writings* (London: Faber, 1988), 91–108 at 94–96; *Beowulf*, trans. Heaney, p. ix.

[5] Heaney, 'Envies and Identifications,' 16.

[6] On 'Mandelstam's Dante' as represented by Heaney as 'Heaney's Dante,' see O'Donoghue, *Seamus Heaney and the Language of Poetry*, 139; on Dante, via Mandelstam, as a figure of artistic freedom, see O'Donoghue, 'Dante's Versatility,' 255–56.

[7] Heaney, 'Envies and Identifications,' 18.

authorizing figure for Heaney's appropriation of the *Commedia* to an Irish context, and the representation of Dante as a figure of artistic freedom allows Heaney to engage with questions of artistic responsibility and liberty in *Station Island*. 'Station Island' has debts to Eliot also, explicitly so, but a construction of Dante as the embodiment of authority is of little use to Heaney in this context. Mandelstam's construction of a vernacular Dante continues to be important for the subsequent translation of *Beowulf*: here, too, Heaney is trying to rescue a canonical poem from the widespread impression that it is written 'on official paper' (p. ix).

Lough Derg in medieval literature

Heaney's decision to relocate Dante's otherworld journey to an Irish context may seem an audacious one, but it is not an unprecedented move. In 'Envies and Identifications,' Heaney notes Thomas Kinsella's 'Downstream' as a poem that uses Dante's *terza rima* to link the description of a boat trip through the Irish midlands with Dante's descent into the underworld,[1] and there are justifications elsewhere in Irish writing for borrowing from canonical works of literature to describe the local and the everyday. Patrick Kavanagh's short poem 'Epic,' for instance, asserts the power of poetry to transform local arguments into great events, comparing a confrontation over a patch of Monaghan farmland with the historical disputes that spawned the *Iliad*;[2] a similar justification for the use of the epic to describe the ordinary is offered by Joyce's *Ulysses*. Perhaps the greatest justification, though, is that offered by Dante himself: Heaney says what he first loved in the *Commedia* was its local intensity, its ability to describe a historical world while submitting that world to a transcendent scrutiny,[3] and his reading of Dante via Mandelstam offers a further validation of this sense of a Dante both local and vernacular.

Heaney's move to rework Dante in a local Donegal context is perhaps less startling in the light of the long literary history of the Lough Derg pilgrimage site and the importance of that literary history in the formulation of the idea of purgatory. Heaney acknowledges Lough Derg's previous literary history, but he directly mentions, as he himself says, 'only the

[1] Heaney, 'Envies and Identifications,' 18.

[2] Patrick Kavanagh, *Selected Poems*, ed. Antoinette Quinn (Harmondsworth: Penguin, 1996), 101–2. Heaney's 'The Ministry of Fear' (*North*, 63) echoes 'Epic' in its opening lines; Heaney invokes the localness of Dante as a prelude to discussing Kavanagh in 'The Sense of Place,' 136–37.

[3] Heaney, 'Envies and Identifications,' 18–19.

English language forerunners' – listing William Carleton, Sean O'Faolain, Patrick Kavanagh, and Denis Devlin as writers who have been to Lough Derg before him. Two of these forerunners (Carleton and Kavanagh) put in appearances as revenants in the 'Station Island' sequence, and were part of the inspiration for Heaney in setting to work on this adaptation of Dante to an Irish context.[1]

Carleton and Kavanagh have received a fair amount of attention from commentators on 'Station Island' as previous chroniclers of the Lough Derg pilgrimage, but the literary history of St Patrick's Purgatory extends back much further than the nineteenth-century Carleton, and begins with a medieval Latin text, the *Tractatus de Purgatorio Sancti Patricii*,[2] composed about 1180–84 by H. de Saltrey, a monk in the Cistercian abbey of Saltrey in Huntingdonshire.[3] H. tells his readers that he heard his story from another monk, Gilbert, who had been sent to Ireland by Gervase, abbot of the Cistercian monastery of Louth Park in the diocese of Lincoln.[4] The story that H. de Saltrey tells is that of Gilbert's companion, a knight named Owein, who journeys to purgatory through an entrance to the otherworld at Lough Derg.

The knight Owein is a fictional character, one borrowed from medieval romances about the knight Ywain, who is himself related to the character Owein from the medieval Welsh *Mabinogion*.[5] But if the tale's protagonist is a creation of the medieval imagination, so too is his destination. Jacques Le Goff suggests that the idea of purgatory as an actual place, intermediate between heaven and hell, did not appear in Christian thought until the twelfth century, subsequently receiving pontifical sanction from Pope

[1] Heaney, 'Envies and Identifications,' 18. While it might seem likely that Irish writing on Lough Derg would validate Heaney's appropriation of Dante, in fact the sense in 'Envies and Identifications' seems the opposite: that Dante (read via Mandelstam) is an exemplar who allows Heaney to overcome the fact that other Irish writers have preceded him to Lough Derg.

[2] The Latin text is in *St Patrick's Purgatory: Two Versions of Owayne Miles and The Vision of William of Stranton together with the long text of the Tractatus de Purgatorio Sancti Patricii*, ed. Robert Easting, EETS no. 298 (Oxford: Oxford University Press, 1991), 119–54; *Saint Patrick's Purgatory: A Twelfth Century Tale of a Journey to the Other World*, trans. Jean-Michel Picard with an introduction by Yolande de Pontfarcy (Dublin: Four Courts, 1985) is a modern English translation. Further references are to this edition and translation.

[3] Easting, *St Patrick's Purgatory*, p. xvii; Picard and Pontfarcy, *Saint Patrick's Purgatory*, 16–18.

[4] Easting, *St Patrick's Purgatory*, 149; Picard and Pontfarcy, *Saint Patrick's Purgatory*, 72 and n.

[5] See Chrétien de Troyes's 'Yvain' in Chrétien, *Arthurian Romances*, trans. D. D. R. Owen (London: Dent, 1993), 281–373, and 'The Lady of the Fountain' in *The Mabinogion*, trans. Gwyn Jones and Thomas Jones (London: Dent, 1993), 129–51.

Innocent IV in 1254 and becoming Church doctrine at the Second Council of Lyons in 1274.[1] This notion of a third place, Le Goff argues, appeared in two different milieus during the twelfth century – among the intellectuals of Paris, and those of the Cistercian order.[2] The new idea was indebted both to the thinking of earlier Christian writers, especially Augustine, and to early-medieval visions of the otherworld, which were themselves indebted to Judaeo-Christian apocalyptic writings and to Germanic and Celtic accounts of otherworld voyages.[3] But the doctrine of purgatory, and the word itself, is a creation of the late twelfth century. As Le Goff puts it: 'some time between 1170 and 1200 – possibly as early as 1170–80 and surely by the last decade of the century – purgatory first emerged.'[4] The emergence of the idea of purgatory, then, is virtually contemporaneous with the composition of the *Tractatus de Purgatorio Sancti Patricii* by the English Cistercian H. de Saltrey, and for Jacques Le Goff 'this brief work occupies an essential place in the history of Purgatory, in whose success it played an important, if not decisive, role.'[5]

The *Tractatus* opens with a prologue that invokes previous writings on the questions of both the fate of the soul after death, and the topography of the otherworld. The prologue invokes both St Augustine and St Gregory by name, and alludes to the writings of others, in its concern to demonstrate that the account to follow is in keeping with previous doctrine. On the crucial question of a place for purgation, the prologue reads:

> Et licet usque ad mortem maneat meritum et post mortem reddatur premium, pena tamen post mortem esse dicitur, que purgatoria nominatur, in qua hii, qui in hac uita in quibusdam culpis, iusti tamen et ad uitam eternam predestinati, uixerunt, ad tempus cruciabuntur, ut purgentur. Vnde, quemadmodum a Deo corporales pene dicuntur preparate, ita ipsis penis loca corporalia, in quibus sunt, dicuntur esse distincta. (p. 122)

> And although the value of merit remains until death and the reward is repaid after death, we are however told that there is a punishment after death, called purgatorial. Here those who have lived in this life with some sins, but are nevertheless just and destined for eternal life, will be tormented for a time in order to be purified. Thus, as it is said

---

[1] Jacques Le Goff, *The Birth of Purgatory*, trans. Arthur Goldhammer (Chicago: University of Chicago Press, 1984), 283–86.
[2] Le Goff, *The Birth of Purgatory*, 167–68.
[3] Le Goff, *The Birth of Purgatory*, 52–127.
[4] Le Goff, *The Birth of Purgatory*, 168.
[5] Le Goff, *The Birth of Purgatory*, 193.

that physical punishments have been prepared by God, so it is also said that physical places have been arranged where these punishments can take place. (p. 44)

Here, H. de Saltrey draws upon existing doctrine regarding the purgation of souls after death to justify the existence of a place where purgation can occur, the subject of the narrative to follow.

Before proceeding to the narrative of Owein's journey to Lough Derg, however, the *Tractatus* first (following a brief excursus on the savagery of the Irish) gives an account of the revelation of the Purgatory to Patrick:

Sanctum uero Patricium Dominus in locum desertum eduxit, et unam fossam rotundam et intrinsecus obscuram ibidem ei ostendit, dicens, quia quisquis ueraciter penitens uera fide armatus fossam eandem ingressus unius diei ac noctis spacio moram in ea faceret, ab omnibus purgaretur tocius uite sue peccatis, sed et per illam transiens non solum uisurus esset tormenta malorum uerum etiam, si in fide constanter egisset, gaudia beatorum. (p. 124)

So the Lord took saint Patrick to a deserted place. There he showed to him a round pit, dark inside, and said to him that whoever, being truly repentant and armed with true faith, would enter this pit and remain for the duration of one day and one night, would be purged of all the sins of his life. Moreover, while going through it, he would see not only the torments of the wicked, but also, if he acted constantly according to the faith, the joys of the blessed. (pp. 47–48)

The *Tractatus* then establishes a history of penitential practice at Lough Derg. Patrick builds a church on the site, and the place becomes a place of pilgrimage for those who wish to be purged of their sins; many pilgrims, however, do not return, and both the bishop of the diocese and the prior of the church attempt to persuade those who wish to enter the pit not to do so, warning them of the many penitents who have been lost.

The narrative now turns to the story proper, and to the knight, Owein, who undertakes the journey to the otherworld, 'in the days of King Stephen,' i.e. in the mid twelfth century. Having undertaken to enter the Purgatory despite the attempts of both the bishop and the prior to persuade him otherwise, Owein is told by the prior of what lies ahead of him. On entering the pit, he passes through an underground cavern until he emerges into a large field, dimly lit, in which he finds a hall. There, as predicted by the prior, Owein is met by fifteen messengers from God, who advise him that to endure his journey through purgatory, he must place his faith in God in the face of the tortures, threats, and promises of the demons who will carry him through purgatory.

Following the departure of these messengers, there is a terrifying noise, and the hall is filled with demons. These demons carry Owein through successive locations, each with a new torment.[1] Each location is filled with suffering people, and Owein is forced to suffer each torment, being released only when he remembers to invoke the name of Jesus Christ. The narrative focuses on the torments suffered by the souls in purgatory, and while it notes in passing that Owein recognizes some of his former companions, this point, so crucial in literary accounts of the otherworld journey by Virgil, Dante, and others, is passed over without further elaboration:

> Alii suspendebantur cathenis igneis per pedes, alii per manus, alii per capillos, alii per brachia, alii per tibias, capitibus ad ima uersis et sulphureis flammis inmersis. Alii in ignibus pendebant, uncis ferreis in oculis fixis, uel auribus, uel naribus, uel faucibus, uel mamillis, aut genitalibus. Alii fornacibus sulphureis cremabantur; alii quasi super sartagines urebantur. Alii uerubus igneis transfixi ad ignem assabantur, quos demonum alii uertunt, alii diuersis metallis liquescentibus deguttauerunt, quos tamen omnes discurrentes demones flagris ciciderunt. Omnia genera tormentorum que excogitari possunt ibidem uisa sunt. Ibi etiam uidit quosdam de suis quondam sociis et eos bene cognouit. (p. 132)

> Some were hanging from blazing chains by the feet, others by the hands, others by the hair, others by the arms, others by the legs, with their heads turned upside down and immersed in sulphurous flames. Some were suspended in fires with iron nails stuck in their eyes, or ears or nostrils or throats or breasts or genitals. Others were burning in furnaces of sulphur; yet others were frying as if on pans; others were roasting on a fire, skewered on blazing spits which were turned by demons. Others were dripping with various molten metals and moreover they were all beaten with whips by demons running in every direction. There one could see all the kinds of torture that one could imagine. Also Owein saw some of his former companions there and he recognized them well. (p. 60)

The final torment Owein endures involves crossing a seemingly impassible

---

[1] The account of the otherworld given in the *Tractatus* is indebted to other literary sources: the writings of SS Augustine and Gregory, the *Vision of Saint Paul*, the *Vision of Drythelm* (as recounted by Bede), and possibly others (Picard and de Pontfarcy, *Saint Patrick's Purgatory*, 29–31). For a general account of medieval otherworld narratives, see Howard R. Patch, *The Other World according to Descriptions in Medieval Literature* (1950; repr. New York: Octagon, 1970).

bridge, beneath which is a burning river that covers the depths of hell. Having crossed the bridge through invoking the name of Jesus, Owein reaches the earthly paradise, the Garden of Eden, where purged souls await their transition to the heavenly paradise. There, two archbishops explain to him the purpose of purgatory in purging the sins of those who will later ascend to paradise; a purgation that may be abbreviated by the masses, psalms, prayers, and alms of the living, made for the benefit of the dead. The story of Owein then concludes with his return to the world and a brief account of his pious life thereafter. The *Tractatus* itself draws to a close with a number of brief accounts appended to the main narrative testifying to the accuracy of the account and the temptations posed by demons – as Stephen Greenblatt comments, the text asserts the existence of the entrance to purgatory at Lough Derg in the face of disbelief articulated within the text.[1] This is even stronger in one of the Middle English translations, where the initial revelation of the Purgatory at Lough Derg to Patrick is prompted by the refusal of Patrick's audience to believe in either hell or purgatory unless someone were able to go and see these places for himself.[2]

The *Tractatus de Purgatorio Sancti Patricii* was enormously influential. Marie de France's adaptation in her *Espurgatoire S. Patrice* is one of several French translations in verse and prose;[3] there are three Middle English versions, one in the thirteenth century *South English Legendary*, and two later verse translations, both called *Owayne Miles*;[4] and there are further translations into German, Italian, Welsh, Bohemian, and other languages.[5] 150 manuscripts of the Latin original, and an equal number of copies in translation, survive throughout Europe.[6] Other medieval writers take up the story: Roger of Wendover includes it in his *Flores Historiarum*; Matthew Paris, in his continuation of Roger's work, does likewise in his *Chronica majora*; Jacques de Vitry, Vincent of Beauvais, Stephen of Bourbon, Humbert of Romans, and Jacobus de Voragine all mention St Patrick's

---

[1] Stephen Greenblatt, *Hamlet in Purgatory* (Princeton: Princeton University Press, 2001), 76; Greenblatt discusses the *Tractatus* and its vernacular translations on 73–101.

[2] Easting, *St Patrick's Purgatory*, 36–39.

[3] The Latin and French texts are printed in parallel in *Das Buch vom Espurgatoire S. Patrice der Marie de France und seine Quelle*, ed. Karl Warnke (Halle: Max Niemeyer, 1938); for a text and English translation of Marie's poem, see *Saint Patrick's Purgatory: A Poem by Marie de France*, trans. Michael Curley (Binghamton, NY: Medieval & Renaissance Texts & Studies, 1993).

[4] Both of the latter are edited in Easting, *St Patrick's Purgatory*.

[5] Marie de France, *Saint Patrick's Purgatory*, trans. Curley, 2.

[6] Picard and de Pontfarcy, *Saint Patrick's Purgatory*, 33.

Purgatory.[1] Pilgrims made the journey to Lough Derg from across Europe during the later Middle Ages: Froissart recounts the (sceptical) account of one such pilgrim, Sir William Lisle.[2] The site's literary history continues with mentions in Erasmus, in Ariosto's *Orlando Furioso*, in Rabelais, and in Robert Burton's *Anatomy of Melancholy*. Calderón wrote a play based indirectly on the story, called *El Purgatorio de San Patricio*, in 1636, and as late as 1798, a young Robert Southey retells the story of Owen's journey to purgatory.[3] As well as its substantial literary influence, the Purgatory also continued to be a place of pilgrimage, despite several post-Reformation attempts to destroy the Lough Derg site.

Lough Derg may even find an echo in *Hamlet*. Horatio's comment to the prince, 'There's no offence, my lord,' draws the following reply from Hamlet:

> Yes, by Saint Patrick, but there is, Horatio,
> And much offence, too. Touching this vision here,
> It is an honest ghost, that let me tell you. (*Hamlet*, I. v. 142–44)[4]

The reference to St Patrick here would seem to be in reference to that saint's association with purgatory, an association derived from the Lough Derg site and the literature surrounding it.[5] As Stephen Greenblatt argues, there are two problems with this possible reference to purgatory in *Hamlet*. Firstly, the cultural context in which the play is first staged is one where the Church of England had rejected the Catholic concept of purgatory almost forty years previously. Secondly, the Ghost's call for revenge is an impetus to murder; an unlikely message from a saved soul enduring purgation, but much more plausible coming from a damned soul in the depths of Hell.[6] The allusions to purgatory in *Hamlet*, then, do not solve the problem of the ghost of Hamlet's father, who remains an ambiguous, unsettling, and powerful figure. For our purposes, however, these references demonstrate something compelling about the influence exercised by

---

[1] Le Goff, *The Birth of Purgatory*, 199.

[2] Shane Leslie, *Saint Patrick's Purgatory: A Record from History and Literature* (London: Burns Oates & Washbourne, 1932), 21–22.

[3] Leslie, *Saint Patrick's Purgatory*, pp. xx, 187–91.

[4] Reference to *Hamlet* is to William Shakespeare, *Hamlet*, ed. Harold Jenkins (London: Methuen, 1982; repr. Surrey: Nelson, 1997).

[5] This is one of a number of potential references to Purgatory in this scene traced by Greenblatt, *Hamlet in Purgatory*, 230–37; the others are contained in the Ghost's assertion that he is 'doomed for a certain term' until his crimes 'are burnt and purged away' (I. v. 10, 13) and the Latin tag '*Hic et ubique?*' at I. v. 164.

[6] Greenblatt, *Hamlet in Purgatory*, 235, 237.

the literature of Lough Derg: that it extends to the heart of the canon of English literature.

If the literary history of purgatory has one of its beginnings at Lough Derg, that history reaches its high point in Dante's *Purgatorio*. Some twentieth-century commentators have suggested that Dante may have been influenced by the literature of Lough Derg. Jacques Le Goff asserts that 'Dante studied the *Tractatus* of H. de Saltrey quite closely,'[1] but there is no direct evidence in Dante for the influence of the *Tractatus*. There are elements in common: Shane Leslie notes parallels between the fourteenth canto of *Inferno* and the twenty-eighth and twenty-ninth cantos of *Purgatorio* and the *Tractatus*,[2] but these do not establish influence. Parallels between Dante's account of the otherworld and the legends that surrounded Lough Derg were apparent during the Middle Ages: in 1412, the Florentine Antonio Mannini's account of his pilgrimage to St Patrick's Purgatory contains a reference to Dante.[3] Direct influence notwithstanding, St Patrick's Purgatory and the literature that surrounded it played an important role in establishing the idea of purgatory in medieval European thought. In adapting Dante's *Commedia* to a local Donegal context in 'Station Island,' then, Heaney is not just appropriating Dante to a local context, but relocating Dante to the site of an earlier medieval purgatory in Ulster; an opportunity he uses to address themes both personal and political.

'Station Island': politics, purgation, and artistic freedom

Heaney's purposes in the 'Station Island' sequence are complex. The motivation of personal purgation for the poet is visibly present as Heaney expresses multiple regrets: asking forgiveness from the ghost of William Strathearn in section VII, condemning himself in section VIII both for his last meeting with Tom Delaney and his account of the death of Colum MacCartney, repenting in section IX 'my unweaned life that kept me competent / To sleepwalk with connivance and mistrust.'[4] In this sense the sequence is 'a *purgatorio* in itself'[5] (although it is not exclusively that), and it's worth bearing in mind the relationship that these poems have to *Sweeney Astray*, a work where, as we have seen, questions of the guilt borne by the artist loom large.

---

[1] Le Goff, *The Birth of Purgatory*, 200.
[2] Leslie, *Saint Patrick's Purgatory*, p. xxiii.
[3] Leslie, *Saint Patrick's Purgatory*, p. xxii–xxiii.
[4] Heaney, *Station Island*, 85; Heaney, *Opened Ground*, 262.
[5] Heaney, 'Envies and Identifications,' 18.

Further to the sequence's purposes in relation to personal purgation, the literature of the otherworld encounter that Heaney invokes here usually has an ethical imperative: those encountered in the world below have a message to convey to readers in the world above. This is the case in the *Tractatus'* promise of punishments in the next world for the sins committed in this; in the *Commedia*, where Beatrice directs Dante in the *Purgatorio* to write 'in pro del mondo che mal vive,' 'for the world's good which lives ill' (*Purgatorio*, XXXII. 103);[1] and even in *Hamlet*, where the ambiguous Ghost has come to convey an unambiguous call to action. In 'Station Island,' what the dead describe to Heaney has nothing to do with the otherworld from which their shades now speak, and everything to do with the contemporary Ireland in which they died. Here, Heaney is indebted to Patrick Kavanagh as much as Dante, for Kavanagh's representation of the Lough Derg pilgrimage is explicitly a piece of social satire. The pieties of Irish Catholicism and the terrors of sectarian conflict are among Heaney's topics here, as they were for Kavanagh and William Carleton respectively. In some ways, as the question posed by Carleton's ghost to the pilgrim Heaney implies, nothing changes; likewise, the shade of Kavanagh can assure Heaney that, forty-two years on, he has got no further than Kavanagh himself had in 1942.

'Station Island' combines these themes of personal purgation and social and political comment in that Heaney's literary pilgrimage is a search for an appropriate personal stance in relation to social and political circumstance. One potential model for a writer is search of such a stance is, of course, Dante. Another, encountered at the end of 'Station Island,' is a further example of the writer in exile: James Joyce.[2] Joyce appears in all three sections of *Station Island*, and in all three there is a reminder of the arc of Heaney's biography in relation to the Joycean model. When writing *Station Island*, Heaney is living in Sandymount, whose Martello tower is the setting for the opening of *Ulysses*, and both 'Granite Chip' from 'Shelf Life' and 'In Illo Tempore' from 'Sweeney Redivivus' are reminders that Heaney's biography has now intersected with Joyce's on Sandymount strand.[3] At the conclusion of 'Station Island' Heaney assumes (briefly, and not without irony) the role of Stephen Dedalus, in associating the date of a crucial entry in Stephen's diary at the end of the *Portrait* with his own

---

[1] Dante, *Divine Comedy*, ed. and trans. Sinclair, ii, 422, 423.

[2] For a discussion of Heaney and Joyce, in 'Station Island' and elsewhere in Heaney's work, see Neil Corcoran, 'Examples of Heaney,' in Corcoran, *Poets of Modern Ireland: Text, Context, Intertext* (Cardiff: University of Wales Press, 1999), 95–120 at 110–19.

[3] Heaney, *Station Island*, 21, 118; Heaney, *Opened Ground*, 218, 285.

birthday.[1] The irony, however, is that Heaney's exile has brought him not to the point of Joyce's eventual arrival, but merely the point he departs from: the role he lays claim to is that of Stephen Dedalus, Joyce's younger self before his departure into exile. As a consequence, the Joycean revenant's response to Heaney's identification with Stephen is one of rebuke.

Joyce has been of use to Heaney in several ways: like Dante, he has served as a figure of the artist in exile, and as an authority for the literary demolition of divisions constructed through linguistic registers. Here, at the conclusion of a literary pilgrimage, he may also serve as a figure for the loss of faith, as Heaney articulates his own *non serviam*.[2] Most of all he serves, like Dante, as a figure of artistic freedom. Stephen Dedalus says in the *Portrait*:

> I will tell you what I will do and what I will not do. I will not serve in that in which I no longer believe whether it call itself my home, my fatherland or my church: and I will try to express myself in some mode of life or art as freely as I can and as wholly as I can, using for myself the only arms I allow myself to use – silence, exile, and cunning.[3]

'Station Island' is similarly a renunciation of affinities in favour of artistic independence: as Heaney declares in 'The Flight Path,' recalling a conversation from 1979, 'If I do write something, / Whatever it is, I'll be writing for myself.'[4] That particular declaration of independence might have been premature, for Heaney has subsequently continued to balance the responsibility of writing for himself with that of speaking up for others, but 'Station Island' nonetheless makes use of the figures of Joyce and Dante in trying to clear some room for the possibility of self-expression.

Revenants and recognitions

'Station Island' is in part an adaptation in miniature of the entire *Commedia*: Heaney seems to suggest as much in describing the sequence as 'a dark night and a bright morning, a departure from the world and a return to it,'

---

[1] Heaney, *Station Island*, 93; this is an association omitted from a reworked 'Station Island' in Heaney's subsequent selections of his work: see Patrick Crotty, 'All I Believe that Happened There was Revision: *Selected Poems 1965–75* and *New Selected Poems 1966–1987*,' in *The Art of Seamus Heaney*, ed. Tony Curtis, 4th edn (Bridgend: Seren, 2001), 193–204 at 202–3.

[2] Cf. Corcoran, 'Examples of Heaney,' 115–19.

[3] James Joyce, *A Portrait of the Artist as a Young Man* (London: Cape, 1964), 254.

[4] Heaney, *The Spirit Level*, 25; Heaney, *Opened Ground*, 413.

and Maria Cristina Fumagalli notes that the allusions to Dante from the *Inferno* in particular must draw into question any reading of the sequence as simply a version of the *Purgatorio* alone.[1] The 'Station Island' collection as a whole also follows the tripartite sequence of the *Commedia*, beginning with a descent (in 'The Underground'), moving through a purgatorial pilgrimage in its middle sequence ('Station Island'), and ending with an upward motion in Heaney's adoption of the figure of Sweeney, the bird-man (in 'Sweeney Redivivus'). As in the *Commedia*, Heaney's progress on his pilgrimage is a series of recognition scenes: all of the poet's visionary interlocutors are based on actual persons – figures from Heaney's family and his upbringing, teachers, friends, other writers, victims of sectarian conflict. Some figures are named, and Carleton, Kavanagh, and Joyce are identified in Heaney's notes to the poem. Others, although based on actual persons named in the discussion below, are abstracted to take on an archetypal character.

As well as adapting Dante and relocating the *Commedia* to an Irish context, Heaney's procedure here involves a complex deployment of quotation and allusion to a much wider range of writing in order to produce composite layers of intertextual reference. The sequence opens with the sound of bells, a call to Sunday prayer that is also reminiscent of Ronan's bell-ringing at the opening of *Sweeney Astray*, an echo reinforced by the appearance of Simon Sweeney a few lines later. This figure of Simon Sweeney is, like the medieval Ulster king, an outcast heretic, a breaker of the Sabbath. He is also the first in a line of Dantesque revenants to be encountered in the sequence, a figure of fear from Heaney's childhood, reminiscent of the similar figure invoked in the poem 'The King of the Ditchbacks,' which closes part one of *Station Island*. With his bow-saw that resembles a lyre, Simon Sweeney is also a figure both of Apollo, the god of poetry, and of Hermes, the psychopomp.[2] Further to that, Sweeney's trade as a woodcutter is a reminder of Heaney's description of Mandelstam's Dante, a 'woodcutter singing at his work in the dark wood of the larynx.' The poem's opening, while reminiscent of *Sweeney Astray*, also recalls William Langland's *Piers Plowman* in its description of a field full of half-remembered faces,[3] an allusion that links 'Station Island' to the tradition of

---

[1] Heaney, 'Envies and Identifications,' 18; Maria Cristina Fumagalli, '"Station Island": Seamus Heaney's *Divina Commedia*,' *Irish University Review* 26/1 (1996), 127–42; Fumagalli, *Flight of the Vernacular*, 135–36.

[2] Fumagalli, '"Station Island",' 137–41; Fumagalli, *Flight of the Vernacular*, 146–49.

[3] The allusion is to *Piers Plowman*, B Prologue, l. 17: 'A fair feeld ful of folk fond I ther bitwene.' See William Langland, *The Vision of Piers Plowman*, ed. A. V. C. Schmidt (London: Dent, 1987). Heaney elsewhere detects the influence of Langland's opening

medieval dream-vision in English. This procedure of creating compound allusions is in keeping with Heaney's practice, already seen, of revisiting and reworking the same material across different poems in diverse ways: both procedures produce complex layers of comparison. If, earlier in the discussion here, we have already seen Sweeney as a Heaney-like poet in exile, a version of the Anglo-Saxon Wanderer, a version of Ulysses, and a version of Icarus, he appears again here in different, multiple, guises.

Comparisons between Sweeney and Dante go beyond 'Station Island,' for Heaney's translation of the early sections of the *Inferno* contains a remarkable echo of his translation of *Buile Suibhne*. In the opening lines, Dante finds himself 'astray in a dark wood.'[1] Here Dante, like Sweeney before him, is astray: the word is repeated in the translation of canto two, where Virgil reports to Dante how Beatrice feared that he might already be 'so far astray' that it would be too late to help him.[2] Like Sweeney, Dante is an exile: he composes his poem having been driven out of his homeland by the civil war between the Ghibellines and Guelfs in his native Florence, to which there are several references in the *Commedia*. Indeed, the setting of the *Commedia* during the days of Easter 1300 may contain, beneath its overt celebration of the possibility of Christian salvation, a grim reference to the Florentine feud that began with the murder of Bondelmonte de' Bondelmonti on Easter Sunday 1215.[3] As Heaney weighs up his own position in relation to social and political circumstance in 'Station Island,' he draws parallels between his own situation and that of two different medieval figures of the poet driven into exile by war.[4]

Following the initial encounter with Simon Sweeney, the next shade encountered on the pilgrimage is the nineteenth-century writer William Carleton, a predecessor of Heaney's in writing about the Lough Derg pilgrimage. Although he rejects for himself the angry role implicitly ascribed to Carleton here, Heaney finds much in common with the figure of the earlier writer. *Traits and Stories of the Irish Peasantry*, mentioned in Heaney's notes to 'Station Island' as Carleton's major work, is an early attempt to

---

lines behind Derek Walcott's 'The Schooner Flight': Seamus Heaney, 'The Murmur of Malvern,' in Heaney, *The Government of the Tongue*, 23–29.

[1] *Dante's Inferno*, ed. Halpern, 3; other translators (H. F. Cary, for instance) use the word 'astray' here, but Heaney's choice is significant given the other comparisons drawn between Sweeney and Dante.

[2] *Dante's Inferno*, ed. Halpern, 8.

[3] Eric Griffiths, 'Introduction,' in *Dante in English*, ed. Griffiths and Reynolds, p. lxxxvi.

[4] The Dante/Sweeney comparison may be strengthened by the suggestion that Dante's surname, Alighieri, may mean 'the wing-bearer': Ciaran Carson, *The Inferno of Dante Alighieri* (London: Granta, 2002), p. xvii.

record a Hiberno-English vernacular: a commitment to the local and vernacular evident in 'Station Island' also.[1] The third encounter is less with an individual than an absence. Heaney has in mind here Agnes Heaney, the sister of Heaney's father, who had died of TB in the 1920s,[2] but what comes into view is a memorial object, not the child herself.

Section IV opens with Heaney, his back turned to the cross, uttering an incomplete renunciation, not of the world, the flesh, and the devil but, it's implied, of Catholicism and its rituals. The revenant here is Terry Keenan, a young missionary priest.[3] When Heaney accuses him of being the prisoner of social convention, Keenan defends himself on grounds of youth and *naïveté*, and turns the accusation back at Heaney, who is himself, Keenan contends, going through the motions. Keenan's last words, however, suggest something else: that the process of going through the motions is one that is coming to an end, and that this pilgrimage is a final look at what is soon to be abandoned.

The next section brings three teachers. The first, Barney Murphy, Heaney's teacher at Anahorish school, is named in the text; the last is explicitly the poet Patrick Kavanagh, named as such in Heaney's notes to the 'Station Island' sequence. The middle figure is identified by Stefan Hawlin as Michael McLaverty,[4] who was both a writer and the principal of the school in Ballymurphy where Heaney first taught, the subject of 'Fosterage' in *North* (alluded to here in the description of Kavanagh as 'a third fosterer').[5] The association of water imagery with creativity is one common in Heaney, and evident in the downpour of rain around the ghost of James Joyce at the end of the 'Station Island' sequence.[6] That imagery occurs here at first in the context of dryness: Barney Murphy's voice lapses (in an echo of the language that Heaney uses to describe Mandelstam's Dante) 'in the limbo and dry urn of the larynx'; when the figure of Master Murphy vanishes, Heaney is refreshed by morning mist; following this, Michael McLaverty's quotation from Gerard Manley Hopkins on love is juxtaposed with the image of water drunk from a well. The final 'fosterer' in this sequence of three, Patrick Kavanagh, is again a precursor of Heaney's in writing about the Lough Derg pilgrimage. This Kavanagh figure is scornful of Heaney, who continues to follow in his footsteps: in this,

[1] See the entries for 'Carleton, William (1794–1869)' and 'Hiberno-English' in *The Concise Oxford Companion to Irish Literature*, ed. Welch.

[2] Parker, *Seamus Heaney: The Making of the Poet*, 195.

[3] Parker, *Seamus Heaney: The Making of the Poet*, 196.

[4] Stefan Hawlin, 'Seamus Heaney's "Station Island": The Shaping of a Modern Purgatory,' *English Studies* (1992), 35–50.

[5] On McLaverty, see Parker, *Seamus Heaney: The Making of the Poet*, 29–30, 149.

[6] On water and wells in Heaney, see Corcoran, *Poetry of Seamus Heaney*, 202–03.

Kavanagh's comments are in line with Carleton's rhetorical question about nothing ever changing. His suggestion that there's hardly any alternative is somewhat ironic, however: in asking what other direction Heaney might take (he might, Kavanagh suggests witheringly, go to Iceland, or maybe the Dordogne), the Kavanagh figure in fact points towards the direction that *Station Island* will adopt at its end point, for the book closes with the figure of Sweeney meditating before the cave paintings at Lascaux, in the Dordogne. Kavanagh's parting shot, a comment that in his day some men made the Lough Derg pilgrimage with an eye out for women, offers a segue into the exploration of sexuality in section VI, a sexuality represented here as repressed by Catholicism, but affirmed in the closing deployment of a quotation from *Inferno* II.

That quotation from the *Inferno* is also a preparation for section VII, for if the previous sections have offered critical reflections on Irish society, and the failings of Irish Catholicism in particular, it is at this point in the sequence that contemporary Ireland really begins to resemble hell. Heaney now encounters the ghost of William Strathearn, with whom he had played football when young, who had been killed by two off-duty policemen.[1] The first sight of the murdered man is presented as a shock:

> And though I was reluctant
> I turned to meet his face and the shock
>
> is still in me at what I saw. His brow
> was blown open above the eye and blood
> had dried on his neck and cheek. 'Easy now,'
>
> he said, 'it's only me. You've seen men as raw
> after a football match [...].'[2]

The poem then goes on to give a step-by-step account of the minutes leading up to the death, as told by the victim himself: the knock on the door in the middle of the night, the two men on the doorstep calling him to open the shop, his wife's panic, his own fear, the sense of tension. The narrative is given in the everyday language of the Ulster vernacular, shaped to Dante's *terza rima*.[3] This account ends before describing the murder, for, as the ghost says, we know as much about that as he does: when questioned, he simply indicates that the men waiting outside were undisguised, barefaced killers, and Heaney responds by telling him what followed, that

---

[1] Parker, *Seamus Heaney: The Making of the Poet*, 198–99.
[2] Heaney, *Station Island*, 77; Heaney, *Opened Ground*, 255.
[3] On which see O'Donoghue, *Seamus Heaney and the Language of Poetry*, 98–100; cf. Corcoran, *Poetry of Seamus Heaney*, 124–25 and nn. 7, 8.

both were caught and jailed. The poem's tone then softens, as William Strathearn's ghost gently gibes at Heaney for being heavier than his youthful self, but turns sorrowful as Heaney observes that the murdered man himself, his injury aside, had hardly aged. Here, for the first time, Heaney asks forgiveness for his own actions; the ghost brushes his words away, then vanishes.

This sense of personal purgation in light of the premature passing of contemporaries endures into section VIII, where there are two encounters, the first with Tom Delaney, an archaeologist friend of Heaney's who died in his early thirties, the second with Colum MacCartney, Heaney's murdered second cousin who was commemorated in 'The Strand at Lough Beg.' Both portraits focus on Heaney's own failings in the face of the deaths of Delaney and MacCartney. In the first encounter, Heaney accuses himself of not meeting his obligations in his last meeting with Delaney in a Dublin hospital; in the second, it is MacCartney who serves as Heaney's accuser, suggesting that the earlier elegy disguised the ugliness of the murder. Here again, Heaney displays guilt at his vocation: the Delaney figure calls him 'lucky poet,' and MacCartney's ghost accuses him both for being absent in the company of poets, and for the poem he writes in remembrance of his cousin's death. Helen Vendler has suggested that all of the direct interlocutors encountered in 'Station Island' are, to some extent, alter egos of Heaney;[1] if so, the three contemporary figures represented in sections VII and VIII in particular have been prematurely deprived of the life the 'lucky poet' continues to enjoy.

The opening lines of section IX, spoken in the first person, could be taken to relate to the pilgrim poet's own purgatorial fast on Station Island, before it becomes clear that another voice is speaking:

> My brain dried like spread turf, my stomach
> Shrank to a cinder and tightened and cracked.[2]

The voice is that of Francis Hughes, a hunger striker: here again, the Northern Ireland troubles are the focus as the sequence descends to its lowest point. Hughes's voice is a voice 'from blight and hunger' – the contemporary incident, Hughes's death by starvation as political protest, is also a reminder of things past, the potato blight that led to the death of a million people in the famine of 1845–47. Francis Hughes was from Bellaghy, a neighbour whose family were known to Heaney, and Heaney outlines the complexities of his feelings on Hughes's death in one of his

---

[1] Vendler, *Seamus Heaney*, 92–94.
[2] Heaney, *Station Island*, 84; Heaney, *Opened Ground*, 261.

subsequent Oxford lectures.[1] Here, descriptions of the natural landscape familiar from Heaney's nature poetry, the landscape of both Heaney's childhood and Hughes', are entwined with descriptions of violence to make a 'maimed music.'[2]

If 'Station Island' is, like the *Commedia*, structured as a descent and resurrection, section IX represents the lowest point: the poetry sinks into despair and self-accusation, before reaching its nadir midway through the section. After this, there is a revival of spirits: 'No more adrift, / My feet touched bottom and my heart revived.' There is more self-accusation to follow, but section IX closes on an optimistic note:

> Then I thought of the tribe whose dances never fail
> For they keep dancing till they sight the deer.[3]

The deer motif here is another look forward towards the cave paintings at Lascaux at the end of the book, the second such gesture in the sequence. This deployment of the deer motif is perhaps another reference to the figure of Sweeney, who is described as stag-headed, and is also, as 'Sweeney Redivivus,' the figure we will meet later in contemplation at Lascaux. The interplay with the Sweeney story endures into section X, where the rescue of Ronan's drowned psalter by an otter is embraced as an example of the 'dazzle of the impossible.' In the reference here, however, the figure of the deer is also invoked in a context suggestive of Native American culture. Parallels between Native American culture and *Sweeney Astray* can be drawn: Heaney comments that he began to translate *Buile Suibhne* at a time when questions of identity and cultural difference raised in the United States for Afro-Americans and Native Americans in the late 1960s and early 1970s had their parallels in similar questions of identity and cultural difference visible in Ulster, and writers sought 'images and analogies that could ease the strain of the present.'[4] There are, then, similar imperatives in Heaney's search for images from medieval Irish culture and a like search by other indigenous peoples in postcolonial societies. The parallel between Irish and Native American circumstance, and the relevance of this for translating *Buile Suibhne*, is carried further by John Montague, who suggests that 'an Irishman of Gaelic background is, in a sense, a White Indian [...]. The poet-king Sweeny, who was translated into a bird, might be

[1] Seamus Heaney, 'Frontiers of Writing,' 186–88.
[2] Heaney, *Station Island*, 84; Heaney, *Opened Ground*, 262; the phrase seems to echo some of the poems in part one of *Station Island*: both 'Widgeon' and the final line of 'Sheelagh na Gig' describe other sorts of 'maimed music' (Heaney, *Station Island*, 48, 50; Heaney, *Opened Ground*, 233, 236).
[3] Heaney, *Station Island*, 86; Heaney, *Opened Ground*, 263.
[4] Heaney, 'Earning a Rhyme,' 60.

a figure – Raven, Crow – from Haida legend.'[1] Here, again, then, Heaney creates a complex series of allusions, where the reference to the deer points to Native American culture, but also to the figure of Sweeney, and so to potential connections between the two, all in the context of an adaptation of Dante.

No revenants are encountered in section x, which instead continues a focus on objects which begins in section IX and extends through XI: here, a brass trumpet, a mug decorated with cornflowers, and a kaleidoscope all serve as images of possibility. In section XI, an unnamed monk from Heaney's past urges him to penitence not through prayer, but through poetry, and specifically by translating something by Juan de la Cruz. The translation that follows, which Heaney's notes identify as 'Cantar del alma que se huelga de conoscer a Diós por fe,'[2] is a description of God as an eternal fountain, a source of nourishment in the night. As elsewhere in Heaney's translation practice, there are echoes of his original poetry here. The lines describing the bottomless nature of the fountain are strongly reminiscent of the end of 'Bogland' from *Door into the Dark*:

> I know no sounding-line can find its bottom,
> nobody ford or plumb its deepest fathom
> although it is the night.[3]

The imagery of water as replenishment connects to a strong current of imagery in Heaney's original work, and in this sequence prepares us for the downpouring of rain that brings the 'Station Island' sequence to a close, following the final encounter in section XII with the figure of James Joyce.

The appearance of the Joyce figure at the end of the sequence is another example of Heaney's compounding of allusions. Although Denis Donoghue criticizes Heaney for invoking the individual figure of Joyce in contrast with the 'familiar compound ghost' of Eliot's 'Little Gidding,'[4] this Joycean figure is, perhaps, not so singular. Heaney has made it clear in

[1] John Montague, 'A Slow Dance,' in Montague, *The Figure in the Cave and other Essays*, 52–53 at 52.

[2] Heaney, *Station Island*, 122.

[3] Heaney, *Station Island*, 90; Heaney, *Opened Ground*, 266.

[4] Donoghue, *We Irish*, 11; T. S. Eliot, *Collected Poems, 1909–1962* (London: Faber, 1974), 214. That Heaney invokes Joyce here rather than Yeats has occasionally been the subject of comment; it's interesting therefore that, as Neil Corcoran notes ('Examples of Heaney,' 119–20), Eliot's drafts portray the 'familiar compound ghost' as an explicitly Yeatsian figure. Similarly, Richard Ellmann (*Ulysses on the Liffey*, 147–48) argues that in *Ulysses*, quotations from Yeats are deliberately deployed to make Yeats a Virgil figure to Joyce's Dante.

his own commentary on 'Station Island' that there are debts here to Eliot, Mandelstam, and, of course, Dante.[1] Further to that, this Joycean figure sounds, in some places at least, less like Joyce than Heaney himself.[2] Joyce is also, like both Dante and Sweeney, a figure of the artist in exile, and *Ulysses* a sort of *Commedia*; the invocation of *A Portrait of the Artist as a Young Man* reminds us that Joyce's autobiographical character, Stephen Dedalus, appropriated by Heaney to himself here, is also a (Sweeney-like) figure of Icarus, the birdman. The figure that Heaney meets at the conclusion of his pilgrimage, then, is like the figure in Eliot, 'both one and many': less James Joyce *per se* than another version of the figure of Joyce/Dante/Sweeney/Heaney, a compound portrait of the artist at a tangent to society who appears in various recombinations through the *Station Island* collection.[3]

Echoes of Dante

The 'Station Island' sequence engages with Dante in terms of its broad structure: it is a narrative of multiple encounters with the dead, told for reasons personal and political, which follows a trajectory that moves gradually downwards before recovery and ascent. But it also engages with Dante in other ways. 'Station Island' is filled with intertextual references: Heaney quotes from or alludes to *Buile Suibhne*, the Catholic liturgy, William Carleton, Gerard Manley Hopkins, Patrick Kavanagh, Horace's *Odes*, his own poems 'The Strand at Lough Beg' and 'Bogland,' Juan de la Cruz, and Joyce's *Portrait of the Artist as a Young Man*. It's no surprise, then, to find that there are also numerous references to Dante in 'Station Island,' made through quotation, intertextual suggestion, and, in some sections, through metre.

Two explicit references to Dante occur earlier in the *Station Island* collection. 'Sandstone Keepsake' alludes to the story of Guy de Montfort in *Inferno* XII, and the note to the poem directs us to the relevant passage in Dante.[4] 'The Loaning' also contains a reference to the *Inferno*, here to the story of Pier delle Vigne in *Inferno* XIII.[5] Both references are to political victims – the first to the murder of Prince Henry, nephew of Henry III, the second to the suicide of Emperor Frederick II's chief counsellor

---

[1] Heaney, 'Envies and Identifications,' 19.
[2] Corcoran, 'Examples of Heaney,' 114.
[3] Cf. Fumagalli, *Flight of the Vernacular*, 149, who also reads Joyce as a 'compound ghost.'
[4] Heaney, *Station Island*, 20 and 122; Heaney, *Opened Ground*, 217.
[5] Heaney, *Station Island*, 52.

following an allegation of conspiracy and subsequent imprisonment, torture, and blinding.[1] Both poems portray a militarized Northern Ireland in the depths of the Troubles: the reference to Dante in 'The Loaning' precedes a scene of interrogation and torture; that in 'Sandstone Keepsake' portrays the poet as a marginal figure, under surveillance from the Magilligan internment camp, which he views from the other side of the border, holding a stone in his hand, but as a memento, not a weapon.

Further to these two direct references to Dante in the first section of *Station Island*, there may also be an indirect allusion to Dante in 'Widgeon.'[2] This much-praised short poem has been read as a gloss upon Heaney's giving voice to the dead, which he does both in translating and adapting *Buile Suibhne* and the *Commedia* in his own voice, and in returning a voice to the prematurely departed shades met on Station Island.[3] If 'Widgeon' does gloss Heaney's ventriloquism for the departed, it does so in a way that recalls other poems. Bernard O'Donoghue observes that the poem, dedicated to Paul Muldoon, reads very much like a Muldoon poem,[4] and if giving voice to the dead through a bird's voice-box reminds us of Heaney's ventriloquism of Sweeney, the bird-man, it may also remind us of a link to Dante via Yeats. Heaney's discussion of Yeats in his 1978 essay 'Yeats as an Example?' ends with a discussion of Yeats's poem 'Cuchulain Comforted,' a poem in *terza rima* about the descent to the underworld, which ends with the bird music of the dead:

> They sang, but had nor human tunes nor words,
> Though all was done in common as before;
>
> They changed their throats and had the throats of birds.[5]

Heaney's procedure throughout *Station Island* is a procedure of composite allusion, where a single line or passage can evoke multiple intertextual echoes. If 'Widgeon' does recall this poem by Yeats, it may also be read as alluding to Dante at one remove.

In the 'Station Island' sequence itself, the influence of Dante is directly evident in Heaney's verse through the use of *terza rima* in some of the sections – II, IV, VII, XII and the opening of XI. There are echoes elsewhere: Heaney's addressing of his teacher, Barney Murphy, as 'Master Murphy' in 'Station Island' V may be reminiscent of Dante's 'Ser Brunetto' in *Inferno*

---

[1] Fumagalli, *Flight of the Vernacular*, 134–35.

[2] Heaney, *Station Island*, 48; Heaney, *Opened Ground*, 233.

[3] Corcoran, *Poetry of Seamus Heaney*, 111; Carson, '*Sweeney Astray*: Escaping from Limbo,' 147–48.

[4] O'Donoghue, *Seamus Heaney and the Language of Poetry*, 66.

[5] Yeats, *Poems*, 380.

xv.[1] Section v also contains a quotation from Gerard Manley Hopkins that can be read as serving multiple purposes, some of them related to Dante. The lines from Hopkins read: 'For what is the great moving power and spring of verse? Feeling, and in particular, love.'[2] They serve in part to identify the speaker (Michael McLaverty was a great enthusiast for Hopkins's work; 'Fosterage' from *North* recalls McLaverty's gift of Hopkins's *Journals*),[3] and perhaps also to suggest indirectly that the purgatorial self-examination in poetry that Heaney undertakes in 'Station Island' bears a similarity to Hopkins's own terrible sonnets. Within the sequence itself, the description of love as a 'spring' points forward to the deluge of water imagery in sections XI and XII. Furthermore, the description of love as the great moving power and spring of verse is also, as Maria Cristina Fumagalli suggests, in tune with the sentiments of Dante, who sees human love as a manifestation of the divine love which moves the Universe.[4]

Towards the end of section VI we have the sequence's single direct quotation from Dante, its presence in the text signalled by the use of italics:

> *As little flowers that were all bowed and shut*
> *By the night chills rise on their stems and open*
> *As soon as they have felt the touch of sunlight,*
> *So I revived in my own wilting powers*
> *And my heart flushed, like somebody set free.*[5]

This is a translation of Dante's:

> Quali i fioretti, dal notturno gelo
> chinati e chiusi, poi che 'l sol li 'mbianca
> si drizzan tutti aperti in loro stelo,
>
> tal mi fec'io di mia virtute stanca,
> e tanto buono ardire al cor mi corse,
> ch'i' cominciai come persona franca. (*Inferno* II. 127–32)[6]

As included here in section VI, this passage is about sexuality, an affirmation of sexual love set against the repressiveness of Irish Catholic attitudes from the preceding descriptions; in its description of 'somebody set free' ('come persona franca') it also presages the liberation from affinities

---

[1] As suggested by O'Donoghue, 'Dante's Versatility,' 247; Heaney, *Station Island*, p.72; Heaney, *Opened Ground*, 251.

[2] Quoted in Heaney, *Station Island*, 73; Heaney, *Opened Ground*, 253.

[3] Heaney, *North*, 71; Heaney, *Opened Ground*, 142.

[4] Fumagalli, *Flight of the Vernacular*, 140.

[5] Heaney, *Station Island*, 76; Heaney, *Opened Ground*, 255.

[6] Dante, *Divine Comedy*, ed. and trans. Sinclair, i, 40.

prescribed by the Joycean revenant in section XII. In Dante's text, the passage follows Virgil's account of Beatrice, and so in the original, as in Heaney's adaptation, the lines describe a response to love. It also serves here, however, as a signal that, as in Dante, the descent into the *Inferno* proper is about to begin.

The next reference to the *Commedia* comes in 'Station Island' VIII, indirectly via Heaney's 'The Strand at Lough Beg,' when the shade of Colum MacCartney accuses Heaney of using the *Purgatorio* to soften the reality of his murder.[1] There is another borrowing in section IX, where Bernard O'Donoghue identifies the lines describing the lighted candle as indebted to the flame of Ulysses in *Inferno* XXVI.[2] Further to this, Maria Cristina Fumagalli suggests that the description of God as an eternal fountain in the translation from Juan de la Cruz in section XI resonates with Dante's description of God as an eternal fountain in *Paradiso* XXXI. 93.[3]

Finally, there is a substantial resonance between Heaney's description of James Joyce and the figure of Cacciaguida encountered in *Paradiso* XV, XVI, and XVII.[4] Cacciaguida is Dante's great-great-grandfather: 'io fui la tua radice,' as he tells Dante, 'I was thy root,' and Dante he calls 'fronda mia,' 'my branch' (*Paradiso* XV. 88, 89).[5] Dante responds in kind: 'Voi siete il padre mio,' he says, 'you are my father' (*Paradiso* XVI. 16).[6] In 'Station Island,' Heaney acknowledges Joyce as a (literary) forefather, addressing him as 'Old father,' an address that is itself a quotation from Joyce as well as a possible allusion to Dante, since Stephen Dedalus addresses his father in the final line of the *Portrait* as 'old father, old artificer.'[7]

Cacciaguida predicts Dante's future for him, and what it contains is exile:

> Tu lascerai ogni cosa diletta
> più caramente; e questo è quello strale
> che l'arco dello essilio pria saetta.
>
> Tu proverai sì come sa di sale

[1] Heaney, *Station Island*, 83; Heaney, *Opened Ground*, 261.

[2] O'Donoghue, 'Dante's Versatility,' 247.

[3] Fumagalli, *Flight of the Vernacular*, 139.

[4] The discussion here is indebted to Fumagalli, *Flight of the Vernacular*, 142–43; other commentators (Donoghue, *We Irish*, 11) have also drawn a comparison with the Brunetto Latini passage in *Inferno* XV, an influence that is at least indirectly present, since the passage in Eliot's 'Little Gidding' to which Heaney is indebted here is based on the portrayal of Brunetto.

[5] Dante, *Divine Comedy*, ed. and trans. Sinclair, iii, 218, 219.

[6] Dante, *Divine Comedy*, ed. and trans. Sinclair, iii, 228, 229.

[7] Heaney, *Station Island*, 93; Joyce, *Portrait*, 257.

> lo pane altrui, e come è duro calle
> lo scendere e 'l salir per l'altrui scale. (*Paradiso* XVII. 55–60)

Thou shalt leave everything loved most dearly, and this is the shaft which the bow of exile shoots first. Thou shalt prove how salt is the taste of another man's bread and how hard is the way up and down another man's stairs.[1]

As a consequence, he advises Dante to make himself alone his faction (*Paradiso* XVII. 69), advice which may lie behind that of Joyce to Heaney at the end of 'Station Island,' one exile to another, to keep at a tangent to others, and strike out on his own.[2]

This sequence of poems describing encounters with the departed on a Donegal pilgrimage, then, is heavily indebted to Dante not only in relation to theme and structure, but also through the inscription of multiple echoes of Dante into the text itself. The echoes are, however, complex and layered: the Joyce figure, for instance, is a version of Cacciaguida, certainly, but also of Heaney and Sweeney, with echoes from T. S. Eliot and Osip Mandelstam as well as Dante. Rather than creating simple equivalences between the contemporary and the medieval, Heaney creates multiple, complex evocations of resonances between figures from the past and those of the present.

Station Island does not end with the downpour of rain into which the ghost of James Joyce disappears at the end of the title sequence; the book then moves to recount the flight of a revivified Sweeney, already discussed in the previous chapter. If the 'Station Island' sequence comes to a close with a revivifying downpour, Sweeney's return to flight, as we have seen, does not end with such certainty. Rather, at the end of 'Sweeney Redivivus,' which is also the end of the *Station Island* collection, the figure of Heaney/Sweeney/Icarus comes to rest in expectation of a patient wait at a dried-up source. As we have seen, this does not represent the end of Heaney's engagement with Dante, which continues to be substantial, particularly in *Field Work*, and persists to some degree as far as Heaney's most recent work. But the volume that follows *Station Island*, 1987's *The Haw Lantern*, also gives an indication of Heaney's next substantial engagement with a medieval text, containing as it does a first fragment of the *Beowulf* translation that would not be completed for many years to come.

---

[1] Dante, *Divine Comedy*, ed. and trans. Sinclair, iii, 244, 245.

[2] Heaney, *Station Island*, 93–94; Heaney, *Opened Ground*, 268.

3

Beowulf

SEAMUS Heaney's translation of *Beowulf*, published in 1999, was his first full-length translation of a substantial medieval text since *Sweeney Astray*, and, like *Sweeney Astray*, it was a long time coming. The commission to translate the poem came in the early 1980s from the editors of *The Norton Anthology of English Literature*, and a portion of Heaney's early work on the translation appeared as 'The Ship of Death' in his 1987 collection, *The Haw Lantern*. By this time, however, the translation project had been put to one side – Heaney comments in a 1988 interview that 'The Ship of Death' 'was born out of an opportunity, which I sadly didn't have the stamina to carry through, to translate *Beowulf*.'[1] In his introduction to the completed translation, published eleven years after this comment, Heaney indicated that although the difficulties inherent in the project caused him to set it aside, he had an instinct nonetheless that the translation should not be abandoned (pp. xxii–xxiii). In the acknowledgements that follow the published version, he says that he 'got going in earnest four years ago' (p. 105), in the mid nineties.[2]

When the translation did appear, it appeared to wide acclaim, winning the Whitbread Book of the Year award for 1999, and becoming what Frank Kermode termed 'a slightly surprising best-seller.'[3] Some Old English specialists expressed reservations: partly, it seems, on the grounds that Heaney, as a Nobel Prize-winner whose translation was to appear in the *Norton Anthology*, was to a certain extent likely to overshadow the poem

[1] Brandes, 'Seamus Heaney: An Interview,' 13; for the influence of 'The Ship of Death' on other poems in *The Haw Lantern*, see Jones, *Strange Likeness*, 225–28.

[2] Except where noted, page references are to *Beowulf*, translated by Seamus Heaney (London: Faber, 1999). Line references are to the Old English text; these and glosses of Old English words refer to *Beowulf with the Finnesburg Fragment*, ed. C. L. Wrenn and W. F. Bolton, 5th edn (Exeter: University of Exeter Press, 1996).

[3] Frank Kermode, 'The Modern Beowulf,' in Kermode, *Pleasing Myself: From Beowulf to Philip Roth* (London: Penguin, 2001), 1–12 at 10, first published in *The New York Review of Books*.

that he was translating, to say nothing of all previous translations put together. 'Like it or not,' wrote Tom Shippey, 'Heaney's Beowulf is the poem now, for probably two generations.'[1] Other medievalists offered praise: juxtaposing Heaney with the poem's most eminent critic, Andy Orchard commented that 'surely Seamus Heaney and J. R. R. Tolkien have and will continue to serve the poem well.'[2] Helen Phillips praised Heaney's translation as 'both a service to, and an inventive and intelligent dialogue with, his predecessors' art.'[3]

Notwithstanding the difficulties of its language, and the uncertainty surrounding the poem's subject, theme, and date and place of origin, *Beowulf* is an important work, the most complex and substantial surviving work of Old English literature, much taught (in the original or in translation) as part of English literature courses, and the subject of an enormous critical industry. But *Beowulf*'s foundational status in the English literary canon is open to question, in part because of the lack of a continuous literary tradition in English between the early and the later Middle Ages. The construction of Chaucer as the 'father of English poetry' (discussed in Chapter 4 below in relation to Dryden) is a process that begins in the fifteenth century, as English writers defer to a literary father figure,[4] and the later discovery of an earlier English literary tradition has not entirely dislodged this sense that English literature begins in the second half of the fourteenth century. Hence Frank Kermode: 'If you are prepared to admit that it was written in English, *Beowulf* is by far the oldest poem of its length in our language. When struggling through it as a student I preferred to call its language Anglo-Saxon, regarding the official description, Old English, as a trick, a means of getting into an English literature course a work in a remote Germanic dialect.'[5] Despite its claims to foundational status, *Beowulf* does not rate a mention in the text of Harold Bloom's *The Western Canon*, which opens with Shakespeare, the foundational writer for Bloom's version of the canon, before moving backwards to what he calls 'the strangeness of Dante,' and then forward to Chaucer. *Beowulf* (in Charles Kennedy's translation) makes it into Bloom's bibliography of canonical works in Appendix A, under the heading 'The Middle Ages: Latin, Arabic, and the Vernacular before Dante,' one of thirteen works

---

[1] Tom Shippey, 'Beowulf for the Big-Voiced Scullions,' *TLS* (1 Oct. 1999).

[2] Andy Orchard, *A Critical Companion to 'Beowulf'* (Cambridge: Brewer, 2003), 267.

[3] Helen Phillips, 'Seamus Heaney's *Beowulf*,' in *The Art of Seamus Heaney*, ed. Curtis, 265–85 at 284.

[4] See Seth Lerer, *Chaucer and his Readers: Imagining the Author in Late Medieval England* (Princeton: Princeton University Press, 1993).

[5] Kermode, 'The Modern Beowulf,' 2.

here.[1] For some, then, *Beowulf* is located so deep in the foundations of English literature as to be lost from sight. Heaney, however, has no such doubts about the poem's foundational status in English (p. ix) or, for that matter, its place in world art (p. xii). Those who see *Beowulf* as non-foundational do so on the grounds that its premodernity makes it alien to us; Heaney challenges this in undertaking a remaking of the poem that suggests its relevance for contemporary concerns. That he does so is not due to anything lacking in the original that requires the supplement of the contemporary, but rather the opposite: the original is 'equal to our knowledge of reality in the present time' (p. ix), and so has something to tell us about our contemporary existence.

To a certain extent, some of the difficulties that this new translation might be thought to pose could stem from the multiple purposes that this new version of *Beowulf* was meant to serve. Heaney's introduction to the translation makes it clear that he sought to offer advocacy of the poem as poetry, to rescue it from the impression that it had been written 'on official paper.' In order to do so, he offers a translation that matches the rest of his poetry in its departures from standard English. But because the poem was to exist, not just as a thing in itself, but also in order to serve a pedagogical function as part of the *Norton Anthology*, it required a certain clarity for the parts of its readership who would come to it, via the anthology, in the classroom. As Heaney himself comments:

> 'Literary' does not mean 'lofty.' The proper translation – 'proper' in the Latin sense of belonging, belonging recognizably to the original and to the œuvre of the translator – exists half-way between a crib and an appropriation. For the truth is, as Eliot Weinberger has said, one of the big motives for translating at all is in order to write vicariously, and for that vicariousness to be complete, the writing has to include those quickenings and homecomings that accompany successful original composition. What keeps the translator in a state of near (but never quite complete) fulfilment is this tension between the impulse to use the work in its first language as a stimulus and the obligation to give it a fair hearing in the second. And because of the strong pedagogical function served by the Norton Anthology, I was more than usually subject to that tension. Indeed, there could be no better illustration of the fact of the tension itself than the footnotes in the new volume. At certain points, it is the very translation that

---

[1] Harold Bloom, *The Western Canon: The Books and School of the Ages* (New York: Harcourt Brace, 1994), 533.

has to be translated for the benefit of the worldwide audience of English-speakers to whom the anthology is directed.[1]

The multiple ways in which we might be expected to take this *Beowulf* are suggested in part by its appearance in four different versions, to a number of slightly different purposes. As published by Faber, the translation stands on its own, accompanied by Heaney's introduction and acknowledgements, a note on names by Alfred David reprinted from the Norton Anthology, a genealogical diagram to help the reader keep track of who's who in the world of the poem, and a single page of the original text facing the opening page of the translation, an accompaniment that fades out quickly as the translation gets going. Here, then, the translation is largely to be read as a thing in itself. The US edition, published by Farrar, Straus & Giroux, is almost, but not quite, identical to the Faber edition.[2] It contains all of the elements listed above, but publishes Heaney's translation in parallel to the original text, on facing pages (here using the Wrenn and Bolton edition of the original, rather than that of George Jack printed by Faber). Here the translation exists in dialogue with the original text to a greater extent than is possible in the Faber version. The third context in which the translation (or, here, extracts from the translation) appears is in the *Norton Anthology*, to explicitly pedagogical purpose. Here, as Heaney notes, the text of the translation is accompanied by explanatory footnotes to gloss his gloss on the Old English original: *tholed, bothies, graith, boltered, bawn, session, keens, brehon, wean,* and *hoked* are all found in need of clarificatory comment.[3] Finally, there is the Norton critical edition, an edition of Heaney's translation by Daniel Donoghue, which prints the entire translation, again to pedagogical purpose and with explanatory footnotes, surrounded by a critical apparatus that provides exegetical comment on both the Old English text and Heaney's translation.[4]

More substantial than this question of how a translation should be pitched in relation to different audiences is the question of the appropriateness of translating an Old English poem into a modern English inflected with Hiberno-English dialect. Both Heaney himself, in his introduction to the translation and in two subsequent essays, and the translation's many commentators and reviewers, have felt it necessary to discuss

---

[1] Seamus Heaney, 'The Drag of the Golden Chain,' *TLS* (12 Nov. 1999).

[2] *Beowulf: A New Verse Translation*, trans. Seamus Heaney (New York: Farrar, Strauss and Giroux, 2000).

[3] *The Norton Anthology of English Literature*, ed. M. H. Abrams, Stephen Greenblatt, et al., 7th edn, 2 vols (New York and London: Norton, 2000).

[4] *Beowulf: A Verse Translation*, trans. Seamus Heaney, ed. Daniel Donoghue (New York and London: Norton, 2002).

the implications of an Irish poet translating an Anglo-Saxon poem into an Irish-inflected English. To quote Nicholas Howe, reviewing the translation for *The New Republic*: 'What complicates Heaney's translation, and in many ways makes it deeply interesting as a contemporary statement on literature and politics, as a redress of poetry, is that he sets out to make the poem Irish.'[1]

Hiberno-Anglo-Saxon and the language of 'Beowulf'

The potential difficulties for an Irish writer facing an Anglo-Saxon text are two-sided. On the one side, there is a tendency for the narrowest and most protective limitations on the expressive possibilities of English to be tied up with a sense of Anglo-Saxon origins, something suggested perhaps by Heaney's mention of 'the prejudice in favour of Anglo-Saxon over Latinate diction in translations of the poem' in the acknowledgements that follow his translation (p. 105). That sense that a modern English translation of an Anglo-Saxon text should be conservative in staying as close as possible to an Anglo-Saxon vocabulary suggests a problematic notion of linguistic purity. Further to that, the study of Anglo-Saxon literature, including *Beowulf*, has been historically connected with ideas of Anglo-Saxon racial identity: in the past, the desire for both linguistic and national points of origin have been closely entwined.[2] That such notions present difficulties for an Irish poet approaching an Anglo-Saxon poem, for reasons cultural and political, is made clear by Heaney in his introduction to his *Beowulf* translation. It took a while, he says, for him to come to the conclusion that *Beowulf* was 'part of my voice-right' (p. xxiii).

On the other side of the problem is an Irish feeling of unease with the English language. The issue is, as Robert Welch puts it, that 'Irish literature is one of those literatures which changed its language, a circumstance

---

[1] Nicholas Howe, 'Scullionspeak,' *The New Republic* (28 Feb. 2000). There are several readings of the original poem that make *Beowulf* Irish by suggesting Irish influence (see most recently R. Mark Scowcroft, 'The Irish Analogues to *Beowulf*,' *Speculum* 74 (1999), 22–64; more generally, Martin Puhvel, '*Beowulf*' and Celtic Tradition (Waterloo, Ont.: Wilfred Laurier University Press, 1979)); Contemporary commentators, in keeping with the poem's setting, continue to emphasise the parallels between the Old English poem and Scandinavian literature, and here Heaney is no different.

[2] Eric Gerard Stanley, *In the Foreground: 'Beowulf'* (Cambridge: Brewer, 1994), 64; Allen J. Frantzen, *Desire for Origins: New Language, Old English, and Teaching the Tradition* (New Brunswick, NJ, and London: Rutgers University Press, 1990), 18, 55, 66, 74, 208, 215.

of enormous difficulty, challenge, and opportunity.'¹ The difficulty can be in part a sense of a language lost – something that finds forceful expression in that stock phrase of Irish cultural nationalism, *tír gan teanga, tír gan anam*: 'a country without a language is a country without a soul.' Heaney conveys a sense of this problem in the introduction to his translation, where he explains a sense that Irish was 'the language that I should by rights have been speaking but I had been robbed of' (p. xxiv). Further to this sense of dispossession from a language lost is a sense of difficulty with the language gained. Because the change of language was an imposition, Irish writers whose heritage is politically nationalist but who write in English necessarily feel a difficulty with the linguistic heritage of the language that they write in. James Joyce's Stephen Dedalus expresses this aspect of the problem like this:

> – The language in which we are speaking is his before it is mine. How different are the words *home, Christ, ale, master*, on his lips and on mine! I cannot speak or write these words without unrest of spirit. His language, so familiar and so foreign, will always be for me an acquired speech. I have not made or accepted its words. My voice holds them at bay. My soul frets in the shadow of his language.²

Heaney quotes part of this passage from Joyce in his poem, 'The Wool Trade,'³ and discusses it again, this time in relation to the *Beowulf* translation, in his essay 'The Drag of the Golden Chain.'⁴ This Irish sense of the English language as a difficulty to be negotiated is one associated with that sense of a connection between linguistic and national origins, this time seen from inside the language but outside the nation. It's a difficulty that can only be increased by an insistence upon ideas of Anglo-Saxon linguistic purity in English. This two-sided thing – an Irish feeling of unease with the English language, and a tendency for the narrowest limitations on the expressive possibilities of the English language to be tied up with a sense of Anglo-Saxon origins – are the difficulties that confront Heaney (as they did Joyce) in 'dealing with the whole vexed question – the question, that is, of the relationship between nationality, language, history and literary tradition in Ireland' (p. xxiv).

These potential adversities between Irish and English were brought into sharp focus during the Northern Ireland conflict, where political adversity

---

¹ Robert Welch, Preface to *The Oxford Companion to Irish Literature*, ed. Welch (Oxford: Oxford University Press, 1996), p. xiii.
² Joyce, *Portrait of the Artist*, 194.
³ Heaney, *Wintering Out*, 37.
⁴ Heaney, 'The Drag of the Golden Chain.'

could lead to cultural adversity, and Irish and English cultures could be seen as oppositional and hostile.[1] This is explicit in 'The Ministry of Fear,' from *North*:

> And heading back for home, the summer's
> Freedom dwindling night by night, the air
> All moonlight and a scent of hay, policemen
> Swung their crimson flashlamps, crowding round
> The car like black cattle, snuffing and pointing
> The muzzle of a Sten gun in my eye:
> 'What's your name, driver?'
>   'Seamus ...'
>   *Seamus?*
>   ('The Ministry of Fear')[2]

If Heaney's right to his Irish heritage (expressed here by his Irish name, Seamus) in a British state is challenged here by policemen with Sten guns, the poem then goes on to problematize any claim that he might have on English literary culture: 'Ulster was British, but with no rights on / The English lyric.'[3]

'The Ministry of Fear' raises the question of the 'rights' that non-English speakers of the English language may have to the English literary heritage, especially in their own, non-standard, voice, and this is a problem that arises again in translating *Beowulf*. Heaney is able to describe the point of view that the Irish language was the language that he should 'by rights have been speaking' (p. xxiv), and can say elsewhere of his translation of *Buile Suibhne* that 'of course I felt I had the right to it.'[4] But the notion that Beowulf was part of his 'voice-right,' as he terms it in his introduction (p. xxiii), or 'an inheritance' that he might claim (as the epigraph taken from his poem 'The Settle Bed' (p. ix) suggests), takes some time to arrive at. In 'The Drag of the Golden Chain,' he draws a parallel between his discovery of the word 'thole' (a favourite Ulster dialect word, used previously in both *Sweeney Astray* and *The Midnight Verdict*)[5] in the original Old English text of *Beowulf*, and Stephen Dedalus's discovery that the word 'tundish,' the source of his earlier outpourings of anguish,

---

[1] Terry Eagleton seems to ignore this in commenting in his review of Heaney's *Beowulf*, 'Hasped and Hooped and Hirpling,' *London Review of Books* (11 Nov. 1999), that 'the "partitioned intellect" in Ireland is not one which sees Irish and British culture as rigidly adversarial. On the contrary, it is one which sees them as intimately interwoven.'
[2] Heaney, *North*, 64; Heaney, *Opened Ground*, 136.
[3] Heaney, *North*, 65; Heaney, *Opened Ground*, 136.
[4] Brandes, 'Seamus Heaney: An Interview,' 12.
[5] O'Donoghue, *Seamus Heaney and the Language of Poetry*, 90.

was both part of his Dublin vocabulary and 'good old blunt English.' As Heaney comments, 'By finding that his Dublin vernacular is related to the old English base, Stephen discovers that his own linguistic rights to English are, as it were, prenatal. He may not be the true-born English man, but he is the new-born English speaker.'[1] Here, Joyce is of use to Heaney in making a point that his revenant self makes towards the end of 'Station Island': that Irish writers, too, may claim ownership of the English language.[2]

If Heaney revisits the problem of potential cultural adversities between Irish and English in the introduction to the *Beowulf* translation, he does so, I think, because of that aforementioned prejudice in previous translations of Old English texts in favour of a diction of Anglo-Saxon origin. Notwithstanding the occasional misreading that sees Heaney's translation of *Beowulf* as a continuation of cultural animosities,[3] it's clear that in fact the translation is a gesture towards breaking down the barriers that are perceived to exist between Irish and English. Discussing the *Beowulf* translation in his essay 'Through-Other Places, Through-Other Times: The Irish Poet and Britain,' Heaney points to Paul Muldoon's translation of Nuala Ní Dhomhnaill's poem 'Ceist na Teangan,' literally 'The Language Question,' as 'The Language Issue,' where the additional resonances of 'issue' means that 'what was problematic has become productive'.[4] Heaney himself does something similar in the same essay by claiming the phrase 'through-other,' meaning 'physically untidy or mentally confused' in an echo of the Irish *trí na céile*. Heaney appropriates this as a positive term to short-circuit the oppositional sense of 'otherness,' saying:

> In the post-colonial phase of our criticism and cultural studies, we have heard much about 'the other', but perhaps the moment of the through-other should now be proclaimed, if only because it seems to have arrived. Translation, among other things, has seen to that.[5]

A translation of *Beowulf* by an Irish poet will be a 'through-other' enterprise, but that is a positive step towards breaking down the otherness that has been constructed between Irish and English. If Heaney declares in this essay that *Beowulf* can now be a book from Ireland, he hopes that it can be

[1] Heaney, 'The Drag of the Golden Chain.'

[2] Heaney, *Station Island*, 93; Heaney, *Opened Ground*, 268.

[3] Loren C. Gruber, '"So." So What? It's a Culture War. That's Hwæt!' *In Geardagum* 23 (2002), 67–84.

[4] Seamus Heaney, 'Through-Other Places, Through-Other Times: The Irish Poet and Britain,' in *Finders Keepers*, 364–82 at 380. Heaney also comments of Stephen Dedalus in 'The Drag of the Golden Chain' that he is 'freed of the language question to become part of the language issue.'

[5] Heaney, 'Through-Other Places, Through-Other Times,' 379.

one similar to those books from Ireland described by the Venerable Bede in the eighth century; a book with the power to heal. Heaney quotes a passage from Bede describing the lack of snakes on the neighbouring island. Bede comments that almost everything in Ireland confers immunity to poison: indeed he has heard that drinking water in which scrapings from Irish books have been steeped is a remedy for those suffering from snakebite.[1] Heaney acknowledges that this account of books from Ireland which have the power to draw poison and heal wounds may be a rare example of humour in Bede;[2] he himself, however, is entirely serious. If he has written an Irish *Beowulf*, that is an effort towards healing differences, not continuing them.

Heaney's sense of a solution to the problem of the 'Irish/English duality' (p. xxiv) gives a nod towards Joyce's own solution to that problem:

> in my mind the stream was suddenly turned into a kind of linguistic river of rivers issuing from a pristine Celto-British Land of Cockaigne, a riverrun of Finnegans Wakespeak pouring out of the cleft rock of some prepolitical, prelapsarian, ur-philological Big Rock Candy Mountain − and all of this had a wonderfully sweetening effect upon me. (p. xxiv)

In *Finnegans Wake*, Joyce tries to create, as Umberto Eco has suggested, a language that precedes Babel, a perfect, universal language that re-enacts the perfect language of Adam:[3] as Heaney says here, a 'prelapsarian, ur-philological' language. But *Finnegans Wake* hardly stands as a useful model for the language in Heaney's own poems, even if it might stand behind them as the flood sweeping through the partitions between Irish and English. Heaney's mention of the Land of Cockaigne is more suggestive: for the late medieval poem *The Land of Cockaigne* is not just a poem about an exuberant fantasyland, a 'cloud-cuckoo-land of sensual bliss,'[4] but also the first major Hiberno-English poem, identifiable as such from its vocabulary. In the lines:

---

[1] Bede, *A History of the English Church and People*, trans. Leo Sherley-Price (Harmondsworth: Penguin, 1955), 39; Heaney, 'Through-Other Places, Through-Other Times,' 381.

[2] Heaney, 'Through-Other Places, Through-Other Times,' 381.

[3] Umberto Eco, 'A Portrait of the Artist as a Bachelor,' in Eco and Liberato Santoro-Brienza, *Talking of Joyce*, ed. J. C. Mays (Dublin: UCD Press, 1998).

[4] *Early Middle English Verse and Prose*, ed. J. A. W. Bennett and G. V. Smithers with Norman Davis, 2nd edn (Oxford: Oxford University Press, 1968), 136.

Þe met is trie, þe drink is clere,
To none, russin, and sopper. (19–20)[1]

The food is excellent, the drink is clear,
For lunch, snack and supper.

the word *russin* (a light meal between dinner and supper) is the Irish word *ruisín*.[2] The incorporation of the local into language is very much Heaney's own style, both in the *Beowulf* translation and elsewhere, and in Ireland the local is inevitably a blending of languages.

In his introduction to *Beowulf*, Heaney points to his use in the poem of the word 'thole,' from Old English *þolian*, 'endure, suffer, hold out,' not as an archaism but as a word linking the Ulster vernacular and the language of the Old English text. That it is not to be seen as an archaism, as an example of that preference for Anglo-Saxon diction that this translation rejects, is clear both from the space in the introduction that Heaney devotes to discussing its resonances and from the way that he uses the word in the poem. For if Heaney uses 'thole,' it is not to translate *þolian*. In Heaney's half-line:

He knew what they had tholed. (p. 3)

'tholed' here does not translate the verb *þolian*, which is not present in the text at this point, but rather the noun *fyren-ðearfe*, 'grievous distress, distress caused by wickedness' (14).[3] Where *þolian* does appear in the poem at line 832, Heaney does not translate it as 'thole.' Where the original has:

ond for þrea-nydum   þolian scoldon
torn unlytel. (832–33a)

Heaney's version has:

the hard fate they'd been forced to undergo,
no small affliction. (p. 27)

where 'to undergo' here translates *þolian*. Furthermore, 'thole' is a word that Heaney uses elsewhere in his poetry: he uses it, of all places, in *Sweeney Astray*, his translation of the medieval Irish *Buile Suibhne*, and later in *The Midnight Verdict*, a partial translation of Brian Merriman's

---

[1] *Early Middle English Verse and Prose*, ed. Bennett and Smithers, 139.
[2] *Early Middle English Verse and Prose*, ed. Bennett and Smithers, 337.
[3] Shippey's *TLS* review suggests that 'tholed' here translates *drugon* in line 15. I take it that the subsequent lines in Heaney, 'the long times and troubles they'd come through / without a leader' translate 15–16a, 'þæt hie ær drugon aldor-lease / lange hwile.' Either way, *þolian* is not present in the original text at this point.

eighteenth-century Irish poem *Cúirt an Mheán Oíche*. These uses of 'thole' are a sign that Heaney's commitment to linguistic pluralism does not come into play only when translating from Old English. Heaney's desire to find 'an escape route [...] away into some unpartitioned linguistic country, a region where one's language would not be simply a badge of ethnicity or a matter of cultural preference or an official imposition, but an entry into further language' (p. xxv) is a desire for multiculturalism, and the word 'thole,' rather than being a sign of an exclusive Anglo-Saxonness, becomes instead a symbol of that multiculturalism, as Heaney finds it in the Ulster dialect of his aunt, in the American English of John Crowe Ransom, and in the centuries-old poem that he is translating (p. xxv). But if Heaney is looking for multiculturalism, it is clear that he expects that multicultural-ism to have *roots*. What he feels, he tells us, quoting Mandelstam, is 'a nos-talgia for world culture' (p. xxvi). It is the word *nostalgia* that is worth noting here: a world culture is something that may be built not out of historical amnesia, but by looking again at the past.

Thanes and septs

If some of the language of the translation has been chosen to find the 'middle voice' between standard and vernacular as the voice of the poem, some of it is there, as Heaney tells us, for reasons of historical suggestive-ness (p. xxx). A possible example is the Danish coastguard's speech to Beowulf's troop on their arrival in Denmark. The coastguard notes that Beowulf's force has not asked 'if the sentries allowed them safe passage / or the clan had consented' (p. 10). The phrase 'the clan had consented,' using a particularly Gaelic social term, translates *maga gemedu*, 'the consent of the kinsmen' (247).[1] Another Gaelic term is used to describe Unferth, who is called a 'brehon' (p. 48), translating *ðyle*, 'orator, spokesman, principal court officer' (1456).[2] Later in the narrative, Beowulf tells Hrothgar that he need not fear 'for a single thane of your sept or nation' (p. 54). Here 'of your sept or nation' translates *þinra leoda* (1673b), where *leod* is glossed by Wrenn and Bolton as 'tribe, nation, people.'[3] Terms like 'clan,' 'brehon,' 'sept' – terms defining social units or social positions from medieval Gaelic society – seem perhaps an odd choice of language here. It's not a constant thing in the translation: Heaney uses 'thane' throughout for *þegn*, the term

---

[1] For 'clan,' see *OED*, s.v. *clan*; cf. *DIL*, s.v. *clann*, '(c) children, family, offspring; a single child; descendants, race, clan.'

[2] See *OED*, s.v. *brehon*; cf. *DIL*, s.v. *breithen*, 'judge.'

[3] For 'sept,' see *OED*, s.v. *sept*.

for a noble retainer. It is, however, suggestive of a comparable social structure, and perhaps of the historical links between Gaelic and Scandinavian
society.

'Beyond the pale'

One of the most telling pieces of evidence for the hint in Heaney's translation at the connections between medieval Irish history and the world
of the poem's Scandinavian narrative comes in the lines where Hrothgar
is speaking after Grendel's mother has attacked Heorot. There Hrothgar
describes Grendel as follows:

> the other, warped
> in the shape of a man, moves beyond the pale (p. 45)

where the Old English text reads:

> oðer earm-sceapen
> on weres wæstmum wræc-lastas træd. (1351b–52)

The phrase 'beyond the pale,' here translating *wræc-lastas*, 'the paths of
exile' (1352), is a term resonant with meaning from colonial Ireland. The
pale was the dividing line between the territory safely occupied by the
English colonisers, where English law applied, and the less certain territory of predominantly Gaelic habitation. 'Beyond the pale' was beyond
the security of the English fortifications. Although the area enclosed by
the pale varied historically, it was always centred on Dublin (the other
English pale, in France, centred on Calais), and Dublin is still known colloquially in contemporary Ireland as 'the pale.' In Heaney's poem, then,
'beyond the pale' can be read first of all (as the original would demand)
as simply meaning 'in exile,' or 'beyond the safe haven of civilised settlement.' It also gives a sense of the Danes being besieged, for if Grendel
is exiled beyond the pale, the Danes are equally hemmed in inside it. If
Heaney explicitly uses the word 'bawn' in the poem to make a connection between Hrothgar's 'embattled keep' and Elizabethan forts in Ireland,
conveying among other things this sense of an isolated group in a fortified
building placed in a hostile landscape (p. xxx), the reference to the pale
does something similar. Further to that, however, to a contemporary Irish
reader, the phrase 'beyond the pale' must inevitably call Dublin to mind.

The phrase makes a number of appearances in Heaney's work, some
with exactly this reference to an Anglicised Dublin. In his discussion of
Brian Merriman's *Cúirt an Mheán-Oíche*, which he describes as 'a poem
from beyond the Pale in all senses,' Heaney is explicit about the literal

sense of the phrase: 'In Ireland, the Pale was that area around Dublin where the English language and an Anglocentric culture had longest been established.'[1] In another Oxford lecture, he quotes some lines from Marlowe's *Edward II* that use the phrase in the same way: 'The wild O'Neill, with swarms of Irish kerns / lives uncontrolled within the English pale.'[2] It occurs in a broader sense in a quotation from R. H. Barrow's *The Romans* that prefaces 'Freedman,' from *North*:

> Indeed, slavery comes nearest its justification in the early Roman Empire: for a man from a 'backward' race might be brought within the pale of civilization, educated and trained in a craft or profession and turned into a useful member of society.[3]

These lines are quoted ironically: if Heaney portrays himself here as the representative of a backward race brought within the pale of civilization, the poem that follows shows him willing to verbally bite the hand that fed him. Post-*Beowulf*, too, in another translation from a medieval text, Cresseid will also be exiled 'beyond the pale.'[4]

An allusion to Dublin within the poem may serve as another pointer back to earlier Heaney poems that explore the Viking foundation of Dublin – poems such as 'North,' or 'Viking Dublin: Trial Pieces.' These are poems that look at Dublin's Scandinavian heritage: if 'Funeral Rites' from *North* references *Njal's Saga*, *Njal's Saga* contains an account of the Battle of Clontarf, fought in 1014 in what is now suburban Dublin.[5] These poems in *North* also nod to the intermingling of Scandinavian and English cultures, as in the lines where Heaney, sifting poetically through Viking skulls, compares himself to an explicitly Shakespearean Hamlet the Dane.[6] The suggestion of Dublin in the phrase 'beyond the pale,' and the use of medieval Gaelic social terms such as 'clan,' 'brehon,' and 'sept,' suggest perhaps that Heaney, a modern Irish writer, obtains another layer of engagement with the poem by finding historical roots in the poem's Scandinavian narrative, just as the medieval English *Beowulf*-poet could. He finds roots both in the language of the English poet and in the Scandinavian story that the poet relates.

[1] Seamus Heaney, 'Orpheus in Ireland: On Brian Merriman's *The Midnight Court*,' in Seamus Heaney, *The Redress of Poetry: Oxford Lectures* (London: Faber, 1995), 38–62 at 38.

[2] Seamus Heaney, 'Extending the Alphabet: On Christopher Marlowe's "Hero and Leander",' in *The Redress of Poetry: Oxford Lectures*, 17–37 at 23.

[3] Heaney, *North*, 61.

[4] Heaney, *Testament*, 27.

[5] Heaney, *North*, 15–18; Heaney, *Opened Ground*, 96–99; *Njal's Saga*, trans. Magnus Magnusson and Hermann Pálsson (Harmondsworth: Penguin, 1960), 341–52.

[6] Heaney, *North*, 23; Heaney, *Opened Ground*, 104.

Retrospectives: 'North'

In his introduction to the *Beowulf* translation, Heaney observes that one of his early poems, 'Digging,' contains some lines that conform to Old English metrical rules, with two balancing half-lines of two stressed syllables each linked by alliteration. 'Digging' is something of a foundational poem for Heaney in that it is the opening poem of his first collection, *Death of a Naturalist*, and the opening poem too of subsequent selections from his work, including the 1998 gathering, *Opened Ground*.[1] But it is also foundational in a broader sense, in that it introduces a thematic parallel between the art of writing and the act of digging that will underpin Heaney's archaeological explorations of past and present in his bog poems. In drawing the reader's attention to these debts to Old English poetry unconsciously inscribed into the beginning of his first book, Heaney tells us that 'part of me, in other words, had been writing Anglo-Saxon from the start' (p. xxiii).[2]

If Heaney's *Beowulf* translation looks back not only to the Old English text, but also to earlier works by Heaney himself, there is one collection in particular with which it has significant affinities: 1975's *North*, the collection of Heaney's that Joseph McGowan describes as 'most fully indebted to the early medieval world of Anglo-Saxon, Norse, and Celt.'[3] *North* is not exclusively focused on the medieval: when, in 'Bone Dreams,' the narrator peels away layers of language to reach 'the scop's / twang, the iron / flash of consonants / cleaving the line,' this is merely a stop on a journey past 'philology and kennings.'[4] This excavation is archaeological rather than philological: the short lines seek to drill back through past language to the point where language runs out, and only the earth itself can offer evidence.

North anticipates Heaney's *Beowulf* translation in that it draws parallels between the violence of early Germanic societies and that of Northern Ireland during the height of the troubles. The end of the poem 'Kinship' directly addresses the Roman historian Tacitus, whose *Germania* describes Germanic society at the end of the first century.[5] The goddess alluded to in the poem's closing lines is Nerthus, the Iron Age fertility goddess to

---

[1] Seamus Heaney, *Death of a Naturalist* (London: Faber, 1966), 13–14; Heaney, *Opened Ground*, 3–4.

[2] Cf. the discussion of Heaney's claim here in Jones, *Strange Likeness*, 198–99.

[3] Joseph McGowan, 'Heaney, Caedmon, *Beowulf*,' *New Hibernia Review / Iris Éireannach Nua* 6/2 (Summer/Samhraidh 2002), 25–42 at 27.

[4] Heaney, *North*, 28, 29; Heaney, *Opened Ground*, 108, 109.

[5] Heaney, *North*, 45; Heaney, *Opened Ground*, 125–26.

whom human sacrifices were made and the subject of Heaney's short poem 'Nerthus' in *Wintering Out*,[1] but she is also Kathleen Ní Houlihán, the embodiment of Ireland in female form, who inspired an endless line of Irish revolutionary martyrs (here with a tinge of Mariolatry in the reference to the Catholic icon of the sacred heart). Kathleen Ní Houlihán is directly compared to Nerthus by Heaney in his essay 'Feeling Into Words,'[2] and the comparison between the two is implicit here and elsewhere in the bog poems. The descriptions in 'Kinship' of legions on ramparts, casualties and victims, and slaughter for the common good have obvious contemporary resonances in 1975, and the shaven heads of the notorious remind us of the 'little adulteress' of 'Punishment' with her 'shaved head / like a stubble of black corn,' and the comparison that that poem draws between her punishment and that of women 'cauled in tar' in 1970s Northern Ireland.[3] Finally, if these lines are directly addressed to Tacitus, they are also implicitly addressed to W. B. Yeats in the line 'where nothing will suffice' – Heaney's answer to the question posed by Yeats in 'Easter 1916.'[4]

In drawing parallels between the violence of early Germanic societies and that of late twentieth-century Northern Ireland, *North* draws on a number of medieval sources, including archaeological material from Viking Dublin (in 'Viking Dublin: Trial Pieces'),[5] medieval texts such as *Lebor Gabála Érenn* and *The Battle of Maldon* (in 'Hercules and Antaeus'),[6] Bede's *Ecclesiastical History* (in 'Bone Dreams'),[7] and *Njal's Saga* (in 'Funeral Rites').[8] The vocabulary of the poems also includes some fragments of Old English and Old Norse – words like *althing*, *scop*, and *ban-hus*.[9] 'Funeral Rites' in particular draws on a medieval text in discussing the cyclical nature of violence: a theme important in *Beowulf*. The poem opens by imagining a laying to rest of the feuds afflicting Ireland through an enormous

---

[1] Heaney, *Wintering Out*, 49; Heaney, *Opened Ground*, 66; Corcoran, *Poetry of Seamus Heaney*, 34.

[2] Seamus Heaney, 'Feeling Into Words,' in *Preoccupations*, 41–60 at 57.

[3] Heaney, *North*, 37–38; Heaney, *Opened Ground*, 117–18.

[4] Stallworthy, 'The Poet as Archaeologist,' 169; on Yeats and Heaney, cf. Adrian Frazier, 'Anger and Nostalgia: Seamus Heaney and the Ghost of the Father,' *Eire–Ireland: A Journal of Irish Studies* 36 (Fall–Winter 2001), 7–38; for Yeats's 'Easter 1916,' see Yeats, *Poems*, 228–30.

[5] Heaney, *North*, 21–24; Heaney, *Opened Ground*, 102–106; Finn, *Past Poetic*, 94–96.

[6] Heaney, *North*, 52–53; Heaney, *Opened Ground*, 129–30; McGowan, 'Heaney, Caedmon, *Beowulf*,' 28.

[7] Heaney, *North*, 27–30; Heaney, *Opened Ground*, 107–111; McGowan, 'Heaney, Caedmon, *Beowulf*,' 30.

[8] Heaney, *North*, 15–18; Heaney, *Opened Ground*, 96–99; McGowan, 'Heaney, Caedmon, *Beowulf*,' 33–34.

[9] Heaney, *North*, 20, 28; Heaney, *Opened Ground*, 101, 108.

funeral at the megalithic tombs in the Boyne valley. The Boyne valley is both a prehistoric burial site, and, ironically, a cradle of the recent conflict, the site of the Battle of the Boyne where in 1690 William of Orange defeated the Catholic James Stuart to win the throne, an event commemorated annually by Orange marches on the battle's anniversary, the twelfth of July. Although Heaney imagines this funeral resulting in 'the cud of memory / allayed for once, arbitration / of the feud placated,'[1] the poem concludes with an episode from *Njal's Saga* that may undercut any hopeful reading:

> imagining those under the hill
>
> disposed like Gunnar
> who lay beautiful
> inside his burial mound,
> though dead by violence
>
> and unavenged.
> Men said that he was chanting
> verses about honour
> and that four lights burned
>
> in corners of the chamber:
> which opened then, as he turned
> with a joyful face
> to look at the moon.[2]

This is a retelling of *Njal's Saga*, chapter 78:

> One night, Skarp-Hedin and Hogni were standing outside, to the south of Gunnar's burial mound. The moonlight was bright but fitful. Suddenly it seemed to them that the mound was open; Gunnar had turned round to face the moon. There seemed to be four lights burning inside the mound, illuminating the whole chamber. They could see that Gunnar was happy; his face was exultant. He chanted a verse so loudly that they could have heard it clearly from much farther away:
>
> > 'Hogni's generous father
> > Rich in daring exploits,
> > Who so lavishly gave battle

---

[1] Jones, *Strange Likeness*, 205, notes that the phrase 'the cud of memory' derives from Bede's telling of the story of Cædmon.

[2] Heaney, *North*, 17–18; Heaney, *Opened Ground*, 98–99.

> Distributing wounds gladly,
> Claims that in his helmet,
> Towering like an oak-tree
> In the forest of battle,
> He would rather die than yield,
> Much rather die than yield.'

Then the mound closed again.[1]

Heaney's poem concludes here, but if Gunnar is unavenged at this point in the narrative of *Njal's Saga*, he does not remain so for long. Skarp-Hedin and Hogni take what they have seen as an imperative to revenge, which they carry out immediately.[2] If the renewal of violence is implicit in Heaney's version also,[3] this is in keeping with the general theme of *North*, which points to recurring cycles of violence from the prehistoric to the present day. Later on in *North*, we see 'berserks' (a word with Norse etymology) club each other to death 'for honour's sake' in what seems to be an echo of the allusion to honour towards the end of 'Funeral Rites.'[4]

The recurrent nature of violence and feud is something also found within *Beowulf*: as Heaney says in his introduction, 'vengeance for the dead becomes an ethic for the living, bloodshed begets further bloodshed' (p. xiv). This is something most obvious in the 'Finnsburg episode,' a fragmentary portion of another narrative that fills an interlude in the poem's main action, one recounted by the scop in Heorot; Heaney gives the episode considerable prominence in his introductory discussion, suggesting that the passage is 'central to the historical and imaginative worlds of the poem as a whole' (p. xiv).[5]

Although the Finnsburg story was presumably well-known to the audience of the Old English poem, only parts of it survive to us, in two separate texts: one is the episode in *Beowulf*, the other a fragmentary Old English poem, the 'Finnsburg Fragment.' The Finnsburg episode in *Beowulf* describes the aftermath of a battle which takes place when Finn, a Frisian leader who has married a Danish princess, Hildeburh, receives a visit from his wife's brother, Hnæf. The 'Finnsburg Fragment' describes part of the battle itself. It appears from that poem that perhaps Finn attempts

---

[1] *Njal's Saga*, 173.

[2] *Njal's Saga*, 173–75.

[3] McGowan, 'Heaney, Caedmon, *Beowulf*,' 34.

[4] Heaney, *North*, 70; Heaney, *Opened Ground*, 141; Bernard O'Donoghue, 'Seamus Heaney: *North*,' in *A Companion to Twentieth Century Poetry*, ed. Neil Roberts (Oxford: Blackwell, 2001), 524–35 at 531.

[5] Phillips, 'Seamus Heaney's *Beowulf*,' 267, suggests that Heaney's interpretation over-emphasises the importance of revenge-killing in the original.

to ambush his brother-in-law while his guest. The poem begins with the words '… gables burning.' But the next lines imply that something else is happening. The poem continues:

> Hleoþrode ða   heaþo-geong cyning:
> 'Ne ðis ne dagað eastan,   ne her draca ne fleogeð,
> ne her ðisse healle   hornas ne byrnað;
> ac her forþ berað,   fugelas singað,
> gylleð græg-hama,   guð-wudu hlynneð,
> scyld scefte oncwyð.   Nu scyneð þes mona,
> waðol under wolcnum;   nu arisað wea-dæda,
> ðe ðisne folces nið   fremman willað.
> Ac onwacnigeað nu,   wigend mine,
> habbað eowre linda,   hicgeaþ on ellen,
> windað on orde,   wesað an-mode!'[1]

Then Hnæf, the young warrior king cried aloud: 'This is no dawn that breaks in the east, nor is there a dragon flying here, nor are this hall's gables burning! Nay, men bear weapons hither, the birds sing and the grey-coated wolf is howling, the spear rings out, the shield echoes to the shaft. Now the moon is shining, wandering through the clouds; now shall arise such deeds of woe as will satisfy the deadly spite of this race. So awake now, my fighting men, take up your shields, set your minds upon valour, fight your way in the van, keep your courage high!'[2]

The two sides fight each other to a standstill after five days, and both sides are too depleted to consider victory possible. A peace is arranged between Finn and Hengest, who is now the leader of the Danes since Hnæf has been killed. This peace lasts for a single winter, but is broken when one of Hengest's followers places a sword in his lap as a reminder of the need for revenge. Hengest and the Danes then slaughter Finn and his followers, and take Hildeburh back to Denmark. All of this demonstrates that feuds are hard to settle, but suggests also the outcome of the proposed peace between the Danes and the Heathobards, which takes place in the background of the poem's main narrative. The revenge described in the Finnsburg episode is prompted by the sight of a weapon; Beowulf's prediction of the collapse of the peace between Heathobards and Danes, between Hrothgar and Ingeld, contains exactly the same motif. This parallel

---

[1] *Beowulf with the Finnesburg Fragment*, ed. Wrenn and Bolton, 216.
[2] *Beowulf and its Analogues*, trans. G. N. Garmonsway and Jacqueline Simpson (London, 1980), 248–49.

with the Finnsburg episode suggests that here, too, a painful slaughter will follow. *Beowulf* does not describe the conflict that follows the collapse of the truce between Hrothgar and Ingeld – that lies outside the scope of the poem – but it does describe the pain and suffering involved in the Finnsburg episode, and the parallels between the two allow the reader to draw the appropriate conclusions.

Likewise, the parallels between the descent into cycles of revenge in this story and the similar descent in the Northern Ireland conflict are not explicitly spelled out – the relevance to Northern Ireland perhaps hinted at in the very early use of the word 'troubles' (p. 3)[1] – but, as in the original, the reader can make the connection. In Heaney's *Beowulf*, as in *North*, the recurrent nature of violence again offers parallels with Northern Ireland.

Heaney's means of finding roots in the original, then, are not merely linguistic and historical, but most likely emotional as well. In his introduction, he comments of the original that 'as a consequence of his doctrinal certitude, which is as composed as it is ardent, the poet can view the story-time of his poem with a certain historical detachment and even censure the ways of those who lived *in illo tempore*' (p. xvi), and he quotes in illustration of his point the passage where the poem describes, with Christian disapproval, the Danes' return to their heathen religious practices. But a few lines later, Heaney translates the following lines in a tone that gives a sense of anything *but* historical detachment, and there is less a sense of didactic censure in these lines than a sense of lament and regret:

> Oh, cursed is he
> who in time of trouble has to thrust his soul
> in the fire's embrace, forfeiting help;
> he has nowhere to turn. But blessed is he
> who after death can approach the Lord
> and find friendship in the Father's embrace. (p. 8)

The original reads:

> Wa bið þæm ðe sceal
> þurh sliðne nið   sawle bescufan
> in fyres fæþm,   frofre ne wenan,
> wihte gewendan!   Wel bið þæm þe mot
> æfter deað-dæge   Drihten secean
> ond to Fæder fæþmum   freoðo wilnian! (183b–188)

The biblical syntax here in the phrases 'cursed is he' and 'blessed is he'

---

[1] As noted by Thomas McGuire, 'Violence and Vernacular in Seamus Heaney's *Beowulf*,' *New Hibernia Review / Iris Éireannach Nua* 10/1 (Spring/Earrach 2006), 79–99 at 84.

keeps the doctrinal certitude of the *Beowulf*-poet embedded in the translation,[1] but the addition of the exclamation 'oh' sounds like painful regret.
Heaney has a greater insight than most of what may happen in times of
trouble to drive desperate men towards evil, and a clearer awareness of the
consequences. Other lines contain a painful optimism, as when Hrothgar
tells Beowulf:

> What you have done is to draw two peoples,
> the Geat nation and us neighbouring Danes,
> into shared peace and a pact of friendship
> in spite of hatreds we have harboured in the past. (p. 60)

Where the original has:

> Hafast þu gefered   þæt þam folcum sceal,
> Geata leodum   ond Gar-Denum,
> sib gemæne   ond sacu restan,
> inwit-niþas,   þe hie ær drugon. (1855–58)

The optimism expressed here may also be read as applicable to another pair
of neighbouring nations trying to settle their differences in the late twentieth century. The poem as a whole, however, shows a repeated conviction
that feuds are difficult to settle; many an optimistic settlement is shown to
be simply a lull before the recurrence of slaughter; and if the translation
contains its moments of optimism, it holds those in balance with an awareness of just how easily cycles of violence can be set in motion yet again.

Foundational moments (1): 'Beowulf', Scyld Scefing, and the book of Genesis

In some ways, in translating *Beowulf*, Heaney can be seen to be both writing himself into the foundations of English literature – he describes the
poem as 'one of the foundation works of poetry in English' (p. ix) – and
also writing those foundations into his own work: he initially accepts the
commission to undertake the translation as a means of staying anchored
to 'the Anglo-Saxon sea floor' while exposed to the 'unmoored speech' of
contemporary American poetry (p. xxii). The poem itself lends weight to
a sense of its foundational status, opening as it does with three narratives
concerned with distant origins: the mythical tale of the founder of the
Danish dynasty – Scyld Scefing ('Shield Sheafson' in Heaney), the story

---

[1] Echoing perhaps the syntax of passages such as the Authorized Version of Matthew
5: 3–11, for example, where the verses begin 'Blessed are the poor in spirit,' 'Blessed are
they that mourn,' 'Blessed are the meek,' and so on.

of the establishment of Hrothgar's hall at Heorot, and within that, a reference back to the biblical narrative of the creation of the world in Genesis.
Scyld is the legendary founder of the Danish kingdom, and he appears in
the poem's opening lines as the progenitor of a line of Danish kings that
leads down to Hrothgar, an historical figure, who is king of Denmark at
the time when the poem is set.

This practice of tracing back the genealogies of real kings to legendary
ancestors is a common one in the early Middle Ages, and Scef, Scyld's father, also appears in the genealogies of the Anglo-Saxon kings of Wessex.
Æþelweard's *Chronicle* lists a genealogy which runs: Godwulf, the son of
Geat, the son of Tetwa, the son of Beo, the son of Scyld, the son of Scef.
The chronicle tells how Scef was driven ashore on an island, on a boat
filled with weapons; the foundling was adopted by the people who found
him, later becoming their king, and the chronicle tells us that it is from this
boy, Scef, that King Æþelwulf is descended.[1] This story is a folk-myth:
a boy arrives from nowhere in a boat, is adopted, and brings prosperity to
the people. Sometimes that prosperity is prophesised by the sign of a sheaf
of wheat in the boat with the boy, and Scef's name (Sheaf) suggests this
element of the myth. In the version of the story here, however, the boy
arrives in a warship with a boatload of weapons, suggesting perhaps that
prosperity will come less through farming than warfare.

What happens at the beginning of *Beowulf* is that the stories of father
and son, Scyld and Scef, are combined in one figure. Scyld Scefing is both
the mythical founder of the *Scyldingas*, the Danish kings, and the boy who
arrives from nowhere in a boat, signalling the bringing of prosperity. The
story of the boat and the child is not discussed directly, but described ret-
rospectively as part of the description of Scyld's funeral (43–46). The pack-
ing of the funeral ship with weapons echoes the boy's arrival with a similar
shipload of weapons: events have come full circle. There's a retrospective
description here of the myth of origin, a sidelong glance at the founding
of the dynasty.

The poem then lists Scyld's heirs: Beow, Halfdane, and Halfdane's four
children, Heorogar, Hrothgar, Halga, and a daughter who marries Onela,
the Swedish king. It is Hrothgar's narrative that the poem now turns to,
and his establishment of a mead-hall, Heorot. In keeping with the emphasis on transience so common in Old English poetry, the description
of the hall's construction also looks forward to its eventual destruction,
and genesis implies apocalypse (81b–83a). The description of this second
foundational moment, the foundation of Heorot, also recalls a third, fundamental, narrative of origin: the biblical narrative of the foundation of

---

[1] *Beowulf and its Analogues*, 119.

the world in Genesis. The *scop*'s song in Heorot, telling how the Almighty made the earth (92), aligns the raising of Heorot's walls with the origins of the world itself. The appearance of Grendel, the monster who attacks Heorot, is associated with another part of the Genesis narrative – Grendel is descended from Cain, the first murderer, outcast for the killing of his brother Abel (102–08).

Beowulf's beginning, then, is profoundly retrospective – it looks back towards points of origin, both for the Danes and for mankind. If Heaney responds to the poem as foundational in itself, as 'one of the foundation works of poetry in English' (p. ix), that is in keeping with the poem's status as the most substantial surviving work of Old English literature, but also with the poem's own sense of foundedness. Heaney's response to this sense of the poem as foundational has an important effect in this translation, for what Heaney does is to write his own roots into this foundational work.

Foundational moments (2): 'Mossbawn'

Heaney's inclusion in *Beowulf* of the Elizabethan English word 'bawn,' from the Irish *bó-dhún*, 'a fort for cattle,' is due, he tells us, to reasons of historical suggestiveness (p. xxx). Using the word allows Heaney to suggest a parallel between Heorot, the Danish hall besieged by Grendel and his mother, and 'the fortified dwellings that the English planters built in Ireland to keep the dispossessed natives at bay' (p. xxx). The word also has resonances with Heaney's own biography, for 'Mossbawn' is the name of the farm in County Derry where Heaney spent his early childhood, a place he describes as his *omphalos*,[1] and the inclusion of the word 'bawn' in the *Beowulf* translation writes not just Irish colonial history but also Heaney's personal history into the poem.[2] It also looks back to *North*, for the two poems in dedication to Heaney's aunt Mary that open that book are collectively titled 'Mossbawn,'[3] and the poem 'Belderg' discusses the etymology of the placename, with its debts to Norse, English, and Irish.[4] In part, the discussion of the placename in 'Belderg' looks forward to the way that 'bawn' is used in the *Beowulf* translation – it is 'an English fort / a planter's walled-in mound.'[5] There is another discussion of the place name in the essay 'Belfast':

---

[1] Heaney, 'Mossbawn,' 17.
[2] Phillips, 'Seamus Heaney's *Beowulf*,' 272.
[3] Heaney, *North*, 8–10; Heaney, *Opened Ground*, 93–95.
[4] Heaney, *North*, 14.
[5] Heaney, *North*, 14.

Our farm was called Mossbawn. *Moss*, a Scots word probably carried to Ulster by the Planters, and *bawn*, the name the English colonists gave to their fortified farmhouses. Mossbawn, the planter's house on the bog. Yet in spite of this Ordnance Survey spelling, we pronounced it Moss bann, and *bán* is the Gaelic word for white. So might not the thing mean the white moss, the moss of bog-cotton? In the syllables of my home I see a metaphor of the split culture of Ulster.[1]

If 'Mossbawn' inscribes the historical division of plantation farmstead and native bogland into Heaney's own point of origin, this same division is then written into the *Beowulf* translation. For Heaney not only inserts a 'bawn' into *Beowulf*: he juxtaposes the description of Hrothgar's hall as bawn with suggestions of Grendel's mere as bog.

In his *TLS* essay discussing the *Beowulf* translation, Heaney is explicit about his recollection of his own earlier poetry in his description of Grendel's mere. In his initial translation of lines 1365–72a, he tells us, his version began:

> At night there, something uncanny happens:
> the water burns. And the water is bottomless.
> Nobody alive has ever fathomed it.[2]

The Old English text here reads:

> Þær mæg nihta gehwæm   nið-wundor seon,
> fyr on flode;   no þæs frod leofað
> gumena bearna   þæt þone grund wite. (1365–67)

What Heaney had in mind here, in the phrasing 'the water is bottomless,' was the concluding line of 'Bogland,' from *Door Into the Dark*, which reads: 'The wet centre is bottomless.'[3] Although this allusion to 'Bogland' does not survive into the final text, the rewritten version nonetheless includes another echo of a different bog poem:

> At night there, something uncanny happens:
> the water burns. And the mere-bottom
> has never been sounded by the sons of men. (p. 45)

Although the echo of 'Bogland' has gone from this version, the description of the mere-bottom that 'has never been sounded' introduces a new

[1] Heaney, 'Belfast,' 35.
[2] Heaney, 'The Drag of the Golden Chain.'
[3] Seamus Heaney, *Door Into the Dark* (London: Faber, 1969), 56; Heaney, *Opened Ground*, 42; Heaney, 'The Drag of the Golden Chain.'

resonance with a related poem, 'Kinship,' from *North*, where bog pools are 'not to be sounded / by the naked eye.'[1]

Other language might have similar resonances: the description of the Grendelkin's habitation uses the word *keshes*, 'causeways' (p. 45) for *fengelad*, 'path over the fen,' in what might be a reference back to another bog poem that uses the word: 'Nerthus,' from *Wintering Out*, where 'kesh and loaning finger out to heather.'[2] In 'Nerthus,' the heather sits atop bogland where, the poem's title suggests, the victims of ritual sacrifice may be found.

If Heaney uses 'bawn' in *Beowulf*, then, he once again juxtaposes the bawn with bog. The divisions inscribed into 'Mossbawn,' plantation farmstead placed against native bog, are reinscribed into the *Beowulf* translation, where bawn and bog are Hrothgar's hall and Grendel's mere respectively, and the divisions written into Heaney's origins are rewritten into *Beowulf*.

Borders, marches, and monsters

In his essay 'Something to Write Home About,' Heaney discusses some of the vocabulary of boundaries. The essay refers specifically to Terminus, the Roman god of boundaries, whose name Heaney uses as the title of a poem about in-betweenness, and to *tearmann*, the Irish equivalent of the Latin *terminus*. It also mentions a term resonant from medieval Ireland in a similar sense to the phrase 'the pale,' a phrase found both in the local vocabulary of Heaney's childhood and in the Old English of *Beowulf*: the word 'march.' Heaney writes:

> The verb meant to meet at the boundary, to be bordered by, to be matched up to and yet marked off from; one farm marched another farm; one field marched another field; and what divided them was the march drain or the march hedge. The word did not mean to walk in a military manner but to be close, to lie alongside, to border upon and be bordered upon. It was a word that acknowledged division, but it contained a definite suggestion of solidarity as well.[3]

Heaney uses the word in the 'Sweeney Redivivus' sequence when, in 'The

---

[1] Heaney, *North*, 41; Heaney, *Opened Ground*, 121; O'Donoghue, 'Seamus Heaney: *North*,' 533.

[2] Heaney, *Wintering Out*, 49; Heaney, *Opened Ground*, 66; cf. the word's use in *Crossings* xxxii, where it calls up memories of Heaney's father (Heaney, *Seeing Things*, 90; Heaney, *Opened Ground*, 377).

[3] Seamus Heaney, 'Something to Write Home About,' in *Finders Keepers*, 48–58 at 51–52.

Cleric,' Sweeney is ousted to the marches.[1] When, in translating *Beowulf,*
Heaney translates the lines:

> Wæs se grimma gæst   Grendel haten,
> mære mearc-stapa (102–103a)

He retains 'march' for Old English *mearc*:

> Grendel was the name of this grim demon
> haunting the marches (p. 6)

The second time the phrase appears in the original (1348a), Heaney will
make a different choice.[2] Here, however, he matches the vocabulary of his
childhood to that the Old English text. If, as Heaney suggests in 'Something to Write Home About,' the word implies both being matched up to
and yet marked off from, both juxtaposition and division, this is a sense
present also in the Old English text.

Grendel and his mother are beyond the pale not just because of where
they are, but because of who (or what) they are. *Beowulf* constructs its
hero's opponents as monstrous – so much so that critics have suggested
that the manuscript that contains the sole surviving text of the poem and
four other works (some or all of which are also interested in the topic of
monstrosity) might have been compiled as a 'Book of monsters.'[3] It also
portrays them as exiles: where Heaney translates Grendel's location as
'beyond the pale,' the original has *wræc-lastas*, 'the paths of exile' (1352);
the poem's use of wolf imagery ('Hie dygel lond / warigeað, wulf-hleoþu'
(1357b–1358a), 'they dwell apart / among wolves on the hills' (p. 45))
conveys a sense of outlawry, and Beowulf's subsequent oath to pursue
Grendel's mother (1392–94) is reminiscent of Norse formulae concerning
the prosecution of outlaws.[4] But, monsters or not, the poem also portrays
Grendel and his mother with sympathy. The word *wræc* in *wræc-lastas* contains some of the sense of its modern descendant, 'wretch': the Old English word means 'misery, distress, oppression, exile.' Although monstrous,
the monsters are also at times given human attributes – Grendel is 'warped
in the shape of a man' (p. 45).[5] And in a balancing move to this humanizing
of the monsters, Beowulf himself has some monstrous attributes.[6]

[1] Heaney, *Station Island*, 107; Heaney, *Opened Ground*, 277.

[2] Heaney, 'The Drag of the Golden Chain,' paraphrases the phrase at 1348a as 'border-
steppers,' but the translation omits this.

[3] Orchard, *Critical Companion*, 24–25.

[4] Orchard, *Critical Companion*, 68.

[5] Andy Orchard, *Pride and Prodigies: Studies in the Monsters of the 'Beowulf'-Manuscript*
(Cambridge: Brewer, 1995), 29–31.

[6] Orchard, *Pride and Prodigies*, 32–33.

It would be a straightforward matter to relate the boundary-lines and representations of monstrousness here to texts about monsters written by Ireland's medieval colonisers: medievalists writing in the context of post-colonial theory, for example, have had much to say on the werewolf story told by Gerald of Wales.[1] But if Heaney's *Beowulf* acknowledges divisions, something clearly signalled by the use of the word *bawn* and the phrase 'beyond the pale,' it's also worth remembering that the act of translation is one that involves the crossing of boundaries, and that this translation's use of words such as *bawn* and *thole* that cross the boundaries between Irish and English seems an imperative to such boundary-crossing. The word *march* seems important in this context, a word 'that acknowledged division' but also contains 'a definite suggestion of solidarity.'

Both 'From the Frontier of Writing' from *The Haw Lantern* and the similarly titled essay 'Frontiers of Writing' from *The Redress of Poetry* suggest an analogy between the work of the imagination and the act of boundary-crossing.[2] Each has a medieval resonance. The poem, which describes crossing through a pair of border checkpoints, the first literal, the second metaphorical, is suggestive of Dante's descent into the underworld in its use of *terza rima*. The essay closes by citing another Heaney poem, one based on a medieval otherworldly vision, from the 'Lightenings' sequence in *Seeing Things*.[3] In 'Frontiers of Writing,' Heaney argues that this poem about a crossing of the boundary between the next world and this (the reverse of Dante's crossing) is an imperative towards the use of imagination in being able to cross other boundaries, and to be in two minds at once. If Heaney's *Beowulf* acknowledges divisions, it would also seem to contain an imperative towards the crossing of boundaries, to translation, to being in two minds. In doing so, it would also seem to be echoing something fundamental about the original Old English text.

---

[1] For the werewolf story, see Gerald of Wales, *History*, 69–72; Catherine E. Karkov, 'Tales of the Ancients: Colonial Werewolves and the Mapping of Postcolonial Ireland,' in *Postcolonial Moves: Medieval Through Modern*, ed. Patricia Clare Ingham and Michelle R. Warren (Basingstoke and New York: Palgrave Macmillan, 2003), 93–109 at 98, argues of the story of the priest and the two werewolves that 'just as Gerald's story was a metaphor for the small-scale conquest of Airgialla, so too it was a metaphor for the larger conquest of Ireland;' cf. Caroline Walker Bynum, 'Metamorphosis, or Gerald and the Werewolf,' *Speculum* 73 (1998), 987–1013; Jeffrey Jerome Cohen, 'Hybrids, Monsters, Borderlands: The Bodies of Gerald of Wales,' in *The Postcolonial Middle Ages*, ed. Cohen (New York: St Martin's Press, 2000), 85–104.

[2] Heaney, *The Haw Lantern*, 6–7; Heaney, *Opened Ground*, 297–98; Heaney, 'Frontiers of Writing,' 203.

[3] Heaney, *Seeing Things*, 62; Heaney, *Opened Ground*, 364.

Dual perspectives

In a reading critical of Heaney's practice in translating *Beowulf*, Loren C. Gruber provides an interesting image for Heaney's use of language suggestive of Irish history in translating the Old English text. Heaney's layering of Irish and Old English materials, he notes, parallels the *Beowulf* poet's retrospective view of a pagan past through Christian eyes. The effect, Gruber suggests, is similar to that achieved visually by a stereoscope. Although my reading of Heaney's *Beowulf* is at odds with Gruber's (his pejorative description of the effect as like that of 'a slightly out-of-focus stereoscope' is, I think, inaccurate and unnecessary),[1] the image of the stereoscope seems a useful one in discussing a modern remaking of a medieval text, especially in the light of Proust's use of the motif of the stereoscope to describe the possibility of seeing past and present in combination. As Roger Shattuck describes Proust's method:

> The visible world reaches us through a double take based on the stereoscopic principle. Two slightly different versions of the same 'object' from our two eyes are combined subjectively with the effect of relief. The binocular nature of human vision is achieved through some of the most delicate adjustments of which our organism is capable. Normally we confine this stereoscopic effect, which gives us an impress of reality in depth to the world around us, to perception in space. Proust undertakes a transposition of spatial vision into a new faculty. The accumulation of optical figures in *A la recherche* gradually removes our depth perception from space and re-erects it in time.[2]

Shattuck goes on to explain that, in Proust, this 'stereoscopic' juxtaposition of simultaneous images from different points in time brings not confusion (or, as Gruber suggests of Heaney, a lack of focus), but depth:

> Multiplicity now brings not confusion but dimensionality and depth. Memory in Proust's sense designates a stereoscopic or 'stereologic' consciousness which sees the world simultaneously (and thus out of time) in relief. Merely to remember something is meaningless unless the remembered image is combined with a moment in the present affording a view of the same object or objects. Like our eyes, our

---

[1] Gruber, '"So." So What?', 69.

[2] Roger Shattuck, *Proust's Binoculars: A Study of Memory, Time and Recognition in 'A la recherche du temps perdu'* (Princeton: Princeton University Press, 1962; repr. 1983), 42–43. I owe references to Proust and to Shattuck's exposition of Proust to Deidre Brollo.

memories must see double; those two images then converge in our minds into a single heightened reality.[1]

While Proust's use of the stereoscopic motif to convey the perception of depth obtained by the simultaneous apprehension of different moments in time relates to individual memory, the motif of the stereoscope also seems a useful means of conceptualizing not just this translation of *Beowulf*, but any reworking of a medieval text that keeps one eye on the source text and another on the present. And while Proust is not among the usual resources brought to bear upon the exposition of either Heaney's work or Old English poetry, its possible to see earlier Heaney poems that draw a parallel between the distant past and the contemporary as working in this way – it is in this sense that Helen Vendler describes Heaney's bog poems as attempting a 'binocular' view of past and present.[2] Furthermore, it's possible to argue that the Old English text of *Beowulf* itself works in a very similar way.

Perspective in *Beowulf* is something conveyed in part through the poem's style. As Andy Orchard puts it, 'the language of *Beowulf* can be said to be based on two opposing principles, namely repetition and variation, which essentially both perform the same function: setting separate elements side by side for the purpose of comparison or contrast.'[3] The stylistic feature of variation, also called 'apposition,' has been seen by Fred C. Robinson, in an influential reading of the poem, as important in conveying some of *Beowulf*'s central thematic features. Literally, apposition requires that two or more elements in a sentence should be the same part of speech, have the same referent, and not be connected except by syntactical parallelism within the sentence where they occur.[4] An example from Heaney's *Beowulf* is:

> There was Shield Sheafson, scourge of many tribes,
> a wrecker of mead benches, rampaging among foes. (p. 3)

Here 'Shield Sheafson,' 'scourge of many tribes,' and 'wrecker of mead benches,' are all in apposition. 'Shield,' 'scourge,' and 'wrecker' all refer to Shield, and none of the three are connected except through being juxtaposed within the sentence. They are in apposition because the poet does not spell out the relationship between them: he does not say 'There was Shield Sheafson *who was* scourge of many tribes *and* a wrecker of mead

---

[1] Shattuck, *Proust's Binoculars*, 47.

[2] Vendler, *Seamus Heaney*, 42, 43.

[3] Orchard, *Critical Companion*, 57–58.

[4] Fred C. Robinson, *'Beowulf' and the Appositive Style* (Knoxville: The University of Tennessee Press, 1985), 3.

benches, rampaging among foes.' Apposition implies a relationship between juxtaposed elements, but does not make that relationship explicit. This juxtaposition of elements which possess an implict (but not overtly stated) relationship is something that Robinson argues is a pattern present throughout *Beowulf*, influencing everything from the smallest elements of style to the broad sweep of the poem's overall structure.[1]

In Robinson's reading, the *Beowulf*-poet wished to provide a dual perspective: to represent the pre-Christian world of the poem sympathetically, while nonetheless conveying a Christian point of view. Robinson argues,

> A poet who, in a deeply Christian age, wants to acknowledge his heroes' damnation while insisting on their dignity must find and exercise in his listeners' minds the powers of inference and the ability to entertain two simultaneous points of view that are necessary for the resolution of poignant cultural tensions.[2]

For Robinson, the dual perspective of *Beowulf* is in part conveyed through an Old English poetic vocabulary that carries double meanings: pre- and post-Caedmonian, which is to say, pre- and post-conversion.[3] Religious terms, in particular, may be taken as meaning one thing for the heathen characters of the poem, another for the Christian audience. For Robinson, these are 'apposed' word-meanings, in that a single word with a dual meaning carries a dual perspective, just as the syntactical apposition of two separate words does. Such double meanings, incidentally, give an indication of how nuanced and subtle the original text is, and how difficult it is to produce a translation of *Beowulf* – no translation can reproduce this sort of verbal ambiguity and potential, conveyed through apposed (and sometimes opposed) word-meanings, in full.

In an extended sense, 'apposition' can be seen to structure the poem on various levels.[4] Characterization is achieved in part through the juxtaposition of character descriptions: for example, Hygd and Thryth, whose narratives are juxtaposed, and whose names, *hygd*, 'forethought, reflection,' and *þryð*, 'force, vehemence,' indicate the contrast between them.[5] And because *Beowulf* is a profoundly retrospective poem, it also juxtaposes elements from different periods of time, both in its narration of a story from pre-Christian Scandinavia for a Christian English audience, and in

---

[1] Robinson, *'Beowulf' and the Appositive Style*, 24–25.
[2] Robinson, *'Beowulf' and the Appositive Style*, 13–14.
[3] Robinson, *'Beowulf' and the Appositive Style*, 30–31.
[4] Robinson, *'Beowulf' and the Appositive Style*, 24–25.
[5] Robinson, *'Beowulf' and the Appositive Style*, 21–22.

its apposition of elements of its narrative with fragments of still older narratives: the story of the mythical founder of the Danish dynasty, Scyld Scefing, Sigemund the dragonslayer, Weland the smith, Eormenric, Hama, all the way back to the stories of Cain and Abel and that of the Creation itself.[1] If a polysemous vocabulary, as Robinson argues, requires the audience to keep pagan past and Christian present simultaneously in mind, the particular pagan past of the direct narrative line is itself layered against fragmentary glimpses of older narratives yet.

In the introduction to his translation, Heaney too makes reference to a dual perspective in the poem, 'a circumference of understanding within which the heroic world is occasionally viewed from a distance and recognized for what it is, an earlier state of consciousness and culture, one that has not been altogether shed but that has now been comprehended as part of another pattern. And this circumference and pattern arise, of course, from the poet's Christianity and from his perspective as an Englishman looking back at places and legends that his ancestors knew before they made their migration from continental Europe to their new home on the island of the Britons' (p. xvi). This is a reading reasonably close to Robinson's in its emphasis on dual perspectives, although it differs from Robinson, perhaps, with the assertion that this is something 'occasionally' visible in the poem. Heaney's discussion of his treatment of 'the appositional nature of the Old English syntax' (p. xxix) is a likely reference to Robinson's work; Tom Shippey's review notes the use of the word 'appositional' here as a sign of 'careful awareness of modern commentary.'[2]

What Heaney says in relation to apposition (or variation) in its primary, syntactical, sense, is that it has been 'somewhat slighted,' and that in relation to weapons in particular he has mainly 'called a sword a sword' (p. xxx). The treatment of apposition is an aspect praised by Tom Shippey's review, questioned by Nicholas Howe's, and discussed at length in Daniel Donoghue's article on the translation, where he finds that while Heaney sometimes removes the appositive syntax of the original, in at least one case he introduces apposition where the original has none.[3] What both Donoghue's discussion and the later discussion by Chris Jones make clear is that Heaney uses Beowulfian apposition not only in *Beowulf*, but

---

[1] See Orchard, *Critical Companion*, 98.

[2] Shippey, 'Beowulf for the Big-Voiced Scullions.'

[3] Shippey, 'Beowulf for the Big-Voiced Scullions'; Howe, 'Scullionspeak'; Daniel Donoghue, 'The Philologer Poet: Seamus Heaney and the Translation of *Beowulf*,' in *Beowulf: A Verse Translation* (Norton, 2002), 237–47 at 244, first published in *Harvard Review*.

elsewhere in his work. Donoghue cites lines such as these, Heaney's description of his relatives in 'The Strand at Lough Beg' as:

> Big-voiced scullions, herders, feelers round
> Haycocks and hindquarters, talkers in byres,
> Slow arbitrators of the burial ground.[1]

These lines, as Donoghue points out, employ something very close to Beowulfian apposition.[2]

So too, I think, does the juxtaposition of past and present in what Helen Vendler's reading of the bog poems calls a 'binocular' view, and what we might alternatively call 'stereoscopic' (after Shattuck's reading of Proust) or 'appositive' (after Robinson's reading of *Beowulf*). In adding new layers to *Beowulf*, in suggesting new resonances, it's possible to argue that Heaney is working with, rather than against, the grain of the original poem. What Heaney gives us is not a fidelity to the original that is literally, word-for-word, resonance-for-resonance, exactly identical to the Old English text: such a thing is an impossibility. But since the original text operates in ways that are retrospective, multilayered, and suggestive, it's possible perhaps to argue that Heaney's translation is faithful to the original in that his version requires of its readers what the Old English text required of its audience: it asks the reader to engage with a poem woven (as Heaney puts it) from two psychic fabrics (p. xvii), and to keep both, apposed, in mind.

Gendering sympathy

Contemporary criticism of *Beowulf* has paid close attention to gender-roles in the poem and their place in the poem's structure. Gale Owen-Crocker draws our attention to what she reads as *Beowulf*'s 'feminist middle':

> The second movement is introduced by Hnæf's funeral at Finnsburg, with its focus on the woman left behind, the failed peaceweaver. In Denmark, much attention is on the queen; and the monster-fight is with a female monster. Beowulf's political discussion with Hygelac focuses on the marriage of Hrothgar's daughter and the narrator focuses on Beowulf's gifts to Hygd.[3]

---

[1] Heaney, *Field Work*, 17; Heaney, *Opened Ground*, 153.

[2] Donoghue, 'The Philologer Poet,' 244; see also Jones, *Strange Likeness*, 215–16, 223–24.

[3] Gale R. Owen-Crocker, *The Four Funerals in 'Beowulf' and the Structure of the Poem* (Manchester and New York: Manchester University Press, 2000), 220.

It is this aspect of *Beowulf* that Helen Phillips sees as most disappointing in Heaney's rendition, and she suggests that the influence of Heaney's earlier work is here a limitation on his treatment of the poem's female characters, pointing to feminist criticism of that earlier writing by Elizabeth Butler Cullingford and Patricia Coughlan.[1] It's true, I think, that Heaney's reading of the female characters in *Beowulf*, both in this mid-section and at the poem's finale, does not focus as strongly as it might on some of the senses in which contemporary critics have shown gender to be an important element in the poem. But the issue of gender is not completely neglected, and the suggestion that the treatment of the female characters is hamstrung by an indebtedness to the positions of earlier poems is not clear-cut. Rather, it's possible to argue that Heaney's treatment of the female characters in *Beowulf* is aligned with a theme visible in his later work: that of the suffering of women in times of conflict.

The treatment of Grendel's mother, the female monster with whom Beowulf clashes in the second of the poem's three battles, is particularly problematic. The difficulty arises because, like Grendel, she is portrayed in the poem as a monster with some human characteristics, and the poem's language plays on this ambiguous status. Phillips points to Heaney's translation of lines 1258b–59 as exemplifying the difference between the portrayal of Grendel's mother in the original text and in Heaney's translation. The lines read 'Grendles modor, / ides, aglæc-wif yrmþe gemunde,' which Phillips translates as 'Grendel's mother, / a lady, a warrior-woman, remembered her misery.' Heaney, in contrast, gives the lines as 'Grendel's mother, monstrous hell-bride, brooded on her wrongs' (p. 42). The difference between the two lies firstly in the omission of *ides* by Heaney, and secondly in the translation of *aglæc-wif*. For Phillips, this latter term is non-pejorative, and means 'warrior-woman': Grendel's mother's role as avenger of her son is a quasi-legal one in Germanic society, and she resembles an honourable male warrior.[2] In another feminist reading of the poem, however, Jane Chance sees the appropriation of the role of avenger by a female character as a breach of Germanic society's sanctioned gender roles: women should be peace-weavers, not avengers, and Grendel's mother is an antitype of appropriate female behaviour just as her son is a parody of the appropriate behaviour of a male warrior. Chance also draws attention to the semantic range of the phrase *aglæc-wif*, which she translates as 'monster-woman' – *aglæca* means 'monster' when describing Grendel or the water-monsters, but also 'fierce combatant' or 'strong adversary'

---

[1] Phillips, 'Seamus Heaney's *Beowulf*,' 275 and n. 21.
[2] Phillips, 'Seamus Heaney's *Beowulf*,' 275–76.

when describing Sigemund, the dragon, and Beowulf himself.[1] Heaney's translation of *aglæc-wif* as 'monstrous hell-bride,' then, can be explained as follows: 'monster' is a valid sense of *aglæca*, and 'bride' is a valid sense of *wif*. 'Hell-bride' is not a sense present in the phrase itself, but is perhaps not invalid in the context of the subsequent lines, which emphasise again the descent of Grendel's mother from the biblical figure of Cain. Heaney's choices here are the most pejorative available – they emphasise the monstrous aspects of Grendel's mother rather than the suggestions of humanity – but they are not entirely at odds with the original text, as Phillips's discussion might suggest. Nor is it easy to appropriate Grendel's mother to a model of 'bog queen' (i.e. a victim of ritual sacrifice)[2] or a 'destructive mother-goddess' like Nerthus or Kathleen Ní Houlihán, as Phillips suggests. If there are representations of monstrousness in the translation, they derive from the Old English text, not from *North*.

If Grendel's mother can be read as an antitype, the ideal model of female behaviour to which she is opposed is that of *freoðu-webbe*, 'peace-weaver'.[3] Phillips argues that by underplaying the role of Grendel's mother as avenger, Heaney lessens the contrast that the poem creates with the Danish queen Wealhtheow, who is a peace-weaver rather than an avenger. In fact, neither of these aspects of character is ignored in the translation. Grendel's mother is explicitly introduced as 'an avenger' (p. 42), she is described as desperate for revenge (p. 43), and Hrothgar describes her attack as motivated by desire to avenge Grendel's death (p. 43). Likewise, although Phillips sees peace-weaving as an underplayed element in Heaney's translations of lines 612–41 and 1162–91, it's a very explicit element in the translation of 1999–2031. Wealhtheow's role as *friðu-sibb folca* (2017a) is translated as 'peace-pledge between nations' (p. 65), and Freawaru's role in making peace through marriage is emphasised; the former distributes treasure, the second moves through the hall with the drinking bowl. Here, explicitly, women are weavers of social cohesion, and the contrast with the preceding story of Thryth (or Modthryth), who fails to act as a *freoðu-webbe* is clear. If, as Phillips suggests, these elements in the original don't get the emphasis they might in the translation, it's not the case that they are dropped entirely.

What Heaney does seem to emphasise in the poem's representation of

---

[1] Jane Chance, *Woman as Hero in Old English Literature* (Syracuse, NY: Syracuse University Press, 1986), 95–97; on the meaning of *aglæca*, see also Orchard, *Pride and Prodigies*, 33.

[2] See 'Bog Queen,' in Heaney, *North*, 32–34; Heaney, *Opened Ground*, 112–14.

[3] See L. John Sklute, '*Freoðuwebbe* in Old English Poetry,' in *New Readings on Women in Old English Literature*, ed. H. Damico and A. H. Olsen (Bloomington, IN, 1990), 204–210.

gender, however, is the suffering of women: something I'll argue in the next chapter to be a continuing theme in his post-ceasefire work, from 'Mycenae Lookout' through *Beowulf* to *The Burial at Thebes* and *The Testament of Cresseid*. It's something present in *Beowulf* in the Finnsburg episode, which opens and closes by describing the effect of the feud on Hildeburh, and also at the poem's conclusion, where the lament of a Geat woman looks forward to a grim future for her and her people both:

> swylce giomor-gyd   Geatisc meowle
> [...]   bunden-heorde
> song sorg-cearig.   Sæde geneahhe,
> þæt hio hyre here-geongas   heardre ondrede
> wæl-fylla worn,   werudes egesan,
> hynðo ond hæft-nyd.   Heofon rece swealg. (3150–55)[1]

In Heaney's version:

> A Geat woman too sang out in grief;
> with hair bound up, she unburdened herself
> of her worst fears, a wild litany
> of nightmare and lament: her nation invaded,
> enemies on the rampage, bodies in piles,
> slavery and abasement. Heaven swallowed the smoke. (p. 98)

This recurrence of the theme of endurance in Heaney's post-ceasefire work is not only focused on women – Heaney describes the passage in Beowulf known as the 'Father's Lament' as being about 'the human capacity to endure' (p. xx), and 'Keeping Going,' a poem about endurance in the face of the Northern Ireland conflict, is for and about Heaney's brother Hugh[2] – but women occupy a prominent place in these poems about endurance. The possibility of a tradition of suffering women in Old English literature is something that has been suggested by critics, and critiqued by Gillian R. Overing, who sees it as construing women as passive.[3] Here, the representation of female suffering is posed as something we might identify with, for Heaney makes it clear in his introduction that this is the sort of scene that can make *Beowulf* contemporary for us, a scene that we might see on a news report from Rwanda or Kosovo (p. xxi). What Heaney is attempting here is to bring the suffering described in ancient texts closer to home for a contemporary audience at a distant remove from the events

---

[1] Manuscript damage makes the text here uncertain.

[2] Heaney, *The Spirit Level*, 10–12; Heaney, *Opened Ground*, 400–402.

[3] Gillian R. Overing, *Language, Sign, and Gender in 'Beowulf'* (Carbondale and Edwardsville: Southern Illinois University Press, 1993), 76–78.

described. It's a topic he comes back to: 'Out of Shot' in *District and Circle* juxtaposes a peaceful Wicklow Bay, site of medieval Viking raids, with footage of a mortar attack in a (presumably Iraqi) city on the previous night's TV news.[1] But if sympathy for past suffering is engendered in Heaney's *Beowulf*, it would also seem to be gendered in its inclination; something that the *Beowulf* translation has in common with several of Heaney's major post-ceasefire works.

Apocalyptic overtones

If *Beowulf* opens with echoes of genesis, it closes with echoes of apocalypse. The narrative of the poem ends with its hero's funeral: Beowulf's people are now left lordless, their enemies will now seek to renew their feuds with the vulnerable Geats, and, as Heaney puts it, 'the poem closes in a mood of sombre expectation' (p. xv). This bleak conclusion, where Beowulf's achievements in leading his people are effective only for a time, is in keeping with a general emphasis in surviving Old English poetry on the transience of all worldly things.[2] The sense of impending disaster at the end of the poem is further underscored by the incorporation of what appear to be euhemerised versions of some of the pagan Scandinavian legends relating to Ragnarök, the Old Norse equivalent of the apocalypse.[3] Toward the end of the poem, we are told the story of Herebeald the Geat, accidentally killed by his brother Haethcyn (2435–71); embedded in Beowulf's retelling of this story is a comparison to a father whose son dies on the gallows (2444–62), the 'Father's Lament.' This pair of stories is usually read as two examples of deaths that cannot be avenged. When one brother accidentally kills another, the dead brother can hardly be avenged

---

[1] Heaney, *District and Circle*, 15; the link to the Vikings is emphasised in the previous publication of 'Out of Shot' alongside 'East Coast,' a brief translation from the 9th-century Irish describing a reprieve from Norse raiders caused by harsh weather: Seamus Heaney, 'Three Poems,' *Salmagundi* 148–49 (Fall 2005 – Winter 2006), 96–99. Kuno Meyer's translation of the same Irish poem appears in *The School Bag*, ed. Seamus Heaney and Ted Hughes (London: Faber, 1997), and is discussed in Heaney, 'Through-Other Places, Through-Other Times,' 379.

[2] On which see Christine Fell, 'Perceptions of Transience,' in *The Cambridge Companion to Old English Literature*, ed. M. Godden and M. Lapidge (Cambridge: Cambridge University Press, 1991), 172–89.

[3] Roberta Frank, 'Skaldic Verse and the Date of Beowulf,' in *The Dating of Beowulf*, ed. Colin Chase (Toronto, 1981), 123–39; Ursula Dronke, 'Beowulf and Ragnarok,' *Saga-book* 17 (1969–70), 302–25; J. R. R. Tolkien, '*Beowulf*: The Monsters and the Critics,' in *An Anthology of Beowulf Criticism*, ed. Louis E. Nicholson (Indiana: University of Notre Dame Press, 1963), 51–103, first published in *Proceedings of the British Academy* 22 (1937), 245–95.

by his kin. Similarly, a father whose son dies on the gallows (whether as a criminal or a suicide) cannot achieve any compensation. Both of these stories are often seen as an indication of Beowulf's regret at his own sonlessness, something he comments upon several times in the later parts of the poem. But more than that, as Roberta Frank points out, both of these stories also bear a substantial resemblance to stories about the Norse god Oðinn, a god closely associated with the Geats, so much so that he is sometimes called 'Geat.' The accidental killing of one of Oðinn's sons by another – the killing of Baldr by Hod because of the treachery of Loki – is one of the events that lead to Ragnarök in the Old Norse *Voluspa*. The story in *Beowulf* reworks the myth, for in the Old English poem, part of the point of the story is that a son killed in this way cannot be avenged, whereas in the Old Norse myth, Oðinn has another son precisely so he can be avenged upon Hod. But the similarity between the two stories, where one son accidentally shoots another with an arrow, may lead us to read the episode in *Beowulf* as a legendary allusion preparing us for an apocalyptic ending. The story of the suicide on the gallows may well be a second allusion to Oðinn, who sacrifices himself to himself by hanging himself on a tree. Even Beowulf's fight against the dragon carries with it overtones of Ragnarök: one of the battles which takes place at Ragnarök is between Oðinn's son Þorr and the world-serpent. Þorr kills the serpent, but at the cost of his own life. So, too, Beowulf kills the dragon but dies himself in the process. One of the things these legendary allusions towards the end of the poem seem to do is to prepare us for an apocalyptic ending through parallels with Ragnarök.[1]

These apocalyptic overtones at the poem's conclusion are tied in with a sense of fatalism. There are a number of passages towards the end of the poem, such as the 'Father's Lament' at 2444–62 and the 'Lay of the Last Survivor' at 2247–66, which echo the 'ruined hall' motif found elsewhere in Old English literature in elegies like *The Wanderer*. The sense of fatalism is one expressed by the characters: Beowulf says before his battle with Grendel that fate always goes as it must (455b), and frequently declares his dependence upon providence (*metod*). He realises the limitations on his own power, and takes an attitude of fatalistic resignation towards his own death: if fate will always go as it must, sooner or later it must turn against everyone, even great kings like Hrothgar and great heroes like Beowulf. One of the important terms in the Old English lexicon from this point of view is the word *edwenden*, which describes a turning of events, a change for the worse. Such things always occur; they are inevitable; and it is just such a reversal of fortune that occurs for the Geats at the poem's

---

[1] Frank, 'Skaldic Verse,' also argues for an anti-Oðinnic sense to these allusions.

end (something that is very clear to them, but, ironically, not to Beowulf himself).

Heaney's account of the way that *wyrd* works in the poem links the metaphysical question of fate and its workings to the mechanics of the blood-feud and its recurring cycles of violence. In doing so, he points to the Finnsburg episode as central to an understanding of how feud and fate are interlinked for the participants:

> The claustrophobic and doom-laden atmosphere of this interlude gives the reader an intense intimation of what *wyrd*, or fate, meant not only to the characters in the Finn story, but to those participating in the main action of *Beowulf* itself. (p. xiv)

Heaney's concern here is not to deal with abstract questions of fatalism, but to give a sense of immediacy; of how it felt to be caught up in the moment when fortune reverses and fate turns against you, in a context of conflict and feud. This sense of a fated recurrence of cycles of violence might once again bring *North* to mind, especially given that Heaney argues for the centrality of the Finnsburg episode and the notion of blood-feud for an understanding of how fate works in the poem – in *North*, too, the eruption of violence seemed part of a long pattern of recurrence.

All of this notwithstanding, Heaney's translation nevertheless seems an optimistic one. If we have read the 'Father's Lament' above as a potential critique of the poem's heirless hero, and as a possible reference to a similar story in Norse myth that intimates apocalypse, Heaney reads it as a lyric expression of 'the human capacity to endure' (p. xx), an important theme in his post-ceasefire work, and one that suggests that use of the word 'thole' in this translation, which has received so much attention, is of thematic as well as linguistic importance. In a subsequent poem in memory of Ted Hughes, where the story of Hrethel's dead son is invoked, and the 'Father's Lament' retold (in a slightly reworded version), Heaney leads us into the retelling of the material from *Beowulf* with the words:

> Passive suffering: who said it was disallowed
> As a theme for poetry? Already in *Beowulf*
> The dumbfounding of woe, the stunt and stress
> Of hurt-in-hiding is the best of it.[1]

So, what might seem apocalyptic in the original is balanced in Heaney's version of the poem with an emphasis on endurance and empathy: endurance in a father's survival to lament his son; empathy in our awareness that a Geat woman's lament might just as well be the lament of our con-

---

[1] Heaney, *Electric Light*, 62.

temporaries on a twentieth-century news report. Most importantly, this translation also affirms that both empathy and endurance are what poetry possesses in the face of what may seem apocalyptic disaster, whether this occurs in early-medieval Scandinavia, late-twentieth-century Rwanda or Kosovo, or the recent history of Northern Ireland.

Poetic optimism

What Heaney calls the 'lovely interlude' that precedes Grendel's attack is a version of the Genesis narrative, a story of creation (89b–98). The Danish *scop* portrayed as telling the story here may be taken as a figure for the *Beowulf*-poet, but in telling a creation-story in vernacular poetic form, he is also reminiscent of Cædmon, whose Old English *Hymn* is both a retelling of the Genesis story and itself a point of genesis, the oldest surviving Old English poem, and so a point of origin of sorts for English literature. As told by Bede, Cædmon is a monastic servant whose gift for retelling biblical material in English verse comes to him in a dream. Cædmon has left the feast to sleep in the stable; a figure appears to him and instructs him to sing; what he sings, in his English vernacular, is the story of the creation of the world.[1] Bede, writing in Latin, points out that he is paraphrasing Cædmon here, making his famous comment on the impossibility of exact translation.[2] Cædmon's English text, however, is also preserved: the English version was added as notes to two eighth-century manuscripts of Bede,[3] and, with perhaps a nod towards Heaney's *Beowulf*, appears in modern English translation in Paul Muldoon's 2002 collection, *Moy Sand and Gravel*.[4] Heaney's identification with Cædmon, whom he represents as a cowherd inspired to poetry, is clear from 'Whitby-sur-Moyola,' the poem's title placing Cædmon's home place together with Heaney's, and the opening line reading: 'Caedmon too I was lucky to have known.'[5]

Less likely as a figure to identify with is Edmund Spenser, but Heaney's

---

[1] Bede, *A History of the English Church and People*, 246.

[2] Bede, *A History of the English Church and People*, 246.

[3] Kevin S. Kiernan, 'Reading Caedmon's "Hymn" with Someone Else's Glosses,' in *Old English Literature: Critical Essays*, ed. R. M. Liuzza (New Haven and London: Yale University Press, 2002), 103–124 at 103, first published in *Representations* 32 (1990), 157–74.

[4] Paul Muldoon, 'Caedmon's Hymn,' in Muldoon, *Moy Sand and Gravel* (London: Faber, 2002), 23.

[5] Heaney, *The Spirit Level*, p, 41; Heaney, *Opened Ground*, 425; McGowan, 'Heaney, Caedmon, *Beowulf*,' 35–37; cf. Howe, 'Scullionspeak.'

introduction is explicit in linking him with the figure of the *scop* in *Beowulf*:

> Indeed, every time I read the lovely interlude that tells of the minstrel singing in Heorot just before the first attacks of Grendel, I cannot help thinking of Edmund Spenser in Kilcolman Castle, reading the early cantos of *The Faerie Queene* to Sir Walter Raleigh, just before the Irish would burn the castle and drive Spenser out of Munster back to the Elizabethan court. (p. xxx)

The comparison of Spenser to the *scop* in Heorot seems, at first sight, an unlikely one, and Spenser has previously been a problematic figure for Heaney. 'Bog Oak,' from *Wintering Out*, quotes some lines from Spenser's notorious *View of the State of Ireland*,[1] and many years later, in his Oxford lectures, Heaney described Spenser's Kilcolman castle as a symbol of 'English conquest and the Anglicization of Ireland, linguistically, culturally, institutionally.'[2] But elsewhere in his Oxford lectures, Heaney makes a case for reading poetry as poetry, notwithstanding the circumstances of its production. His subject here is Marlowe's *Edward II*, but the discussion also takes in Spenser. Heaney does not shy away from Spenser's implication in the troubles of the times he lived in:

> When Spenser settled in Kilcolman, it was in a country almost depopulated by slaughter and famine. Within the previous half-year an estimated 30,000 men, women and children had perished; Spenser himself, indeed, when acting as secretary to Lord Grey, had witnessed a massacre on a large and systematic scale at Smerwick Harbour, where 600 Spaniards and Irish had been butchered.[3]

Although Heaney acknowedges that we have been 'rightly instructed' about the destruction of native populations and cultures in the name of civilization, he argues that 'it still seems an abdication of literary responsibility to be swayed by these desperately overdue correctives to a point

---

[1] Heaney, *Opened Ground*, 45; Edmund Spenser, *A View of the State of Ireland*, ed. Andrew Hadfield and Willy Maley (Oxford: Blackwell, 1997). Jean Brink, 'Constructing a View of the Present State of Ireland,' *Spenser Studies* 11 (1990), 203–28, questions the attribution of *A View* to Spenser.

[2] Heaney, 'Frontiers of Writing,' 199. For the role of Spenser's literary work in promoting an English jurisdiction over what he calls 'the British Islands,' see Nicholas Canny, *Making Ireland British 1580–1650* (Oxford: Oxford University Press, 2001), chap. 1, 'Spenser Sets the Agenda.'

[3] Heaney, 'Extending the Alphabet,' 23.

where imaginative literature is read simply and solely as a function of an oppressive discourse, or as a reprehensible masking.'[1]

What ties together the *scop* in Beowulf, Edmund Spenser, and Heaney himself, is that all are poets writing in a context of conflict. And what connects the *scop* (if the figure of the *scop* is to be taken as a figure for the *Beowulf*-poet) and Spenser is that their poetry has endured: that their cultural legacy is less the violence that they lived through than the words that they wrote. Hence, when Helen Phillips asks whether Heaney is, 'in part, finding it possible to identify with Spenser,'[2] the answer, it seems, in part at least, is yes.

The optimism of Heaney's translation lies not in a conviction that feuds may be settled (although that hope is there), but in a confidence in the power of poetry. There is much in *Beowulf* to justify such an optimism about poetry: if the poem's mood (shared with much other Old English poetry) is one that stresses the transience of worldly things, it is also one that stresses the endurance of memory, of story, of fame. The passage in *Beowulf* that associates the story of Genesis with the construction of the hall of Heorot (and, metaphorically, with the act of poetic creation) comes just before Grendel, the figure of destruction, attacks. But whereas the poem tells us of the eventual destruction of Heorot in the very lines that describe its construction (p. 5), the poem itself, that other act of creation, survives. If this version of *Beowulf* has endurance in the face of suffering as one of its primary concerns, it displays a robust confidence in the ability of poetry itself to endure.

The poem begins with the memory of famous Danes:

> Hwæt we Gar-Dena   in gear-dagum
> þeod-cyninga   þrym gefrunon,
> hu ða æþelingas   ellen fremedon. (1–3)

> So. The Spear-Danes in days gone by
> and the kings who ruled them had courage and greatness.
> We have heard of those princes' heroic campaigns. (p. 3)

And it ends with the assertion that Beowulf was *lof-geornost*:

> cwædon þæt he wære   wyruld-cyninga,
> manna mildust   ond mon-ðwærust,
> leodum liðost   ond lof-geornost. (3180–82)

> They said that of all the kings upon the earth

---

[1] Heaney, 'Extending the Alphabet,' 24.
[2] Phillips, 'Seamus Heaney's *Beowulf*,' 270.

he was the man most gracious and fair-minded,
kindest to his people and keenest to win fame. (p. 99)

Heaney's poetry does not avoid facing the atrocity in history: his lines in
the introduction describing the 'adequacy, dignity and unforgiving truth'
of the way that grief is expressed in *Beowulf* (p. xxi) seems to echo some
of what was said in his Nobel lecture about art being equal to the task of
representing suffering.[1] He also asserted in that lecture that:

> Only the very stupid or the very deprived can any longer help know-
> ing that the documents of civilization have been written in blood and
> tears, blood and tears no less real for being very remote.[2]

Writing a version of *Beowulf* that resonates with Irish history in so many
ways in the language that it uses is one way of making the blood and tears
behind *Beowulf* less remote, closer to home (even uncomfortably so). But
Heaney also points in his introduction to the classic paper by J. R. R. Tolkien, '*Beowulf*: The Monsters and the Critics' (p. xi), a paper that asserted
the primacy of the poetic in *Beowulf* against contemporary readings that
treated it as a historical document.[3] In his Nobel lecture, Heaney argued
for an inherent potency in lyric poetry. He argued for the power of poetry to create beauty in the world while acknowledging destructiveness,
its ability to sing of the suffering that it is born from, but to remain music
nonetheless. The inherent power of poetry, Heaney says, 'has as much
to do with the energy released by linguistic fission and fusion, with the
buoyancy generated by cadence and tone and rhyme and stanza, as it has to
do with the poem's concerns or the poet's truthfulness.'[4] Heaney acknowledges in his introduction that the tone of *Beowulf* is one of 'melancholy
and fortitude' (p. xxii) – indeed, this is part of its appeal for him. Given the
poem's focus on the transience of human happiness, this could hardly be
otherwise. But Heaney's translation, although it does not shy away from
treating these themes, and from giving them fresh resonances, is nevertheless an optimistic work. And it is in this conviction, embedded in *Beowulf*,
of the possibility of the endurance of poetic creation beyond the transience
of the suffering that spawns it, that the optimism in this poem resides.

[1] Heaney, 'Crediting Poetry,' 454.
[2] Heaney, 'Crediting Poetry,' 457.
[3] Tolkien, '*Beowulf*: The Monsters and the Critics,' 53.
[4] Heaney, 'Crediting Poetry,' 465.

4

The Testament of Cresseid

Hiberno-Scots

WILLY Maley, writing in this instance on Joyce, argues that 'there is evidence in recent years of a growing interest in Scottish and Irish relations on a range of fronts – historical, political, cultural – that promises to undo the double bind implicit in traditional Anglo-Scottish and Anglo-Irish perspectives.'[1] An interest in historical links may be ascribed in part to a recent interest in Scottish history in itself, and in part to a new attitude evident in British history that takes account of a four-nation perspective. This is an attitude pioneered by historians like J. G. A. Pocock[2] and Hugh Kearney,[3] visible in writings on the early-modern period by scholars such as Brendan Bradshaw and John Morrill,[4] an influence on the accounts of medieval Britain and Ireland in the work of R. R. Davies and Robin Frame,[5] and writ large in Norman Davies's

---

[1] Willy Maley, '"Kilt by kelt shell kithagain with kinagain": Joyce and Scotland,' in *Semicolonial Joyce*, ed. Derek Attridge and Marjorie Howes (Cambridge: Cambridge University Press, 2000), 201–218 at 201.

[2] J. G. A. Pocock, 'British History: A Plea for a New Subject,' in Pocock, *The Discovery of Islands: Essays in British History* (Cambridge: Cambridge University Press, 2005), 24–43, first published in *New Zealand Journal of History* 8 (1974), 3–21. Pocock, 'The Field Enlarged: An Introduction,' in *The Discovery of Islands*, 47–57 at 48 n. 3, offers a selective list of works indebted to the methods proposed in his 1974 essay.

[3] Hugh Kearney, *The British Isles: A History of Four Nations* (Cambridge: Cambridge University Press, 1989); Heaney, 'Through-Other Places, Through-Other Times,' 378, mentions Kearney's approach.

[4] *The British Problem, c.1534–1707: State Formation in the Atlantic Archipelago*, ed. Brendan Bradshaw and John Morrill (Basingstoke: Macmillan, 1996).

[5] R. R. Davies, *The First English Empire: Power and Identities in the British Isles, 1093–1343* (Oxford: Oxford University Press, 2000); Robin Frame, *The Political Development of the British Isles, 1100–1400* (Oxford: Oxford University Press, 1990; rev. pbk edn, 1995); here, however, the expanded perspective comes with the caveat that these countries are still nascent: as Davies warns, 'to construct the history of the British Isles as the history of

synthesis *The Isles*, which argues that 'the conventional framework of the history of the Isles is in urgent need of revision,' and itself seeks 'to pay due respect to all the nations and cultures in the history of the Isles and to the detriment of none.'[1] Such an interest in a non-Anglocentric perspective on the history of Britain and Ireland may be further modified, for the Middle Ages, by an awareness of transnational links such as those between Ireland and Scotland. Steven Ellis argues that Irish history written from 'a perspective which focuses on interaction between English and Irish within Ireland is too narrow for the pre-1534 period, when interaction was rather between separate English and Gaelic worlds extending well outside Ireland.'[2] Interest in political relations between Ireland and Scotland may have arisen because political changes have made such interest possible: in recent years, peace in Northern Ireland has taken some of the heat out of a previous Irish/British dualism, and devolution in Scotland has drawn attention to a Scottish polity distinct from that of Westminster.[3]

A revival of interest in cultural relations has been visible in projects such as the publication by Canongate in 2002 of *An Leabhar Mòr*, an anthology of verse and artwork from Ireland and Scotland that combined one hundred poems in Gaelic with the work of one hundred visual artists.[4] In his general introduction to *An Leabhar Mòr*, Malcolm Maclean draws attention to the way that political change has created space for a renewed interest in Hiberno-Scottish relations, arguing that 'by devolution in 1999, the Council of the Isles and the Northern Ireland peace process had created a new political context in which the idea of the *Leabhar Mòr* has flourished.' He goes on to give a potted history of the neglected cultural and political links between the countries:

> A language map of Europe reflects cultural realities that bear little resemblance to political boundaries. This is particularly true of Gaelic

four countries is to foreclose on the options that were still possible in the late eleventh century' (p. 61).

[1] Norman Davies, *The Isles: A History* (London: Macmillan, 1999), p. xxxix. Differences do exist between the methodologies of the historians gathered together here: see J. G. A. Pocock, 'The Politics of the New British History,' in Pocock, *The Discovery of Islands*, 289–300 at 298 n. 3.

[2] Steven G. Ellis, *Tudor Ireland: Crown, Community and the Conflict of Cultures, 1470–1603* (London: Longman, 1985), 13.

[3] Political interest has been reciprocal: see Ray Ryan, *Ireland and Scotland: Literature and Culture, State and Nation, 1966–2000* (Oxford: Oxford University Press, 2002), 1–2, 13–15.

[4] *An Leabhar Mòr: The Great Book of Gaelic*, ed. Malcolm Maclean and Theo Dorgan (Edinburgh: Canongate, 2002). Heaney is one of the contemporary poets asked to nominate poems for inclusion in the book: he nominates the medieval Irish poem *Pangur Bán* (p. 44).

Scotland and Ireland. There are no two countries in Europe with more in common. We share a mythology, three languages, a rich music tradition and some significant history, and yet a great deal of this enduring connection has been consistently glossed over or deliberately obscured.

It was the Irish Gaels, known as the Scoti, who migrated into Scotland from the 5th century and gave it its name. The most famous artefact from Ireland's golden age, the Book of Kells, originated on the Scottish Island of Iona. It was the Gaels who united Scotland in the 9th century and made Gaelic the language of the medieval court. The 'Irish' Gaelic culture in the Scottish Highlands survived that in Ireland by a century and a half. The Scots were 'planted' into Ireland from the 17th century and hundreds of thousands of Irish people migrated to Scotland in the 19th and 20th centuries.[1]

There are differing views on how to interpret the historical connections between Scotland and Ireland. Wilson McLeod has argued recently that national distinctions between Ireland and Scotland were important in the period 1200–1650, stating that the 'relationship between Gaelic Scotland and Gaelic Ireland must be considered one of ambiguous connection' during this period, and questioning Steven Ellis's arguments for a pan-Gaelic perspective.[2] While interpretations might be contested, what is not in doubt is the growth of interest in recent years in the subject of Hiberno-Scottish relations.

Seamus Heaney's turn to translate a major work of medieval Scottish literature, then, seems a timely one given a renewed Irish interest in Scotland, and it may be possible to read Heaney's translation (or 'retelling' as the title page has it) of Robert Henryson's *Testament of Cresseid*, published in a limited edition in 2004 by Enitharmon Editions, as participating in this renewed Irish interest in Scotland and its history and culture.[3] It's also true to say, though, that Heaney's sense of affinity with Scotland is long standing. Scotland makes several appearances in the poetry: the introduction to *Sweeney Astray* emphasises that the poem's topography includes western Scotland as well as southern Ireland, holding that affinity with both places,

---

[1] Malcolm Maclean, General Introduction to *An Leabhar Mòr*, 1–5 at 2.

[2] Wilson McLeod, *Divided Gaels: Gaelic Cultural Identities in Scotland and Ireland, c.1200–c.1650* (Oxford: Oxford University Press, 2004), 5, 220–22.

[3] Page references are to Seamus Heaney, *The Testament of Cresseid: A Retelling of Robert Henryson's Poem by Seamus Heaney with Images by Hughie O'Donoghue* (London: Enitharmon Editions, 2004). Line references are to Henryson's original, in *The Poems of Robert Henryson*, ed. Denton Fox (Oxford: Oxford University Press, 1981).

as displayed in the medieval work, is 'exemplary for all men and women
in contemporary Ulster' (p. vi). 'The First Flight' takes a more jaundiced
view of historical Hiberno-Scottish relations (as the whole 'Sweeney Redivivus' sequence does with much of its subject matter) in its passing reference to the levies from Scotland, said levies being the Scottish *gallóglaigh*
or 'gallowglasses' that participated in Irish conflicts.[1] Hugh MacDiarmid
is praised in 'An Invocation' from *The Spirit Level*,[2] and in Heaney's prose,
essays on MacDiarmid, Edwin Muir, and Robert Burns, and reminiscence
for Norman MacCaig (an early influence) demonstrate an immersion in
Scottish writing and a connection with Scottish writers.[3] Norman Mac-
Caig is remembered again alongside Iain MacGabhainn, Sorley MacLean,
and George Mackay Brown in 'Would They Had Stay'd,' from Heaney's
2001 collection, *Electric Light*.[4]

Heaney's first foray into Scottish translation in recent times was to
translate a Gaelic poem, 'Hallaig,' by Sorley MacLean, the twentieth-century's pre-eminent Gaelic poet.[5] Heaney describes the poem as 'haunted
by the great absence that the Highland clearances represent in Scots Gaelic
consciousness. "Hallaig" is at once historical and hallucinatory, a poem
in which the deserted homesteads of a little settlement on the island of
Raasay are repopulated by a vision of "a fair field full of folk".'[6] Heaney's
words here are elegiac for the 'great absence,' but the snippet of quotation

---

[1] Heaney, *Station Island*, 103; Heaney, *Opened Ground*, 274. McLeod, *Divided Gaels*,
40–54, notes that Gaelic Irish chiefs begin hiring Scottish Gaelic mercenaries (*gallóglaigh*,
conventionally 'foreign warrior,' but more specifically, McLeod argues, 'Hebridean warrior') after the mid 13th century; the 15th and 16th centuries saw larger numbers of mercenaries used for shorter periods: these were called 'redshanks' by the English, and simply
Albanaigh, 'Scots,' by the Irish. The contemporary levies are, of course, in the British
army: the Scots Guards served in Northern Ireland during the Troubles (see Peter Taylor,
Brits: The War against the IRA (London: Bloomsbury, 2001), 44).

[2] Heaney, *The Spirit Level*, 27–28; MacDiarmid's advocacy of Henryson is mentioned
by Heaney in his introduction to his translation of the *Testament* (p. 6).

[3] Seamus Heaney, 'Edwin Muir,' 'A Torchlight Procession of One: Hugh Mac-
Diarmid,' 'Burns's Art Speech,' 'Norman MacCaig,' in Heaney, *Finders Keepers*, 246–56,
293–311, 347–63, 399–402; for MacCaig as an early influence on Heaney, see Corcoran,
Poetry of Seamus Heaney, 4.

[4] Heaney, *Electric Light*, 68–69; Bernard O'Donoghue, 'The Pastoral Power Station,'
the Independent (31 March 2001), detects an implicit reference to William Dunbar's *Lament
for the Makars* here alongside the explicit reference to Shakespeare.

[5] MacLean's work is collected in Somhairle MacGill-Eain / Sorley MacLean, *O Choille
gu Bearradh / From Wood to Ridge: Collected Poems in Gaelic and in English Translation* (Manchester: Carcanet; Edinburgh: Birlinn, 1999); for 20th-century Scots Gaelic poetry in
general, see *An Tuil: Anthology of 20th Century Scottish Gaelic Verse*, ed. Ronald I. M. Black
(Edinburgh: Polygon, 1999).

[6] Seamus Heaney, 'The Trance and the Translation,' *The Guardian* (30 Nov. 2002).

from the Middle English *Piers Plowman*[1] here is a subtle reminder that the Gaelic *aisling* tradition that endures in MacLean's poem has its roots in the same medieval dream-vision tradition in which Langland participates, and is a reminder also of Heaney's refusal of the separation of Gaelic and English-language literary traditions.

The alignment of language, culture and politics is one with a long history, however, in Scotland as well as Ireland, an alignment visible in a poem by Robert Henryson's contemporaries, William Dunbar and Walter Kennedy. During the insults exchanged in *The Flyting of Dunbar and Kennedy*, Dunbar calls his counterpart Kennedy, who is from the Gaelic-speaking Highlands, an 'Iersche brybour baird' (a vagabond Irish bard). He tells Kennedy,

> Thy trechour tung hes tane ane Heland strynd,
> Ane Lawland ers wald mak a bettir noyis.[2]

> Your treacherous tongue has taken a Highland strain,
> A Lowland arse would make a better noise.

Dunbar goes on to say,

> Sic eloquence as thay in Erschry vse,
> In sic is sett thy thraward appetyte.
> Thow hes full littill feill of fair indyte.
> I tak on me, ane pair of Lowthiane hippis
> Sall fairar Inglis mak and mair parfyte
> Than thow can blabbar with thy Carrik lippis.[3]

> Such eloquence as they use in the Highlands,
> In that is set your backward appetite.
> You have very little understanding of fair speech:
> I swear a pair of Lothian hips
> Shall fairer English make, and more perfect,
> Than you can blabber with your Carrick lips.

The poem is a *flyting*, a quarrel, 'a contest in abuse and poetic virtuosity,' as Patricia Bawcutt puts it,[4] and so it's not necessarily correct to take the sentiments here at face value. Dunbar's actual affection for Kennedy is visible

---

[1] The reference is to *Piers Plowman*, B Prologue, line 17: 'A fair feeld ful of folk fond I ther bitwene,' also alluded to at the beginning of 'Station Island.'

[2] *The Poems of William Dunbar*, ed. Priscilla Bawcutt, 2 vols., Association for Scottish Literary Studies 27, 28 (Glasgow: Association for Scottish Literary Studies, 1998), i, 201, 202.

[3] *Poems of William Dunbar*, ed. Bawcutt, i, 203–04.

[4] *Poems of William Dunbar*, ed. Bawcutt, ii, 427.

in his roll-call of poets in *Lament for the Makars*, where Dunbar lists 'Gud Maister Walter Kennedy' last in a list of poets that begins with the English poets Chaucer, Lydgate, and Gower, and proceeds through a list of Dunbar's Scottish predecessors (including Henryson) who have passed away, to conclude with Kennedy, now on his deathbed, and Dunbar himself, who will no more escape death than the long list of poets already listed. 'Gret reuth it wer that he suld de' ('It would be a great pity if he should die'), says Dunbar here of Kennedy, a brief tribute that is a far cry from the lengthy torrents of abuse in the *Flyting*, and much more likely to be sincere.[1]

The *Flyting* does, however, align language with politics, where Dunbar places Highland Gaelic in opposition to Lowland English as treacherous, and Kennedy replies in kind:

> Thou lufis nane Irische, elf, I vnderstand,
> Bot it suld be all trew Scottis mennis lede.[2]

> You love no Irish, elf, I understand,
> But it should be all faithful Scotttish men's speech.

This alignment of the English and Irish languages with political positions is one familiar from contemporary Ireland, although the situation is more complex than it might initially appear: contemporary Irish language politics is not something that can be mapped directly onto contemporary (much less medieval) Scotland, and the reverse is also true. As Edna Longley notes (citing Gordon McCoy and Maolcholaim Scott), contemporary Scots Gaelic culture includes features unimaginable in an Irish context, such as ceilidhs held in British Legion halls and Free Presbyterians who worship in Gaelic, and it is in Ulster, rather than Scotland, where there has been a successful campaign for political recognition of Scots (here, specifically Ulster Scots) as a language, rather than a dialect of English.[3] Heaney makes a similar point in relation to Sorley MacLean, saying that 'it disturbed a number of tidy Irish assumptions, north and south, to discover that this Gaelic-speaking Free Presbyterian from Raasay and Skye, a passionate socialist whose heroes included James Connolly, had fought with

---

[1] *Selected Poems of Robert Henryson and William* Dunbar, ed. Douglas Gray (London: Penguin, 1998), 355; *Poems of William Dunbar*, ed. Bawcutt, i, 97 chooses the reading 'so suld be' over 'he suld de.'

[2] *Poems of William Dunbar*, ed. Bawcutt, i, 211.

[3] Edna Longley, 'Multi-Culturalism and Northern Ireland: Making Differences Fruitful,' in Longley and Declan Kiberd, *Multi-Culturalism: The View from the Two Irelands* (Cork: Cork University Press, 2001), 1–44 at 26, 39–40; Ulster Scots is named as a language in the Good Friday Agreement, cited by Longley, 'Multi-Culturalism,' 39.

equally passionate conviction as a British soldier in the Western Desert and had written about the heroism of the common Tommy.'[1]

Heaney, in any case, has been explicit in his rejection of 'binary thinking about language' where English and Irish (or, here, their close relations, Scots Gaelic and Lowland Scots) are seen as 'adversarial tongues, as either/or conditions rather than both/and.'[2] His refusal to separate the Gaelic and English-language literary traditions into opposing camps is evident in *Sweeney Astray*'s allusions to an English literary canon in translating a medieval Irish text, in the *Beowulf* translation's incorporation of Irish-language words in a translation of an Anglo-Saxon poem, and in gestures elsewhere such as the inclusion of Irish, Welsh, and Scottish Gaelic materials in translation alongside materials in English in *The School Bag*, an anthology co-edited with Ted Hughes,[3] where there is a deliberate juxtaposition of Cresseid's lament with Lady Gregory's translation of an eighteenth-century Irishwoman's lament, 'Dónal Óg.'[4] So Heaney is equally able to find himself in tune with a fifteenth-century poet writing in Scots as with a twentieth-century poet writing in Scots Gaelic, just as he was able, in writing about Robert Burns, to compare Burns's poem 'To a Mouse, On turning her up in her Nest, with the Plough, November, 1785,' with the Irish poet Cathal Buí MacGiolla Ghunna's Gaelic poem 'An Bonnán Buí,' and to praise both.[5] In translating Henryson, Heaney tells us, he finds 'the hidden Scotland at the back of my own ear,' a hidden Scotland that for Heaney is 'phonetic rather than ethnic.' 'When I went back to Henryson a few years ago,' he tells us in the introduction to the translation, 'I felt entirely at home with his "sound of sense"; some of his vocabulary I had met in the Scots-influenced vocabulary of mid-Ulster speech, but more important I found myself in tune with his pace and pitch and had a strong inclination to hum along with him' (p. 8).

Heaney's inclination to hum along with Henryson is unsurprising given some of the elements they have in common. Heaney's description of Henryson's poetry as having 'an in-stepness between the colloquial and considered elements of a style that is all his own' (p. 6), reminds us, in that balance of 'colloquial' and 'considered,' of Heaney's own balancing of the standard and the local in his poetic vocabulary. Here, too, Heaney has no

[1] Heaney, 'Through-Other Places, Through-Other Times,' 380.

[2] *Beowulf*, trans. Heaney, p. xxiv.

[3] Heaney's foreword to *The School Bag* (p. xvii) draws attention to inclusions from 'the non-English poetries of Britain and Ireland.'

[4] As Heaney tells us in 'Through-Other Places, Through-Other Times,' 379.

[5] Heaney, 'Burns' Art Speech,' 352–55.

need to season standard English with a sprinkling of Gaelic, for Henryson's original includes words of Gaelic origin:

> Quhen scho ouircome, with siching sair and sad,
> With mony cairfull cry and cald ochane. (*Testament*, 540–41)

'Ochane' here is the Gaelic term of lament *ochón*, retained in Heaney's translation:

> When she came to, she sighed sore and bewailed
> Her woeful plight, and wept and cried 'Ochone.' (p. 39)[1]

The *Testament* also includes Old English words that might be considered important to Heaney: specifically *thole*, from Old English *þolian* 'endure, suffer, hold out,' which previously appeared in Heaney's translations of *Sweeney Astray*, *The Midnight Verdict*, and *Beowulf*, and which makes an appearance here in Henryson's original.[2] Heaney discusses *thole* at length in his introduction to the *Beowulf* translation as a word that provides a link between the Old English of the poem and the Ulster vernacular of his childhood. In his discussion there, Heaney notes that the word reminded him:

> that my aunt's language was not just a self-enclosed family possession but an historical heritage, one that involved the journey *þolian* had made north into Scotland and then across into Ulster with the planters, and then across from the planters to the locals who had originally spoken Irish, and then farther across again when the Scots Irish emigrated to the American South in the eighteenth century.[3]

The journey that *þolian* made into Scotland during the Middle Ages results in the word's appearance in Henryson's poem, in a passage where the poet tells us how his putative source for Cresseid's end describes 'quhat distres scho thoillit, and quhat deid' (*Testament of Cresseid*, 70). Heaney doesn't translate *thoillit* as *tholed* here – he renders the line as 'What she would

---

[1] *Poems of Robert Henryson*, ed. Fox, 379, n. to l. 541, notes the derivation from Scottish and Irish Gaelic, and argues for 'cald' as adjectival 'cold' rather than 'called,' noting however that '*ochane* can be construed either as the first word of Cresseid's speech or as a noun parallel with cry.' Douglas Gray, *Robert Henryson* (Leiden: Brill, 1979), 16, suggests that *ochón* may have been one of the few Gaelic loan words in Middle Scots: see *Dictionary of the Older Scottish Tongue from the Twelfth Century to the End of the Seventeenth*, ed. Sir William Craigie et al., 12 vols. (Oxford: Oxford University Press, 1937–2002), s.v. *ochane*. On the sound of 'och,' see Heaney, 'Burns' Art Speech,' 350.

[2] Heaney, *Sweeney Astray*, 28; Heaney, *The Midnight Verdict*, 28; *Beowulf*, trans. Heaney, 3.

[3] *Beowulf*, trans. Heaney, p. xxv.

endure and how she died' (*Testament of Cresseid*, p. 15) – but this is also his practice in the *Beowulf* translation, where he uses *tholed*, certainly, but not to translate *þolian*. Its presence in Henryson's original here, however, is useful as a twofold reminder. Firstly, it reminds us that the original poem's 'vernacular edge,' as Heaney describes it (p. 8), contains, like Heaney's own poetic vernacular, fragments of both Gaelic and Anglo-Saxon. Secondly, it's a reminder that endurance is a continuing theme in Heaney's post-ceasefire poetry: Helen Vendler argues for stoicism as a key theme in the 1996 collection *The Spirit Level*,[1] and the discussion of *thole* in the introduction to the *Beowulf* translation, while highlighting linguistic issues, also draws attention to the theme of endurance in adversity. *The Testament of Cresseid* seems to mark a further engagement with that theme.

If Henryson's poetic vernacular shares some elements with Heaney's, there are also some possible echoes in this translation of earlier Heaney poems. The sentence passed on Cresseid, that she would live 'beyond the pale' (p. 27), a phrase not present in Henryson's original, is perhaps an echo of that other outcast 'beyond the pale,' Grendel:

> the other, warped
> in the shape of a man, moves beyond the pale.[2]

Bernard O'Donoghue, reviewing this translation in the *TLS*, suggests possible echoes from another Heaney translation, *The Midnight Verdict*, in the description of Saturn. Praising Heaney's retelling, O'Donoghue says that this version of the *Testament* is 'faithful to the language and world of the source text, but in a voice that is unmistakably the translator's own.' A sense of fidelity to both the medieval and the modern is possible here because, while Heaney and Henryson do not always sound alike, there are places where they do. O'Donoghue notes how 'the poem's most famous question fits Heaney's voice with total naturalness: "Who knows if all that Chaucer wrote was true?"'[3] Henryson's Scots vernacular, containing fragments of both Gaelic and Old English within it, anticipates Heaney's own Ulster-Scots and Irish inflected English, and if Henryson in some ways predicts Heaney, Heaney returns the compliment by occasionally having his version of Henryson echo earlier lines of his own.

[1] Vendler, *Seamus Heaney*, 157–68.
[2] *Beowulf*, trans. Heaney, 45.
[3] Bernard O'Donoghue, 'Cider and Pear-Gall,' *TLS* (18 Feb. 2005).

Trojan wars, medieval and modern

If it is possible to view Heaney's reworking of *The Testament of Cresseid* as contextualized by engagement with Scotland, it's also possible to read it as part of a twofold engagement with material relating to the Trojan war, firstly by Heaney himself and other Irish writers, but also by Henryson's medieval antecedents, Chaucer included. Heaney had previously used Trojan material in his play from 1990, *The Cure at Troy*, which is a version of Sophocles' *Philoctetes*,[1] and in the sequence of poems in *The Spirit Level* entitled 'Mycenae Lookout', which reworks material from Aeschylus' *Oresteia*.[2] Other contemporary Irish writers, including Michael Longley, Brendan Kennelly and Ciaran Carson, have also drawn upon Trojan material, often in relation to the Northern Ireland conflict; indeed, contemporary Irish writing has drawn on classical literature to such an extent that Heaney, when invited to translate Sophocles' *Antigone* for the Abbey Theatre, wondered 'how many Antigones could Irish theatre put up with?'[3]

Trojan material is also thematically important for later medieval writers. It features firstly as a subset of one of the three great subjects of medieval romance: the matter of Britain, the matter of France, and the matter of Rome (concerning King Arthur, Charlemagne, and classical material respectively). The story of Troy was also of foundational importance for later medieval European rulers. Medieval English legendary history offered a version of Britain's origins in which the Virgilian account of Aeneas' foundation of Rome is followed by the foundation of Britain by the Trojan exile Brutus, and fourteenth-century London was seen by contemporaries as a 'new Troy'.[4] Henryson, however, is writing a medieval love-narrative set against the backdrop of the fall of Troy, and is not directly concerned with the details of Trojan history. Henryson writes a narrative in which the fate of Cresseid, 'this deceived and deluded young

---

[1] Seamus Heaney, *The Cure at Troy: A Version of Sophocles' 'Philoctetes'* (New York: Farrar Strauss Giroux, 1991).

[2] Heaney, *The Spirit Level*, 29–37; Heaney, *Opened Ground*, 414–22.

[3] Seamus Heaney, 'A Story that Sings down the Centuries,' *Sunday Times* (21 March 2004).

[4] For Brutus' foundation of Britain, see Geoffrey of Monmouth, *The History of the Kings of Britain*, trans. Lewis Thorpe (Harmondsworth: Penguin, 1966), 53–74; for discussion of the influence of the Trojan foundational myth, see Lee Patterson, *Chaucer and the Subject of History* (London: Routledge, 1991), 90–94; cf. Sylvia Federico, *New Troy: Fantasies of Empire in the Late Middle Ages*, Medieval Cultures 36 (Minneapolis and London: University of Minnesota Press, 2003).

woman, who never even existed,' as Derek Pearsall puts it, is seen as more important than questions about the fate of nations, which are relegated to the background.[1] There are other later medieval poems where the appearance of the Trojan story as background material allows it to be read as reflecting upon foreground themes with which it may not be directly connected. *Sir Gawain and the Green Knight* is a regularly invoked example, where the poem opens with the story of the fall of Troy and the foundation of Britain, a story seemingly incidental to the subsequent narrative of Gawain's quest for the Green Knight, but perhaps emblematic of the motif of 'shame and success' that turns out to be central to the poem.[2] Chaucer's *Troilus and Criseyde*, likewise, while focusing on a love story between two individuals rather than the epic tale of the Trojan war, manages to suggest telling parallels between the microcosm of the love narrative and the macrocosm of the epic struggle raging between the Greeks and Trojans. As Barry Windeatt notes, the narrative of Criseyde's betrayal of Troilus is set in the context of political and historical instances of betrayal in the Trojan War, a conflict itself caused by infidelity.[3]

Henryson, however, remains focused on individuals and their sufferings rather than the fate of nations, and this focus is shared by Heaney and other contemporary Irish writers in their engagement with the Trojan story on a human rather than an epic scale. First performed by the Field Day Theatre Company in 1990, Heaney's play *The Cure at Troy* depicts the Greeks Odysseus and Neoptolemus coming to Lemnos to find the injured and outcast Philoctetes. Philoctetes possesses the invincible bow that the Greeks need to win the Trojan war, but his hostility to Odysseus means that Neoptolemus is persuaded, initially at least, to attempt to trick Philoctetes into handing over the bow and returning with the Greeks to Troy to finish the war. Philoctetes bears some resemblance to another outcast figure in Heaney's work, for, like Sweeney, he has become animal-like through exposure and suffering.[4] In contrast to the situation of Sweeney,

---

[1] Derek Pearsall, '"Quha wait gif all that Chaucer wrait was trew?": Henryson's *Testament of Cresseid*,' in *New Perspectives on Middle English Texts: A Festschrift for R. A. Waldron*, ed. Susan Powell and Jeremy J. Smith (Cambridge: Brewer, 2000), 169–82 at 170.

[2] *The Poems of the Pearl Manuscript: Pearl; Cleanness; Patience; Sir Gawain and the Green Knight*, ed. Malcolm Andrew and Ronald Waldron (Exeter: University of Exeter Press, 1987), 207, n. to ll. 3f. Critics differ as to whether the traitor referred to in the poem's opening lines is Antenor or Aeneas himself. Malcolm Andrew, 'The Fall of Troy in *Sir Gawain and the Green Knight* and *Troilus and Crisedye*,' in *The European Tragedy of Troilus*, ed. Piero Boitani (Oxford: Oxford University Press, 1989), 75–93, compares the treatment of the Troy narrative in the two poems.

[3] Barry Windeatt, *Oxford Guides to Chaucer: Troilus and Criseyde* (Oxford: Oxford University Press, 1992), 246.

[4] Heaney, *The Cure at Troy*, 13.

however, Philoctetes's suffering is not accompanied by the compensation of insight, and one of the important themes of the play is the way that Philoctetes's obsession with past wrongs prevents him from looking forward towards the possibility of healing:

> The past is bearable,
> The past's only a scar, but the future –
> Never. Never again can I see myself
> Eye to eye with the sons of Atreus.[1]

That the echo of Sweeney seems deliberate, however, is suggested by Philoctetes's declaration 'I am astray' at the height of his suffering.[2] Philoctetes's earlier description of himself as 'rotting like a leper'[3] might seem to look forward to another outcast figure, Cresseid, but it is 'Mycenae Lookout' rather than *The Cure at Troy* that seems thematically closer to Heaney's reworking of Henryson's *Testament*.

'Mycenae Lookout' also begins with a Sweeney-like figure, the watchman who opens Aeschylus' *Agamemnon*, 'posted and forgotten' (in an echo of the opening line of 'In the Beech' from the 'Sweeney Redivivus' sequence),[4] and, as with Sweeney, here again the sentry-figure is an autobiographical projection for the poet watching from the sidelines through years of warfare. The opening poem of the sequence, which introduces the figure of that watchman-narrator reminiscent of both Sweeney and Heaney, is followed by 'Cassandra,' which describes the pain suffered by women in warfare in one of the most explicit descriptions of suffering to be found anywhere in Heaney's work. The opening of 'Cassandra' recalls an earlier Heaney poem: 'Punishment,' from *North*.[5] There, at the poem's conclusion, the narrator stands by watching women being tarred and feathered. The echoes of 'Punishment' in the later poem are emphasised by the detail of Cassandra's shaved head and the use of severely abbreviated lines, even shorter than those of *North*.

Bernard O'Donoghue has described 'Punishment' as the most controversial poem in *North*, and what makes it controversial is the self-accusation that concludes the poem, drawing a parallel between the poet's voyeuristic gaze at the 'little adultress' exhumed from the bog, and his role as bystander while his own contemporaries, here seen as the betray-

---

[1] Heaney, *The Cure at Troy*, 73.

[2] Heaney, *The Cure at Troy*, 44.

[3] Heaney, *The Cure at Troy*, 17.

[4] Corcoran, *Poetry of Seamus Heaney*, 191; Heaney, *Station Island*, 100; Heaney, *Spirit Level*, 29; Heaney, *Opened Ground*, 271, 414.

[5] As noted by Corcoran, *Poetry of Seamus Heaney*, 201.

ing sisters of the girl exhumed from the bog, are cauled in tar in an act of what's described as intimate revenge.[1] As O'Donoghue notes, the poem itself provides the self-accusation that the poet is an 'artful voyeur,' which Edna Longley uses as half her title in an essay criticising *North*.[2] It seems that what Declan Kiberd says of Heaney is true: 'the worst that can be said against Heaney always turns out to have been said already of himself by the artist within the poems.'[3] If that is so, Heaney is again prepared to repeat the self-accusation from 'Punishment' twenty years later in 'Mycenae Lookout,' at greater length, and in painful detail. In 'Cassandra,' the account of the girl's death again points the finger at those watching:

> And the result-
>
> ant shock desire
> in bystanders
> to do it to her
>
> there and then.
> Little rent
> cunt of their guilt:
>
> in she went
> to the knife,
> to the killer wife,
>
> to the net over
> her and her slaver,
> the Troy reaver.[4]

Helen Vendler sees 'Mycenae Lookout' as an 'afterwards,' 'a summary of troubles concluded,' possible only in the aftermath of the 1994 ceasefires. Only in this context, she argues, does Heaney permit himself such 'unexampled linguistic violence,' something not seen elsewhere in the poetry, and found here in an attempt to draw a line under the suffering of the previous twenty-five years.[5] If 'Mycenae Lookout' is a backward look at something now judged concluded, its use of Trojan material to do so may echo Michael Longley's use of the Trojan myth in 'Ceasefire,' Longley's

---

[1] O'Donoghue, 'Seamus Heaney: *North*,' 534; Heaney, *North*, 38, Heaney, *Opened Ground*, 118.

[2] O'Donoghue, 'Seamus Heaney: *North*,' 534; Edna Longley, '*North*: "Inner Emigré" or "Artful Voyeur"?' in *The Art of Seamus Heaney*, ed. Curtis, 65–95.

[3] Declan Kiberd, *Inventing Ireland: The Literature of the Modern Nation* (London: Cape, 1995; repr. Vintage, 1996), 594–95.

[4] Heaney, *Spirit Level*, 32–33; Heaney, *Opened Ground*, 417–18.

[5] Vendler, *Seamus Heaney*, 157, 168–69.

poem following the IRA ceasefire of 1994, which depicts the painful but necessary reconciliation between Priam and Achilles following the latter's killing of Hector, Priam's son.[1] If 'Mycenae Lookout' takes a backward look, however (both to past events and to previous Heaney poems), it also seems to contain in itself a theme that will continue to concern Heaney in subsequent work, for 'Mycenae Lookout' is one of a number of places where Heaney's post-ceasefire poetry has described the suffering of women against a background of conflict. His introduction to the *Beowulf* translation draws our attention to precisely this theme at the end of the Old English poem, and Heaney suggests that this element in the poem makes it contemporary for us:

> The Geat woman who cries out in dread as the flames consume the body of her dead lord could come straight from a late-twentieth-century news report, from Rwanda or Kosovo; her keen is a nightmare glimpse into the minds of people who have survived traumatic, even monstrous events and who are now being exposed to a comfortless future. We immediately recognize her predicament and the pitch of her grief and find ourselves the better for having them expressed with such adequacy, dignity and unforgiving truth.[2]

The theme of female suffering similarly offers one motivation for his translation of *Antigone*, published in 2004, the same year as *The Testament of Cresseid*:

> I remembered the opening lines of Eibhlín Dubh Ni Chonaill's lament, an outburst of grief and anger from a woman whose husband had been cut down and left bleeding on the roadside in Co. Cork, in much the same way as Polyneices was left outside the walls of Thebes, unburied, desecrated, picked at by the crows. [...] I made a connection between the wife traumatised by the death of her husband at the hands of the English soldiery at Carriganimma and the sister driven wild by the edict of a tyrant in Thebes [...].[3]

In his introduction to his retelling of *The Testament of Cresseid*, Heaney

---

[1] Michael Longley, *The Ghost Orchid* (London: Cape. 1995), 39.

[2] *Beowulf*, trans. Heaney, p. xxi.

[3] Heaney, 'A Story that Sings down the Centuries'; Seamus Heaney, *The Burial at Thebes: Sophocles' 'Antigone'* (London: Faber, 2004). Paul Muldoon translates a fragment of Eibhlín Dubh Ni Chonaill's *Caoineadh Airt Uí Laoghaire* in 'Keen' (Muldoon, *Poems*, 49); part of the poem appears in Irish and English translation in *An Duanaire, 1600–1900: Poems of the Dispossessed*, ed. Seán Ó Tuama, trans. Thomas Kinsella (Portlaoise: Dolmen / Bord na Gaeilge, 1981), 200–219. Heaney discusses the poem briefly at the beginning of his Oxford lecture on Merriman: Heaney, 'Orpheus in Ireland,' 38–39.

points again to the theme of the suffering of women, and what he calls Henryson's 'singular compassion for the character of Cresseid' (p. 9). Whatever of Henryson's compassion for Cresseid (a point I'll return to at some length below), it seems that Heaney's motivation to work on the poem is in part one of sympathy towards its central character and her suffering, and so a continuation of concerns evident in the translation of *Antigone*, the *Beowulf* translation, and (in a previous engagement with Trojan material) in 'Mycenae Lookout.'

Heaney's use of Trojan material here to describe female suffering and endurance seems to chime with the practice of other contemporary Irish writers. In a prefatory comment to the published version of his play *The Trojan Women*, Brendan Kennelly draws attention to the colloquial description of a woman as 'a Trojan' to express admiration for the ability to endure. Kennelly writes:

> Almost fifty years ago, I heard women in the village where I grew up say of another woman, 'She's a Trojan', meaning she had tremendous powers of endurance and survival, was determined to overcome different forms of disappointment and distress, was dogged but never insensitive, obstinate but never blackscowling, and seemed eternally capable of renewing herself.[1]

Ciaran Carson's version of Ovid's *Metamorphoses* xiii. 439–575 also focuses on the suffering of women as it describes Hecuba's mourning for the murder of her children Polyxena and Polydorus, her revenge on Polymestor, and her metamorphosis.[2] Heaney's sympathetic focus on Cresseid in this poem differs from Kennelly and Carson in that it deals with the suffering of a female character against the backdrop of war, rather than (as in the 'Cassandra' poem in 'Mycenae Lookout,' the *Beowulf* translation and *The Burial at Thebes*) the sufferings of women caused directly by war, but it shares that use of Trojan material to describe the experience of female suffering and the endurance of that suffering.

---

[1] Brendan Kennelly, *Euripedes' The Trojan Women: A New Version by Brendan Kennelly* (Newcastle upon Tyne: Bloodaxe, 1993), 5.

[2] Ciaran Carson, 'Ovid: *Metamorphoses*, xiii, 439–575,' in Carson, *First Language* (Oldcastle: Gallery, 1993), 46–48; the poem also appears as 'Hecuba' in *After Ovid: New Metamorphoses*, ed. Michael Hofman and James Lasdun (London: Faber, 1994), 270–72.

Translation and poetic forefathers

Heaney's reworking of Henryson's tale is not simply a tale of two poets, for there is a longer tradition to be taken into account here, one stretching back from Henryson to Chaucer's *Troilus and Criseyde* and beyond. Troilus is a minor figure in classical literature, where he is mentioned in the *Aeneid*, the *Iliad*, and by both Horace and Cicero: a young son of the Trojan king Priam, killed by Achilles.[1] Cresseid appears as 'Briseis' (the name of Achilles' slave-concubine in the *Iliad*) in the *De excidio Troiae historia* of Dares Phrygius, a Latin text from the sixth century, thought to be based on a Greek original from the first century AD. She is not associated here with either Troilus or Calchas, her lover and her father respectively in medieval versions of the Troy narrative.[2] She first appears as the character we know, the lover who betrays Troilus, in the twelfth-century *Roman de Troie* of Benoît de Sainte-Maure, where she is called 'Briseida';[3] Benoît's work was later translated into Latin prose in the thirteenth-century *Historia destructionis troiae* of Guido delle Colonne.[4] The story of Troiolo and Criseida is first extracted from the general narrative of the Trojan war in the fourteenth century by the Italian poet Giovanni Boccaccio in his *Filostrato*, which is indebted to both Benoît and Guido,[5] and it is this Italian poem that is the primary narrative source of Chaucer's version of the story in *Troilus and Criseyde*. Chaucer's version, like Boccaccio's, gives an account of Troilus's love for Criseyde set against the backdrop of the Trojan war. The couple's love is initially successful as a secret relationship inside the besieged city of Troy, but ultimately tragic: the separation of the lovers leads to Criseyde's betrayal of Troilus for the Greek Diomede, and to Troilus's death. Henryson's poem, in turn, presents itself as a response to Chaucer's. It recounts Criseyde's rejection by Diomede and her subsequent suffering and death from leprosy, events not portrayed by Chaucer, and, in the case of Criseyde's leprosy, original to Henryson's account.

---

[1] Piero Boitani, 'Antiquity and Beyond: The Death of Troilus,' in *The European Tragedy of Troilus*, ed. Boitani, 1–19; *Chaucer's Boccaccio: Sources of 'Troilus' and the 'Knight's' and 'Franklin's Tales'*, ed. and trans. N. R. Havely (Cambridge: Brewer, 1980), 164.

[2] Windeatt, *Troilus and Criseyde*, 72–76; *Chaucer's Boccaccio*, ed. and trans. Havely, 164, 165.

[3] Roberto Antonelli, 'The Birth of Criseyde – An Exemplary Triangle: 'Classical' Troilus and the Question of Love at the Anglo-Norman Court,' in *The European Tragedy of Troilus*, ed. Boitani, 21–48; *Chaucer's Boccaccio*, ed. and trans. Havely, 165.

[4] Antonelli, 'The Birth of Criseyde,' 45; *Chaucer's Boccaccio*, ed. and trans. Havely, 165–66.

[5] *Chaucer's Boccaccio*, ed. and trans. Havely, 166.

Heaney's introduction to his translation of Henryson's *Testament* draws Henryson's debt to Chaucer to our attention, saying that 'Chaucer, as author of the universally admired *Troilus and Criseyde*, is obviously the poetic forefather in question here' (p. 5). In doing so, he follows the emphasis in Henryson's own poem, which opens with the narrator reading Chaucer's poem:

> To cut the winter nicht and mak it schort
> I tuik ane quair – and left all vther sport –
> Writtin be worthie Chaucer glorious
> Of fair Creisseid and worthie Troylus. (*Testament*, 39–42)

Heaney's translation, like Henryson's original, draws our attention to the source text at the outset, a book 'written by Chaucer, the great, the glorious' (p. 14). Henryson's narrator goes on to summarize Chaucer's poem, with an account that emphasises the suffering of Troilus (lines 43–60). Henryson's emphasis here is faithful to that of Chaucer's poem, for *Troilus and Criseyde* is predominantly a poem about Troilus, something clear from its opening lines:

> The double sorwe of Troilus to tellen,
> That was the kyng Priamus sone of Troye,
> In lovynge, how his aventures fellen
> Fro wo to wele, and after out of joie,
> My purpos is, er that I parte fro ye.
> (*Troilus and Criseyde*, I. 1–5)

This emphasis on Troilus is also clear from Chaucer's references to the poem as 'the book of Troilus' in the *Retractions* that conclude *The Canterbury Tales* and as 'Troylus' in his short poem *Chaucers Wordes unto Adam, his owne Scriveyn*.[1] Consequently, Henryson's narrator is able to say of Troilus, 'of his distres me neidis nocht reheirs,' for anyone who wishes to read about Troilus and his tale can consult Chaucer. At this point, however, Henryson indicates a departure from Chaucer, to take 'ane vther quair,' in which, he tells us, 'I fand the fatall destenie / Of fair Cresseid, that endit wretchitlie' (*Testament*, 61–63).

This other volume, this 'vther quair' which remains unnamed, calls into question the truth of Chaucer's account, and, as Henryson's poem presents it, may or may not be authoritative in presenting an account of Cresseid's fate:

---

[1] The poem is, however, referred to as 'Crisseyde' in *The Legend of Good Women,* F. 441, G. 344, 431. The reference here may be influenced by the context, where Chaucer is accused by the God of Love of writing antifeminist works.

> Quha wait gif all that Chauceir wrait was trew?
> Nor I wait nocht gif this narratioun
> Be authoreist, or fenʒeit of the new
> Be sum poeit, throw his inuentioun
> Maid to report the lamentatioun
> And wofull end of this lustie Creisseid,
> And quhat distres scho thoillit, and quhat deid.
>
> (*Testament*, 64–71)[1]

Henryson uses very specific language here to invoke the notion of literary authority, important in medieval literary culture, whereas Heaney's version of these lines opts for clarity rather than reproduce Henryson's rather technical terminology: 'Nor do I know if this second version / Was genuine, or maybe something new / Invented by a poet' (p.15). For medieval literary culture, an author is not simply a writer, but also a source of authority,[2] and so Henryson first asks if we can be sure of the truth of Chaucer's version – of its authority – before going on to say that he also cannot be certain whether this second version of the story, the one he is about to tell us, is 'authoreist.' It may be, he says, here flirting with the ancient cliche that all poets are liars, that this is something 'fenʒeit' by 'sum poeit.'[3] If Henryson was drawing on another text, it has never been identified, and the critical consensus is that if 'sum poeit' has 'fenʒeit' the story that Henryson tells, that poet was probably Henryson himself: Denton Fox, Henryson's modern editor, comments that 'it is reasonably certain that this *vther quair* never existed.'[4]

If Henryson has invented an imaginary authority for his text, this is no more than Chaucer does in Henryson's actual source, *Troilus and Criseyde*, for, notwithstanding Chaucer's claims in *Troilus and Criseyde* to be translating from Latin (*Troilus and Criseyde*, II. 13–14) and drawing on a classical source named Lollius (*Troilus and Criseyde*, I. 393, V. 1654), the major source for the narrative of Chaucer's tragedy is Boccaccio's early-fourteenth-century Italian poem, *Il Filostrato*, a source the English poet never names. It is possible that Chaucer may have believed (on the basis of a possible misreading of Horace's *Epistles* I. ii. 1–2) that a classical authority on the Tro-

---

[1] 'Thoillit' in line 71 is 'tholed,' important elsewhere in Heaney, and discussed in Chap. 3 above.

[2] A. J. Minnis, *Medieval Theory of Authorship: Scholastic Literary Attitudes in the later Middle Ages*, 2nd edn (Aldershot: Scolar Press, 1988), 10.

[3] For Boccaccio's defence of poetry against the charge of lying, see *Medieval Literary Theory and Criticism, c.1100–1375: The Commentary Tradition*, ed. A. J. Minnis and A. B. Scott with David Wallace, rev. edn (Oxford: Oxford University Press, 1988), 431–36.

[4] *Poems of Robert Henryson*, ed. Fox, 344, n. to l. 61.

jan War named Lollius did actually exist. It seems clear from the context, though, that Chaucer intends the knowledgeable reader to recognize that this is not really his source.[1] The poem's initial mention of 'Lollius' comes immediately before a translation of a Petrarchan poem, where Chaucer claims (tongue in cheek) to quote Troilus verbatim:

> And of his song naught only the sentence,
> As writ myn auctour called Lollius,
> But pleinly, save oure tonges difference,
> I dar wel seyn, in al, that Troilus
> Seyde in his song, loo, every word right thus
> As I shal seyn; and whoso list it here,
> Loo, next this vers he may it fynden here.
> (*Troilus and Criseyde*, i. 393–99)[2]

It may be, then, as Barry Windeatt suggests, that Chaucer's pretence to attribute his poem to 'Lollius' was always a piece of deliberately transparent artifice.[3] Annotations to manuscripts of Chaucer's poem by early scribes show recognition of Chaucer's use of a variety of sources for different passages of *Troilus*;[4] such awareness of the poem's real authorities would also suggest recognition of the fictional status of the poem's falsified authority, 'Lollius.' If Chaucer's early audience is aware of the artifice in his claims for 'Lollius,' we may assume the same for Henryson. Henryson's claim to be writing from 'ane vther quair,' then, is probably part of a knowing response to the claims for authority made in Chaucer's poem, a claim of his own made with a Chaucerian tongue in cheek.

Henryson's poem calls Chaucer's authority into question, and invokes an imagined alternative source, because its account of events is somewhat at odds with that of *Troilus and Criseyde*. What Heaney says is that 'Henryson's poem takes up where Chaucer's left off' (p. 5). This is true, insofar as Henryson continues the narrative of Cresseid's affair with Diomede, and supplies an account of her death, both topics not treated by Chaucer. It is also true to say that Henryson's poem can be seen a continuation of Chaucer's, in that it enjoyed a long career as an honourary 'sixth book' appended to the five books of Chaucer's *Troilus*. It is not the case, however,

---

[1] *The Riverside Chaucer*, ed. Larry D. Benson (Boston: Houghton Mifflin, 1987), 1022; see Windeatt, *Troilus and Criseyde*, 37–42. Lollius is also mentioned in *The House of Fame*, 1468.

[2] For the Petrarchan poem that Chaucer translates immediately after these lines, see *Petrarch's Lyric Poems: The 'Rime sparse' and Other Lyrics*, ed. and trans. Robert M. Durling (Cambridge, MA, and London: Harvard University Press, 1976), 271.

[3] Windeatt, *Troilus and Criseyde*, 39.

[4] Windeatt, *Troilus and Criseyde*, 42.

that Henryson simply takes up the story where Chaucer leaves it. Rather, in terms of narrative sequence, the events described in Henryson's poem take place between Criseyde's betrayal of Troilus with Diomede and Troilus' subsequent death in battle, both of which occur in the fifth book of Chaucer's poem.

Book five of Chaucer's *Troilus and Criseyde* opens with Criseyde's departure from Troy: she is to be traded in an exchange of prisoners between the Trojans and Greeks that, ironically, will see the return to Troy of Antenor, the man who will betray the city. In the poem's fourth book, Troilus and Criseyde fail to act against the exchange for fear of exposing their secret relationship, and instead agree that Criseyde should secretly return to Troy after ten days have passed. The fifth and final book of the poem sees the gradual realization by each of a truth that neither wishes to admit: that Criseyde's return to Troy will never come. Criseyde turns to the Greek Diomede while continuing to protest to Troilus that she will return, berating herself for her failure to keep her promise. When Troilus finally realizes the truth of the situation, he throws himself into battle against the Greeks, seeking Diomede, and clashing with him several times before his eventual death at the hands of Achilles. The time lines of book five are deliberately fluid – at one point in the narrative, we move from Criseyde's protests that she will try to return surreptitiously to Troy to the narrator's observation that 'er fully monthes two, / She was ful fer fro that entencioun!' (v. 766–67); an account of Diomede's courtship of Criseyde follows, before we return to Troilus, still waiting for the ten days to elapse and Criseyde to return as promised.

When Troilus does finally realize that Criseyde now loves Diomede, the narrative is drastically foreshortened. The period between Troilus's realization of Criseyde's betrayal (v. 1639–1743) and his death (v. 1806) is covered by Chaucer in just over sixty lines. It's clear, however, that a significant period of time elapses – Troilus participates 'in many cruel bataille' (v. 1751) during this time, and he and Diomede 'ofte tyme' meet in battle 'with blody strokes and with wordes grete' (v. 1759). But the story is moving quickly towards Troilus's death, and we hear nothing further of the fate of Criseyde. The last we hear from her in her own voice is in the letter she writes to Troilus, protesting that she will return to him, although we, as readers, know the opposite to be true (v. 1590–1631). The last comment from any of the characters goes to Pandarus, who declares 'I hate, ywis, Criseyde' (v.1732), and wishes for her death (v. 1742–43). This is slightly softened by the narratorial comment that although Criseyde was unfaithful, there are also examples to be found of faithful women and unfaithful men (v. 1772–85), a topic that Chaucer would turn to unsuccessfully in his uncompleted *Legend of Good Women*. Apart from a passing reference at v. 1833, there are no further references to the poem's heroine, and the poem leaves her with Diomede:

> Criseyde loveth the sone of Tideüs,
> And Troilus moot wepe in cares colde.
> (*Troilus and Criseyde*, v. 1746–47)

Henryson's poem, then, takes up this thread of the narrative left unfinished by Chaucer, and inserts his account of Criseyde's fate into this period of time which Chaucer quickly passes over at the end of book five, between the betrayal and Troilus's death.

In doing so, Henryson gives the narrative an ending that contrasts substantially in tone with Chaucer's original conclusion. If Chaucer's poem ends with a heavenly perspective on human folly, Henryson adds a new conclusion for its heroine that provides a graphic account of retribution for misdeeds in this world, not the next. In narrative terms, Henryson's poem is not so much a continuation of Chaucer's poem as a reversal of it. Chaucer's poem tells how Troilus is abandoned by his lover, and later dies; Henryson's tells the same story, but of Cresseid, not Troilus. Chaucer's Troilus, Jill Mann argues, is a 'feminized' hero, 'abandoned and betrayed by his lover, immobilized, frustrated of action and movement, finding relief only in memory, lamentation and fruitless letter-writing.'[1] This reversal of gender roles in Chaucer's narrative is turned around again in Henryson, where Troilus is returned to an active role, and Cresseid takes on the part of the abandoned lover who dies a tragic death. Henryson's narrative (as A. C. Spearing points out) is an ironic reversal of the prophecy that Troilus makes in *Troilus and Crisedye*, when he writes:

> I woot that whan ye next upon me se,
> So lost have I myn hele and ek myn hewe,
> Criseyde shal nought konne knowen me.
> (*Troilus and Criseyde*, v. 1402–4)

In Chaucer, the couple never meet again. In Henryson, they do, but it is Cresseid who is unrecognizable because she has lost her *hele* and *hewe*.[2] Henryson's poem, then, puts itself forward as both an extension of Chaucer's *Troilus* and a revision of it.

Heaney's retelling of Henryson is not a reworking of the same order as Henryson's revision of Chaucer. But if Chaucer is identified by Heaney as Henryson's 'poetic forefather' here (p. 5), he also serves, to some extent,

---

[1] Jill Mann, *Feminizing Chaucer* (Cambridge: Brewer, 2002), 131.
[2] A. C. Spearing, *Medieval to Renaissance in English Poetry* (Cambridge: Cambridge University Press, 1985), 167.

the same function for Heaney. Henryson's praise of 'worthie Chaucer glorious' (line 41) is echoed by Heaney's praise of 'Chaucer, the great, the glorious' (p. 14) – while Heaney is here responding directly to Henryson, like Henryson he too looks back to Chaucer as a 'poetic forefather.' This is the case not least because of John Dryden's labelling of Chaucer as 'the father of English poetry' in the preface to his own Chaucer translation,[1] and Heaney's reference to Dryden's reworking of Chaucer as justification of his own practice in translating Henryson. Heaney, citing Eliot Weinberger, gives three motives for undertaking his translation: advocacy of Henryson's poem, refreshment from the encounter with a different speech and culture (here Middle Scots), and the experience of writing by proxy. 'I had experienced,' Heaney writes, 'what Dryden called (in his preface to *Fables, Ancient and Modern*) a "transfusion," and the fact that Dryden used the term in relation to his own modernizations of Chaucer makes it all the more applicable to my own case' (pp. 7–8).

Dryden's positioning of Chaucer in that same preface as 'the father of English poetry' makes the fourteenth-century poet a notional point of origin for what might be a narrow canon of English literature: Dryden suggests a line of influence that runs from Chaucer through Spenser and Milton, and on to Dryden and his contemporaries.[2] Similarly, if Dryden's preface to his Chaucer translation suggests that the English literary tradition in poetry proceeds in the sequence Chaucer–Spenser–Milton–Dryden, his preface to his play *Troilus and Cressida* posits a line of canonical descent from Latin literature through Chaucer and Shakespeare to himself. Dryden's version of the Troilus story is a reworking of Shakespeare's *Troilus and Cressida*: he states in the preface that 'the original story was written by one Lollius a Lombard, in Latin verse and translated by Chaucer into English,' here taking seriously Chaucer's spurious claim to be following Lollius.[3] If Dryden sees Chaucer as the father of English poetry, the lines of descent from a Chaucerian father figure run through Spenser and Milton on one side, and Shakespeare on the other, before meeting in the person of Dryden himself.

Heaney demonstrates his divergence from any such model of the English canon not least by translating *Beowulf*, the major work of an English literature that precedes Chaucer and problematizes any attempt to claim

---

[1] *The Poems and Fables of John Dryden*, ed. James Kinsley (London: Oxford University Press, 1962), 528.

[2] *Poems and Fables of John Dryden*, ed. Kinsley, 521.

[3] *The Works of John Dryden*, xiii: *Plays: All for Love; Oedipus; Troilus and Cressida*, ed. Maximilian E. Novak et al. (Berkeley, Los Angeles, and London: University of California Press, 1984), 225.

him as a point of origin for a continuous English literary tradition. But
he also problematizes any supposed poetic descent from Chaucer in translating Henryson. In translating the *Testament of Cresseid*, Heaney engages
with 'the father of English poetry' at one remove, by reworking a Scottish poem that is explicitly indebted to, subtly engaged with, but also in
many ways at odds with, a foundational English literary text – a Scottish
poem explicitly descended from 'the father of English poetry,' but left
out of a family tree that sees Chaucer as a direct and unmediated influence
on Shakespeare.[1] If in translating Henryson Heaney follows Henryson in
responding to Chaucer as a 'poetic forefather,' he also draws attention in
doing so to both Scottish and Irish literary traditions within the English
language. These are traditions that might be sidelined by literary genealogies (such as Dryden's) positing a foundational Chaucerian paternity, and,
in the case of Henryson, may still remain marginal to the contemporary
canon of literature in English. Although Henryson and the other 'Scottish
Chaucerians' brought about what Heaney calls 'a significant flowering in
the literary life of Scotland in late medieval times' (p. 5), and their Middle
Scots texts have been rendered reasonably accessible via annotated modern
editions (p. 7), advocacy is still required.

Chaucer, Henryson, and antifeminism

Because Henryson significantly alters the sense of Criseyde's fate that we
might derive from Chaucer, his poem has been open to adverse comment
for its treatment of its heroine. Having asked 'gif all that Chauceir wrait
was trew' (*Testament of Cresseid*, 64), and introduced his supposed alternative source for the life of his heroine, Henryson takes up the narrative as
follows:

> Quhen Diomeid had all his appetyte,
> And mair, fulfillit of this fair ladie,
> Vpon ane vther he set his haill delyte,
> And send to hir ane lybell of repudie
> And hir excludit fra his companie.
> Than desolait scho walkit vp and doun,
> And sum men sayis, into the court, commoun.
>
> O fair Creisseid, the flour and A per se

---

[1] The tradition of Cresseid's leprosy, which originates with Henryson, finds a mention in Shakespeare: in *Henry V* Pistol calls Doll Tearsheet 'a lazar kit of Cressid's kind'
(II. i. 76) (Windeatt, *Troilus and Criseyde*, 371).

Of Troy and Grece, how was thow fortunait
To change in filth all thy feminitie,
And be with fleschelie lust sa maculait.
And go amang the Greikis air and lait,
Sa giglotlike takand thy foull plesance!
I haue pietie thow suld fall sic mischance!

(*Testament*, 71–84)

These lines describe events not contained, or even suggested, in Chaucer, and their interpretation has been controversial. The usual interpretation of line 77 is that *commoun* here means 'promiscuous.'[1] This has been disputed: H. A. Kelly (who takes the general line that Henryson acknowledges but rejects the accusations of sexual promiscuity made against Cresseid) argues that the punctuation should be 'into the court commoun,' and that the translation should be 'into the courtyard,' although he concedes that the next stanza does deal with reports of promiscuity.[2] There has been more extensive critical debate as to whether, taking *commoun* to mean 'promiscuous,' Henryson is implying that Cresseid is engaged in prostitution.[3] The implication of promiscuity seems certain: Cresseid is described at line 83 as 'giglotlike,' and the *Middle English Dictionary* defines *gigelot* as 'a loose woman, a courtesan, a harlot.'[4] It's also possible that Henryson intends to link Cresseid's reported promiscuity here and her subsequent leprosy, since in the Middle Ages leprosy was viewed as transmissible through sexual activity among other means. Henryson may be implicitly linking the two when he describes her in line 81 here as being 'with fleschelie lust sa maculait': the use of the word *maculait* here may foreshadow the physical blemishes of leprosy described later, where the poem describes 'thy lustie lyre ouirspred with spottis blak, / And lumpis haw appeirand in thy face' (*Testament*, 339–40).[5] This possibility is perhaps reinforced by the suggestion that the infliction of leprosy is the revenge of Cupid, the God of Love (*Testament*, 370–71).

Heaney's translation of these lines dealing with Cresseid's promiscuity

---

[1] *Poems of Robert Henryson*, ed. Fox, 345, n. to l. 77.

[2] Henry Ansgar Kelly, *Chaucerian Tragedy* (Cambridge: Brewer, 1997), 227.

[3] For a discussion of late medieval prostitution in relation to the poem, see Susan Aronstein, 'Cresseid reading Cresseid: Redemption and Translation in Henryson's *Testament*,' *Scottish Literary Journal* 21 (1994), 5–22 at 11–13; Lee W. Patterson, 'Christian and Pagan in *The Testament of Cresseid*,' *Philological Quarterly* 52 (1973), 696–714 at 699 n. 7, argues that Cresseid is promiscuous, but not a prostitute; Pearsall, '"Quha wait gif all that Chaucer wrait was trew?",' 179, agrees.

[4] *MED*, s.v. *gigelot*.

[5] *Poems of Robert Henryson*, ed. Fox, pp. lxxxiv and 346, n. to l. 81. Heaney's translation of *maculait* as 'sullied' omits this nuance.

does not shy away from the implications. After Diomede banishes Cresseid from his company, Heaney's version of lines 76–77 reads:

> She went distracted then and would ramble
> And be, as men will say, available. (p. 15)

Heaney's version of line 77 renders the specific general. It's not the case here that some (specific) men say that she became, as Heaney puts it, available: rather, this is something that men (in general) will say. Any potential for agreement with such a judgmental attitude is softened by Heaney's rendering of line 76. For Henryson's 'Than desolait scho walkit vp and doun,' Heaney renders *desolait* as 'distracted' and *walkit vp and doun* as 'ramble' – her desolation is rendered more specifically psychological than is clear from Henryson, and (like that other outcast, Sweeney) it's suggested here that she is both physically and mentally astray.

Heaney doesn't soften the accusation of prostitution, translating lines 81–83:

> And sullied so by lustful appetite
> You'd go among the Greeks early and late
> So obviously, like any common pickup? (p. 16)

Line 83 here picks up the original's earlier description of Cresseid as *commoun*, translating *giglotlike* as 'like any common pickup.' But the introduction of a psychological perspective in the rendering of line 76 is sympathetic to a Cresseid who then takes to the streets.

Henryson's next stanza purports to put up a defence of Criseyde's reputation:

> 3it neuertheles, quhat euer men deme or say
> In scornefull langage of thy brukkilnes,
> I sall excuse als far furth as I may
> Thy womanheid, thy wisdome and fairnes,
> The quhilk fortoun hes put to sic distres
> As hir pleisit, and nathing throw the gilt
> Of the – throw wickit langage to be spilt!
>
> (*Testament*, 85–91)

There are reasons for scepticism regarding this defence. It's equivocal – the narrator will excuse Cresseid 'als far furth as I may' ('to what extent I may' in Heaney (p. 16)), a formula that suggests that the defence may not be completely successful, and reminiscent of the similarly equivocal protests of Chaucer's narrator in *Troilus and Criseyde*, who also attributes blame of Criseyde to others (e.g. *Troilus and Criseyde* v. 1050). This raises at least the possibility of a narratorial figure who is not to be taken at face value.[1] Neither is the charge of *brukkilnes* contested (generally 'brittleness,' here 'moral frailty').[2] Heaney's translation substitutes 'And yet whatever men may think or say / Contemptuously about your quick compliance' (p. 16), which while not substantially changing the implication of Henryson's text, seems to keep the emphasis on Cresseid's passive reaction to circumstance while removing the implication of moral weakness inherent in 'brittleness.'

Because these accusations about Criseyde's taking up with others after Diomede are not to be found in Chaucer, Henryson's primary source, critics formerly argued that Henryson was largely the author of the adverse reputation against which he seems to be defending Cresseid. Gretchen Mieszkowski, however, has demonstrated that the *Testament* is not the source of Cresseid's reputation for fickleness, and that it is Chaucer who is exceptional in not including this in his poem.[3] The possibility that Briseida may be unfaithful to Diomedes is raised in the very first medieval version of the love story, the twelfth-century *Roman de Troie* of Benoît de Sainte-Maure. In Benoît, this possibility is raised by Troilus himself, as he taunts Diomedes on the battlefield, saying that although Diomedes has taken his place, there will be many others to follow before the end of the siege of Troy.[4] What we find here in Benoît is very different from what we find in Henryson: these unpleasant speculations are the jealous comments of a spurned lover, and they suppose that it will be Briseida who will betray Diomedes, a prediction that is not actually fulfilled in Benoît's text. Henryson's version is more sympathetic to Cresseid than this, in the sense that it is Diomede who casts her out, and as an outcast she becomes 'giglotlike'. Where Henryson is less sympathetic than even Benoît, and certainly less sympathetic than Chaucer, is that what is merely suggested as a possibility in Benoît actually comes to pass in Henryson: Cresseid does take other lovers after Diomede. What is notable from Benoît is that the idea does not originate with Henryson: from the very first version of the Troilus–Briseida–Diomedes love triangle, not only does Briseida betray Troilus, but it is suggested she may also have other lovers after Diomedes.[5]

---

[1] On the similarity to Chaucer's narrator here, see *Poems of Robert Henryson*, ed. Fox, 346, n. to ll. 89–91.

[2] *Poems of Robert Henryson*, ed. Fox, 381, n. to l. 569.

[3] Gretchen Mieszkowski, 'The Reputation of Criseyde, 1155–1500,' *Transactions of the Connecticut Academy of Arts and Sciences* 43 (1971), 73–153 at 131.

[4] *Chaucer's Boccaccio*, ed. and trans. Havely, 179; Benoît's characterization of Briseis is discussed in Mieszkowski, 'The Reputation of Criseyde,' 79–87.

[5] While Chaucer is familiar with both Benoît and the Latin prose translation of Benoît by Guido delle Colonne (Windeatt, *Troilus and Criseyde*, 77–90), it's not possible to

It may, then, be possible to take Henryson's claims in Cresseid's defence at lines 85–91 more seriously.

Henryson does, however, have his heroine again accused of lustfulness later in the poem, and while her adverse reputation may be dismissed as gossip early in the poem, subsequent accusations are not so easily set aside. Criseyde is accused by Cupid of 'leuing vnclene and lecherous' (*Testament*, 285), although again, Cupid is hardly presented here as a reliable and unbiased witness. Most damagingly, however, Cresseid accuses herself of lechery in describing her betrayal of Troilus (*Testament*, 547–49, 558–60). In Heaney's translation, these lines are softened somewhat – the 'wantonnes' that Cresseid accuses herself of in Henryson (*Testament*, 549) becomes is softened to the suggestion that she is 'giddy' (p. 39), and although she still describes herself as 'lustful, passionate, and lecherous' (p. 39), the suggestion that her lust is foul, 'fleschelie foull affectioun' (*Testament*, 558) as Henryson puts it, is gone.

Cresseid's *self*-condemnation as lecherous would seem to neuter any possible defence against accusations of lechery; she then further describes herself as fickle:

> 'Louers be war and tak gude heid about
> Quhome that ȝe lufe, for quhome ȝe suffer paine.
> I lat ȝow wit, thair is richt few thairout
> Quhome ȝe may traist to haue trew lufe agane;
> Preif quhen ȝe will, ȝour labour is in vaine.
> Thairfoir I reid ȝe tak thame as ȝe find,
> For thay ar sad as widdercok in wind.

> 'Becaus I knaw the greit vnstabilnes,
> Brukkil as glas, into my self, I say –
> Traisting in vther als greit vnfaithfulnes,
> Als vnconstant, and als vntrew of fay –
> Thocht sum be trew, I wait richt few ar thay;
> Quha findis treuth, lat him his lady ruse;
> Nane but my self as now I will accuse.' (*Testament*, 561–74)

There is a double edge in this final line (Heaney's version reads 'For now, I will only be my own accuser' (p. 40)). Cresseid's statement that she will accuse no-one but herself can be read (as it often is) as symptomatic of a developing self-awareness, a movement from her position earlier in the poem of blaming the gods for her ill fortune in love. But it can also be read

determine whether or not Henryson knows these sources (*Poems of Robert Henryson*, ed. Fox, p. lxxxiii).

another way. This line concludes some lengthy generalisations about how rare it is to find a faithful lover, and can consequently be read as implying that although Cresseid accuses only herself, that there are many others who might be accused as well. Read this way, this line is an example of *occupatio*, the rhetorical figure that says something while refusing to say it, a device common in Chaucer. It's noticeable too that the observation about the inconstancy of lovers is directed to men – 'Quha findis treuth, lat *him his lady ruse*' – it is female lovers, like Cresseid, who are inconstant. The motif of the female character accusing herself of moral frailties is a strategy found elsewhere in medieval antifeminist literature. Jean de Meun's *Roman de la Rose* describes Heloise as an exceptional woman, one whose erudition enabled her to overcome the qualities attributed to women in antifeminist literature, but she is nonetheless portrayed as recognizing these qualities in herself:

> Car les livres avait veüz
> E estudiez e seüz,
> E les meurs femenins savait,
> Car trestouz en sei les avait. (*Roman de la Rose*, 8773–76)

For she had seen and studied and understood the books, and she understood feminine ways, for she had them all in herself.[1]

A male author using a female character's recognition of female frailties to make a general antifeminist point is not something original to Henryson.

Cresseid's self-accusation in Henryson is particularly problematic given the many interpretations of Henryson's poem that see Cresseid as moving towards self-awareness during the course of the poem.[2] Both Derek Pearsall and Douglas Gray make use of the Joycean word 'epiphany' in their discussion of what they see as Cresseid's arrival at self-knowledge.[3] In fact, the character of Criseyde can be seen as at least partly self-aware and self-reflexive from the outset of the tradition – in Benoît and in Chaucer we see Briseida/Criseyde reflecting on what she has done, and what this means for her reputation.[4] Elements of self-consolation remain: in the

---

[1] Guillaume de Lorris and Jean de Meun, *Le Roman de la Rose*, ed. Ernst Langlois, 3 vols. (Paris: Champion, 1914–21), iii, 95; *The Romance of the Rose*, trans. Frances Horgan (Oxford: Oxford University Press, 1994), 135.

[2] Spearing, *Medieval to Renaissance*, 186; Gray, *Robert Henryson*, 205; Pearsall, '"Quha wait gif all that Chaucer wrait was trew?",' 173–74; cf. Aronstein, 'Cresseid reading Cresseid,' 18–19. Pearsall astutely comments (177) that it is not her illness but her encounter with Troilus that brings about the change in Cresseid's perspective.

[3] Pearsall, '"Quha wait gif all that Chaucer wrait was trew?",' 178, Gray, *Robert Henryson*, 205.

[4] *Chaucer's Boccaccio*, ed. and trans. Havely, 180–81; *Troilus and Criseyde*, v. 1058–85.

Chaucerian version, Criseyde tries to diminish the implications of her actions by reassuring herself that at least she will remain true to Diomede (*Troilus and Criseyde*, v. 1071), and perhaps it is this to which Henryson's version offers a corrective. If so, it is possible to argue that Henryson overcorrects; Douglas Gray argues that Cresseid may have overstated the case against herself.[1] It is not clear from the text, however, that we are meant to read her self-condemnation as excessive. When she accuses herself of being motivated by lust, she is repeating what the narrator reported as her motivation at the poem's outset – she is lustful (*Testament*, 81 and 559) and *brukkil*, 'morally frail' (*Testament*, 86 and 569).

If Cresseid is seen here as motivated by lust, this is a motivation entirely different from that of Chaucer's character (although one that is found in the earlier version of the story by Guido delle Colonne).[2] It's something of a cliché of Chaucer criticism to point out that, in Chaucer's poem, fear is Criseyde's primary motivating force. When we first encounter Criseyde, her father Calchas has fled Troy for the Greek camp, and her vulnerability is emphasised:

> For of hire lif she was ful sore in drede,
> As she that nyste what was best to rede;
> For bothe a widewe was she and allone
> Of any frend to whom she dorste hir mone.
> (*Troilus and Criseyde*, I. 95–98)

She is nervous again in her next appearance, both of the Greeks, and of what Pandarus has to say: she is 'the ferfulleste wight / That myghte be' (*Troilus and Criseyde*, II. 450–51). Even after she has begun to incline towards Troilus, there is a long speech detailing her fear of the possible consequences of such a love (*Troilus and Criseyde*, II. 764–812). In book four, when the lovers are threatened with separation, Criseyde will not agree to elope with Troilus for fear of what people should say about them (*Troilus and Criseyde*, IV. 1555–82), and in book five, fear of the dangers involved in an attempt to return to Troy prevent any reunion with Troilus (*Troilus and Criseyde*, v. 701–7). Fear is not the only motivating characteristic in Chaucer's complex portrait of Criseyde, but it is a prominent one. There is, perhaps, something of this in Henryson also. The vulnerable Cresseid's need of male protection, so evident in Chaucer's poem where in the absence of Calchas she depends upon Hector, Pandarus, and Troilus for protection within Troy, and Diomede in turn for support in the Greek camp, is implicit in her desolation when rejected by Diomede in Henryson's account,

---

[1] Gray, *Robert Henryson*, 204.
[2] *Chaucer's Boccaccio*, ed. and trans. Havely, 185.

and her flight, 'friendless and unprotected' in Heaney's words (p. 16), 'but fellowschip or refute' in Henryson's (*Testament*, 94), to her father's house. But if Henryson's character does contain a suggestion of the vulnerability that motivates Chaucer's Criseyde, his characterisation of Cresseid as motivated by lust seems fundamentally at odds with Chaucer's portrayal.

Henryson's unequivocal praise of Troilus in contrast to Cresseid is also at odds with his Chaucerian source, for Chaucer is subtly critical of the excesses of Troilus' lovesickness. As Barry Windeatt puts it:

> Much modern interpretation of the poem and its hero has taken the view that the fundamental error in his understanding of human love is his overcharging it beyond the limits of human nature. The resonant beauty of language conveys the idealizing longing with which Troilus wishes to understand his love as an experience that leads the individual into communion with the ordering principles of the universe, although the developing 'proces' of the poem will come to place Troilus' understanding of love in a different perspective.[1]

That 'different perspective' comes as outright condemnation at the end of the poem of 'the blynde lust, the which that may nat laste, / And sholden al oure herte on heven caste' (*Troilus and Criseyde*, v. 1824–25), but this perspective has been implicit all along. When he first falls in love with Criseyde, she was 'likynge to Troilus / Over alle thing' (*Troilus and Crisedye*, I. 309–10); instead of being in communion with the ordering principles of the universe, as the Middle Ages understood them, Troilus' love is fixed on Criseyde to the disregard of all else. As Gerald Morgan says, 'Chaucer has shown to us in the figure of Troilus a conscious and complete acceptance of a purely earthly ideal of love, and has made us aware of its insufficiency.'[2]

Henryson's version contains no such commentary on the flawed nature of Troilus' love; it simply contrasts 'fals Cresseid' with 'trew knicht Troylus'. This emphasis is itself derived from Chaucer, where Criseyde writes to Troilus 'I kan nat in yow gesse / But alle trouthe and alle gentilesse' (v. 1616–17), but is herself aware that 'for now is clene ago / My name of trouthe in love, for everemo!' (v. 1054–55).[3] Chaucer, however, portrays

---

[1] Windeatt, *Troilus and Criseyde*, 225.

[2] Gerald Morgan, 'Natural and Rational Love in Medieval Literature,' *Yearbook of English Studies* 7 (1977), 43–52 at 51.

[3] On the semantic range of the Middle English word *trouthe*, see Richard Firth Green, *A Crisis of Truth: Literature and Law in Ricardian England* (Philadelphia: University of Pennsylvania Press, 1999), 8–10; for the importance of concepts of *trouthe* in Chaucer's writing, see Green and also George Kane, 'The Liberating Truth,' in Kane, *Chaucer and Langland: Historical and Textual Approaches* (London: Athlone, 1989).

Troilus as faithful in a love that is flawed: Henryson's Troilus is simply praised for his fidelity in contrast with Cresseid.

Finally, if Henryson is not the first to accuse Cresseid of promiscuity, he is certainly innovative in giving his heroine leprosy, described in vivid detail. In Heaney's version, Cynthia decrees:

> Your healthy skin I blacken, blotch and spot.
> With livid lumps I cover your fair face.
> Go where you will, all men will flee the place. (p. 28)

The poem concludes on a moralizing note: it is made for the 'worschip and instructioun' of 'worthie wemen,' who should bear in mind Cresseid's unpleasant end. This might be conventional enough to be disregarded as an empty flourish, were it not that it echoes the message on Cresseid's gravestone, which also addresses itself to 'fair ladyis' (*Testament*, 606), and Cresseid's own lament, which urges 'ladyis fair of Troy and Greece' to see the leprous Cresseid as a mirror of their own potential end (*Testament*, 452–69).

Henryson's tale of Cresseid, then, represents her as promiscuous in a way that preceding versions do not. It portrays her as motivated by lust and weakness, and contrasts her infidelity with the moral steadfastness of Troilus. There are hints in the language of Henryson's poem (though not in Heaney) that her leprosy may be related to her promiscuity. The poem suggests through Cresseid's self condemnation that many women are inconstant, and it draws the attention of women to its narrative of Cresseid's downfall. Heaney's version softens the rhetoric in places, and gives a crucial twist to our sense of Cresseid's state of mind following her rejection of Diomede: 'She went distracted then and would ramble / And be, as men will say, available' (p. 15). Nonetheless, the antifeminist elements in Henryson's original text pose potential difficulties for a contemporary audience asked to read the poem as sympathetic.

'Ane cairfull dyte': the tragedy of Cresseid

The case for reading Henryson's original as antifemist is worth making at such length, because Heaney is explicit in claiming that Henryson's attitude towards the heroine of his poem is a sympathetic one. He writes in his introduction:

> From our perspective, he proves himself more durably by his singular compassion for the character of Cresseid. Available to him all along is the rhetoric of condemnation, the trope of woman as daughter

of Eve, temptress, snare, Jezebel. But while this is the given cultural norm, Henryson never succumbs to it. The preacher's tune is changed to a poet's. Instinctive sympathy rather than high-toned castigation, the pared down truth of heartbreak rather than the high tone of the pulpit [...]. (p. 9)

Heaney is not alone in interpreting *The Testament of Cresseid* as a poem ultimately sympathetic to Cresseid, for many of the poem's critics read it in this way. A. C. Spearing comments that 'it would be difficult not to feel pity for a woman who had suffered this reversal in her earthly situation, whatever she might have done to deserve it, and *The Testament of Cresseid* is a deeply compassionate poem.'[1] Spearing suggests that Henryson 'grasped the paradox of Chaucer's sympathetic portrayal of a notorious female deceiver, and that in his alternative ending to *Troilus and Criseyde*, just as he heightened the moral degradation of Cresseid, the arbitrary cruelty of the gods in punishing her, and the misery of her consequent sufferings, so he also heightened the compassion with which the poem treats her.'[2]

Heaney's point is not that Henryson fails to offer judgment regarding Cresseid. It is that judgment is balanced with sympathy: 'weight of judgement, justness of statement, a tenderness that isn't clammy, a dry-eyed sympathy — these are the attributes of a moral understanding reluctant to moralize, yet one that is naturally and unfailingly instructive,' he says of Henryson (p. 6). In support of his claim that Henryson is sympathetic to his principal character, he cites in the introduction (pp. 9–10) what is undoubtedly the poem's high point, the moment where Troilus and Cresseid meet again. They do not recognize one another, but the sight of the leprous Cresseid reminds Troilus of the woman he once loved. In Heaney's translation, the lines read:

> Upon him then she cast up both her eyes
> And at a glance it came into his thought
> That he some time before had seen her face.
> But she was in such state he knew her not;
> Yet still into his mind her look had brought
> The features and the amorous sweet glancing
> Of fair Cresseid, one time his own, his darling. (p. 36)

There are other such moments. Cresseid's father, Calchas, an almost entirely unsympathetic character in Chaucer, is a much more amenable paternal figure in Henryson, where his sympathy is directed towards his

---

[1] Spearing, *Medieval to Renaissance*, 179.
[2] Spearing, *Medieval to Renaissance*, 181.

daughter. We see him take her in after Diomede has rejected her, with words of welcome that seem cruelly ironic in their optimism given what is to come, suggesting that all may yet have turned out for the best. The language of Calchas's welcome is affectionate – 'Welcum to me; thow art full deir ane gest' (*Testament*, 105) – and that affection is heightened in Heaney's translation, where the line 'You are welcome, daughter dear, my dearest guest' (p. 16) repeats the element 'dear'/'dearest,' giving added emphasis to what is already there in Henryson.

We see Calchas again some time later in the poem, facing his leprosy-stricken daughter, knowing that there can be no cure, and unable to take any action except to grieve with her. Our sympathy for the leprosy-stricken Cresseid is heightened by the dreadful irony of the child's words in calling Cresseid to supper in the immediate aftermath of the gods' cruel judgement, reporting Calchas' words that there's no need to spend so long praying (*Testament*, 358–64). Our response to her lament on her arrival in the leper-house is underscored by the sympathetic reaction of the leper-woman who advises Cresseid to adopt a stoic endurance of her fate (*Testament*, 475–80). The sympathetic reactions of these sympathetic characters lends support to Heaney's interpretation of the poem as one that balances judgement with sympathy.

The point is in part made by the fact that the *Testament of Cresseid* is, as Derek Pearsall says, a poem, and not another sort of text, such as a didactic treatise (Heaney takes a somewhat similar line in saying that 'the preacher's tune is changed to a poet's'(p. 9)).[1] More important still is the sort of poem that it is. The *Testament of Cresseid* is a tragedy, explicitly announced as such in its opening lines:

> Ane doolie sessoun to ane cairfull dyte
> Suld correspond and be equiualent:
> Richt sa it wes quhen I began to wryte
> This tragedie;   (*Testament of Cresseid*, 1–4)

Heaney, as it happens, omits the word 'tragedy' from his version, but he does so because he wants to announce his version as something else, a 're-telling': the sense of 'ane cairfull dyte,' – 'a poem full of hurt,' as Heaney puts it (p. 13) – remains. In describing his poem as a 'tragedie,' Henryson is following Chaucer, who also labelled *Troilus and Criseyde* a tragedy (*Troilus and Criseyde*, v. 1786). Indeed, it is Chaucer who introduces the terms 'tragedy' and 'comedy' into English,[2] and who formulates the definition of tragedy as a story that ends unhappily, a definition that we nowadays

---

[1] Pearsall, '"Quha wait gif all that Chaucer wrait was trew?",' 169.
[2] Derek Brewer, 'Comedy and Tragedy in *Troilus and Crisedye*,' in *The European Tragedy*

take as commonplace, but assume to be Aristotelean in origin.[1] In defining tragedy in his translation of Boethius's *Consolation of Philosophy*, Chaucer asks: 'What other thynge bywaylen the cryinges of tragedyes but oonly the dedes of Fortune, that with an unwar strook overturneth the realmes of greet nobleye? (*Glose. Tragedye is to seyn a dite of a prosperite for a tyme, that endeth in wrecchidnesse)*' (*Boece*, II. pr. 2).[2] But if Chaucer's poem is a tragedy, it is the tragedy of Troilus — it is he who enjoys prosperity for a time, a prosperity that ends in wretchedness. Chaucer's poem does not tell us of Criseyde's end. Henryson's supplement to Chaucer is, therefore, not just the testament, but the tragedy of Cresseid. The severity of Cresseid's downfall and the sympathy of the supporting characters seem appropriate for such a genre.

If the poem is full of sympathetic moments, and the downfall of Cresseid is seen as tragic, the problems of the poem's antifeminism remain nonetheless. Given that these are problems attributable to the source text rather than the translation, the difficulty is in reading Heaney's translation in a way that can balance his emphasis in the introduction on the poem's sympathetic moments with the problem of antifeminism in Henryson's original. A similar problem might be thought to arise for *Sweeney Astray*. The original medieval Irish text, *Buile Suibhne*, also has a strong antifeminist streak to it, and, as here with Henryson's poem, Heaney's translation in *Sweeney Astray* is broadly faithful to the original text. Consequently, it contains antifeminist passages such as that where Sweeney declares that men should beware women, for betrayal is second nature to them (pp. 62–63). The antifeminist streak in *Buile Suibhne* is reasonably prominent, but the difference between this and Henryson's poem is that gender relations are not the major focus of the Irish text. The same cannot be said of *The Testament of Cresseid*.

It also happens that some of the most substantial criticism of Heaney's work has come from feminism. Critics such as Elizabeth Butler Cullingford and Patricia Coughlan have raised questions about the implications of Heaney's use of gender and myth in the earlier poetry.[3] Neil Corcoran has suggested that Heaney's translation of portions of Merriman's *Cúirt*

---

of Troilus, ed. Boitani, 95–109 at 95. Brewer comments (109) that no generic label can fully define Chaucer's poem; similarly Windeatt, *Troilus and Criseyde*, 138–79.

   [1] Kelly, *Chaucerian Tragedy*, 139–40.

   [2] Chaucer's gloss here is from Nicholas Trevet's commentary on Boethius; see Kelly, *Chaucerian Tragedy*, 50–51. Kelly notes (219) that the formula in parentheses isn't an exact description of Henryson's *Testament*; for Henryson's work as tragedy, see Kelly, *Chaucerian Tragedy*, 216–21.

   [3] For a summary of the issues, see Elmer Andrews, 'Gender, Colonialism, Nationalism,' in *The Poetry of Seamus Heaney*, ed. Andrews, 120–41.

an Mheán Oíche with its comic savaging of the Irish male, sandwiched between portions of Ovid in *The Midnight Verdict*, might have been a gesture
in response to feminist criticism of the *Field Day Anthology of Irish Writing*,
which eventually required an additional two volumes to balance its mas-
culinist construction of an Irish literary canon; Heaney was not editorially
involved, but was both a contributor to the anthology and a director of
Field Day.[1] More recently, Helen Phillips, in commenting on the *Beowulf*
translation, argued that 'it is Heaney's treatment of the females in *Beowulf*
that is most disappointing,' drawing comparisons with Heaney's earlier
work and feminist criticism of it.[2]

In seeking a way to square Heaney's sympathy for Cresseid with the elements of antifeminism found in Henryson, it's perhaps worth paying heed
to a reading of Henryson's poem by Felicity Riddy, who links Cresseid's
description of herself as 'abiect odious' (*Testament of Cresseid*, 133) with
Julia Kristeva's notion of the abject.[3] Riddy reads Cresseid as an excluded
figure from beginning to end:

> Throughout the poem Cresseid is an outcast, an 'vnworthie outwaill'
> (129), and the action concerns the processes whereby she is progres-
> sively excluded or excludes herself: socially, morally, spatially, tem-
> porally. She enters the poem as an exile from Troy, and her promised
> 'retour' (51) or 'ganecome' (55) can never take place. She is formally
> reputed by Diomeid and, 'desolait' (76) and 'maculait' (81), passes 'far
> out of the toun' (95) to her father's house, but once she has become a
> leper she cannot stay there either. In the gods's sentence on Cresseid
> the sufferings of leprosy are represented as another form of exclu-
> sion, not only because her repulsive disease means that 'Quhair thou
> cummis, ilk man sall flee the place' (341), but because she is cut off
> from her own former beauty and desire.[4]

[1] Corcoran, *Poetry of Seamus Heaney*, 187; the Merriman translation is in Heaney, *The
Midnight Verdict*; the passages of Ovid's *Metamorphoses* juxtaposed with Merriman were
also published separately in *After Ovid*, ed. Hofmann and Lasdun, 222–29. The anthology
is *The Field Day Anthology of Irish Writing*, ed. Seamus Deane et al., 3 vols. (Derry: Field
Day, 1991), supplemented by *The Field Day Anthology of Irish Writing*, iv–v: *Irish Women's
Writing and Traditions*, ed. Angela Bourke et al. (Cork: Cork University Press in association with Field Day, 2002); for the relationship between the two, see the preface to vol.
iv, pp. xxxii–xxxiii.

[2] Phillips, 'Seamus Heaney's *Beowulf*,' 275–78 and n. 21; cf. the discussion in Chap. 3
above.

[3] Felicity Riddy, '"Abject odious": Feminine and Masculine in Henryson's *Testament
of Cresseid*,' in *The Long Fifteenth Century: Essays for Douglas Gray*, ed. Helen Cooper and
Sally Mapstone (Oxford: Oxford University Press, 1997), 229–48.

[4] Riddy, '"Abject odious",' 232–33.

In Kristeva, the abject is what is excluded to make identity possible; in Riddy's reading of Henryson's poem, the construction of masculine identity requires the exclusion of the feminine.[1] For Riddy, 'Cresseid is made to bear the symbolic weight of the expulsion of the feminine: Troilus's famous truth, his self-consistency, is a version of the "clean and proper body" from which hers, defiled by promiscuity and then disfigured by leprosy, is abjected.'[2]

Heaney is not directly indebted to Riddy or to Kristeva. There is no evidence from the translation that he might be aware of Riddy's reading – quite the contrary, in fact, for the crucial term in Riddy's reading, *abject*, which appears in line 133 with the possible sense of 'outcast,' is not translated as such by Heaney, who renders the lines:

> Quha sall me gyde? Quha sall me now conuoy,
> Sen I fra Diomeid and nobill Troylus
> Am clene excludit, as abiect odious? (*Testament*, 131–33)

as:

> Who's now to guide, accompany or stand by
> Me, so at odds and made so odious
> To Diomede and noble Troilus? (p. 18)

The word 'abject' disappears entirely from the translation – perhaps to avoid a choice between translating the word as either 'object' or 'outcast.'[3] But if Heaney is not thinking in terms of the Kristevan abject, as Riddy is, his Cresseid does nonetheless say that she receives 'a banishment decree' (p. 15), that she is 'completely destitute, / Bereft of comfort and all consolation, / Friendless and unprotected' (p. 16), 'demeaned into an outcast' (p. 18), cursed to live 'beyond the pale / Anathema, diseased, incurable' (p. 27).

If Cresseid is progressively exiled from Troy, from Diomede, from her beauty and health, from her father's home, and ultimately from life itself, it's worth remembering the extent of Heaney's engagement and identification with other outcast figures throughout his poetry. In *Sweeney Astray*, Heaney's description of Sweeney as 'a figure of the artist, displaced, guilty, assuaging himself by his utterance' (p. vi) is in part autobiographical self-

---

[1] Riddy, '"Abject odious",' 234–36, 244–48; citing Julia Kristeva, *Powers of Horror: An Essay on Abjection*, trans. Leon S. Roudiez (New York, 1982).

[2] Riddy, '"Abject odious",' 236.

[3] Denton Fox, *Poems of Robert Henryson*, 348, n. to l. 133, notes that 'abject is a noun, "outcast" (not elsewhere recorded in MSc; first recorded in English in 1534)'; cf. Pearsall, '"Quha wait gif all that Chaucer wrait was trew?",' 180 n. 16 who argues for 'object,' not 'outcast.'

projection, and Heaney's sense of exile after his move south as expressed in *Sweeney Astray* emphasises an existing sense of displacement; through Heaney's work in general the expression of a desire for home is constantly in tension with both a sense of a sense of homelessness and an awareness that the desired 'at-homeness' is already pre-problematized. In *Stations*, the narrator figure is identified with those outside the walls,[1] and there are outcast or marginal figures to be found throughout the poetry: the neighbour excluded from a scene of domestic prayer in 'The Other Side,'[2] the child imprisoned in a hen-house in 'Bye-Child,'[3] the 'inner emigré' of 'Exposure,'[4] the poet Chekhov in 'Chekhov on Sakhalin,'[5] the travellers who live at the edge of settled society in 'The King of the Ditchbacks' and 'Station Island,'[6] the exogamous bride ducking stones thrown by neighbours in 'Clearances,'[7] Sweeney himself, Philoctetes, and Grendel and his mother, to say nothing of the Iron Age victims of ritual murder exhumed from bogs and the many contemporary victims of 'neighbourly murder' who appear in the poems. Sometimes these outcast or marginal figures are projections of the poet; always they are treated with sympathy, even when, as with Grendel and Philoctetes, that sympathy is not unqualified. Like Grendel, Cresseid is 'beyond the pale,' like Sweeney, distracted and rambling, like Cassandra, a woman suffering against the background of the Trojan war. Heaney's advocacy of the outcast is long standing, and it offers a likely explanation of his sympathetic reading of Henryson's Cresseid.

[1] Heaney, *Opened Ground*, 85.
[2] Heaney, *Wintering Out*, 34–36; Heaney, *Opened Ground*, 59–61.
[3] Heaney, *Wintering Out*, 71–72; Heaney, *Opened Ground*, 76–77.
[4] Heaney, *North*, 72–73; Heaney, *Opened Ground*, 143–44.
[5] Heaney, *Station Island*, 18–19; Heaney, *Opened Ground*, 215–16.
[6] Heaney, *Station Island*, 56–58, 61–63; Heaney, *Opened Ground*, 238–41, 242–44.
[7] Heaney, *The Haw Lantern*, 27; Heaney, *Opened Ground*, 307.

Conclusion

Before and after: contexts and canons

SEAMUS Heaney's responses to medieval literature take place in the context of an ongoing engagement with medieval material by twentieth-century predecessors and contemporary writers. Several of the texts discussed above have been a rich source of literary inspiration for previous twentieth-century writers. Certainly *Buile Suibhne* has been a source of inspiration for a long list of twentieth-century Irish writers, both before and after Heaney, although Heaney's is the first full-length English translation for generations. Dante has exerted a substantial influence on English-language poetry from Chaucer to the present; Heaney's own essay 'Envies and Identifications' mentions Yeats, Eliot, and Kinsella as English-language predecessors in their responses to Dante, and another twentieth-century Irish disciple of Dante, James Joyce, is a significant presence in *Station Island*. As discussed in Chapter 2, the literary history of Lough Derg itself begins in the twelfth century and extends to the twentieth, with Heaney acknowledging both in 'Envies and Identifications' and in 'Station Island' itself that many previous writers have traipsed ahead of him on the pilgrimage. There have also been many previous translations of *Beowulf*, albeit mostly for pedagogical purposes, and none by major poets such as Heaney. Finally, Heaney's translation of Henryson can be read as part of an ongoing series of responses to Trojan texts by contemporary Irish writers.

Translations and adaptations of medieval texts that immediately precede Heaney's may have offered a precedent for the work discussed here. Geoffrey Hill's *Mercian Hymns*, Ted Hughes' *Wodwo*, and Thomas Kinsella's *Tain* might all have served as imperatives for Heaney's turn towards the Middle Ages in *Buile Suibhne* and the accompanying 'Sweeney Redivivus' sequence; Robert Lowell's translation practice is an influence directly acknowledged by Heaney in 'Earning a Rhyme.'[1]

---

[1] Heaney, 'Earning a Rhyme,' 63.

There are, in turn, what might be seen as responses to Heaney's translations of medieval texts visible in the work of other Irish poets. Bernard O'Donoghue's work includes a number of responses to the Middle Ages, including a translation of the Old English *Wulf and Eadwacer* in his collection *The Weakness*,[1] and a number of translations and allusions in the subsequent *Here Nor There*: the opening poem 'Nechtan' alludes to the medieval Irish *Imram Brain* (*Voyage of Bran*), 'Not Believing in Crocodiles' opens with a quotation from Mandeville's *Travels*, there are fragments of translation from Langland's *Piers Plowman*, 'The Pleasures of the Circus' may be indebted to the Old English *Maxims II*, and 'Fallout' is a translation from the work of the thirteenth-century troubadour Peire Cardenal.[2] While O'Donoghue has written extensively on Heaney, he is also a medievalist by profession, and so is hardly following in Heaney's wake in his response to medieval literature – his professional output includes translations from medieval European love poetry and a recent translation for Penguin of *Sir Gawain and the Green Knight*.[3]

Two more likely respondents to Heaney's medieval translations are Paul Muldoon and Ciaran Carson, both careful readers of Heaney. Muldoon's 'The More a Man Has the More a Man Wants,' from *Quoof*, contains a stanza that parodies both Heaney's placename poem 'Broagh' and a passage from the end of *Sweeney Astray* that sets the protagonist up for the 'threefold death' where the victim dies by a spear, a fall, and by drowning.[4] Muldoon doesn't only produce responses to the medieval in reaction to Heaney: 'Immram' from Muldoon's previous volume *Why Brownlee Left* has debts to the medieval Irish *Imram Curaig Máile Dúin* (*Voyage of Muldoon*) via Tennyson, and (as Heaney notes) Yeats.[5] There may be another response to Heaney's versions of the medieval in Muldoon's brief poem 'The Briefcase', a poem dedicated to Heaney and a matching pair for Heaney's 'Widgeon' (dedicated to Muldoon).[6] Where Heaney's poem produces music from an inanimate object, Muldoon's has the inanimate

---

[1] Bernard O'Donoghue, *The Weakness* (London: Chatto, 1991), 51.

[2] Bernard O'Donoghue, *Here Nor There* (London: Chatto, 1999), 1, 15, 23–25, 35, 47; the debt to *Maxims II* is suggested by Jones, *Strange Likeness*, 183n.

[3] Bernard O'Donoghue, *The Courtly Love Tradition* (Manchester: Manchester University Press, 1982); *Sir Gawain and the Green Knight*, trans. Bernard O'Donoghue (London: Penguin, 2006).

[4] Muldoon, *Poems*, 135; the parody is discussed in Neil Corcoran, 'A Languorous Cutting Edge: Muldoon versus Heaney?' in *Poets of Modern Ireland: Text, Context, Intertext* (Cardiff: University of Wales Press, 1999), 121–36 at 122–23; Heaney comments on the poem in 'Place and Displacement,' 127. On the motif of the 'threefold death,' see Carney, 'Suibhne Geilt,' 91–94.

[5] Muldoon, *Poems*, 94–102; Heaney, *Finders Keepers*, 240.

[6] Muldoon, *Poems*, 202.

object return to life. The eelskin briefcase recalls the place of eels in several Heaney poems, and perhaps in particular, as Neil Corcoran suggests,
Joyce's Heaneyesque imperative to the pilgrim Heaney at the end of 'Station Island' to produce 'elver-gleams.'[1] But 'The Briefcase' also has a couple of echoes from Dante: the 'obol' that Muldoon is searching for is lifted
from another Heaney poem, but also recalls the fare paid to Charon when
crossing Avernus. Further to that, Muldoon's final reference to the sea as
a quotation-marked 'open' sea might also have a Dantesque provenance: if
the journey up the East River and out into the open sea is the journey back
to Ireland,[2] the journey to the open sea is also that of Ulysses' last voyage
as described in *Inferno* XXVI (a portion of Dante that Heaney alludes to in
'Station Island' IX. 84–85):[3]

> ma misi me per l'alto mare aperto
> sol con un legno e con quello compagna
> picciola dalla qual non fui diserto.
>
> (*Inferno*, XXVI. 100–102)

And I put forth on the open deep with but one ship and with that
little company which had not deserted me.[4]

Here again, then, Muldoon may be offering an intertextual glance towards
a medieval text by way of responding to Heaney.

More recently, Muldoon has taken his medieval material relatively
straight, with a translation of Cædmon's Hymn that might be seen as a brief
nod towards Heaney's epic *Beowulf* (I say 'relatively' straight because there
is a characteristic Muldoonian wit in the choice of Cædmon's poem as
a contribution to a series of poems for the London Underground: as Chris
Jones puts it, 'reconstructing the foundations of English verse beneath the
deepest archaeological strata of the English capital').[5] A more substantial
response to Heaney's *Beowulf* might be Ciaran Carson's *Inferno* translation,
where the dust-jacket blurb on the original hardcover edition claimed that
the translation 'deserves comparison with Heaney's *Beowulf* and Hughes's
Tales from Ovid.' Carson's translation may well deserve comparison with
Beowulf as an Hiberno-English rendering of a major medieval text; it also
merits comparison with Heaney's own extensive engagement with Dante.
Carson's *Inferno* translation is a virtuoso affair: rendering Dante's text in

---

[1] Corcoran, 'A Languorous Cutting Edge,' 131–32.

[2] Corcoran, 'A Languorous Cutting Edge,' 132.

[3] On Heaney's allusion to *Inferno* XXVI here, see O'Donoghue, 'Dante's Versatility,' 247.

[4] Dante, *Divine Comedy*, ed. and trans. Sinclair, i, 324, 325.

[5] Muldoon, *Moy Sand and Gravel*, 23; Jones, *Strange Likeness*, 183–84.

a *terza rima* crossed with Irish ballad, this translation reads very differently from Heaney's translation of portions from the *Inferno*. While Carson acknowledges echoes from other translations, there is little here directly from Heaney: perhaps Beatrice's description of Dante as 'astray' in canto II, and the use of the word 'famine' (albeit not in a manner identical to Heaney) in canto XXXIII, neither of which is significant in a work of such lexical exuberance.[1] Carson's *Inferno* does, however, resemble Heaney's versions of Dante in that it finds parallels between the world of Dante and that of contemporary Northern Ireland, and has a similar commitment to vernacularity. There may also, perhaps, be some echoes of Mandelstam, whose essay on Dante is so influential for Heaney. Carson's descriptions of walking the streets of Belfast during the translation process, while no doubt literal, also seem to recall Mandelstam's question about how many sandals Dante wore out in the course of composition, wandering about on the goat paths of Italy. Carson's use of Hiberno-English ballad as a model for translation, while in keeping with Carson's musical affinities, also seems in tune with Mandelstam's comparison of Dante's Ugolino episode with the ballad form.[2] Heaney's extensive creative engagement with medieval poetry, then, does not take place in isolation: there are both predecessors and successors to be taken into account.

In an academic context (where medieval literature mostly tends to be read), Heaney's *Beowulf* translation was exactly in step with the arrival of postcolonialism in medieval studies in the late 1990s,[3] and there have been some readings of *Beowulf* in the wake of Heaney's translation that seem to read the original Old English text in a way that might indicate the translation's influence: an essay by Alfred K. Siewers published in 2003, for instance, has a passing reference that reads Grendel and his mother as stand-ins for residual Celtic populations in areas marginal to Anglo-Saxon society, and a 2005 essay by Seth Lerer is explicit in its reading of both Heaney's text and the Old English poem as being, each in their own way, postcolonial.[4] But if the *Beowulf* translation is in keeping with an interest in postcolonialism becoming visible in medieval studies, Heaney's advocacy of the 'through-other' has already taken account of and moved

---

[1] Carson, *Inferno*, II, 230.

[2] Carson, *Inferno*, pp. xi, xx–xxi; Mandelstam, 'Conversation about Dante,' 6, 33.

[3] See, for example, *The Postcolonial Middle Ages*, ed. Jeffrey Jerome Cohen (New York: St Martin's Press, 2000).

[4] Alfred K. Siewers, 'Landscapes of Conversion: Guthlac's Mound and Grendel's Mere as Expressions of Anglo-Saxon Nation Building,' *Viator* 34 (2003), 1–39 at 33; Seth Lerer, '"On fagne flor": The Postcolonial *Beowulf*, from Heorot to Heaney,' in *Postcolonial Approaches to the European Middle Ages: Translating Cultures*, ed. Ananya Jahanara Kabir and Deanne Williams (Cambridge: Cambridge University Press, 2005), 77–102.

beyond postcolonial notions of 'otherness': in that sense, literary practice here seems already out in front where academic commentary seems to be just catching up.

In addition to contemporary contexts, Heaney's engagement with the medieval can also be read as engaging with ideas of canonicity. Heaney's work more generally tends both to invoke and to resist the idea of a specific literary tradition: Michael O'Neill describes Heaney's relationship with the Romantic tradition, for instance, as containing both a longing for Romantic authority and an ironic opposition to that longing.[1] As Neil Corcoran comments, Heaney invokes notions such as 'the canon' and 'tradition' while including under these umbrella terms some previously non-canonical writers, works, and readings.[2] In his translations and adaptations of medieval texts, one of the things that Heaney does is to write himself into the canon – as argued in Chapter 3, the *Beowulf* translation sees Heaney quite literally writing his own foundations into the foundations of writing in English. But there is also an impulse here towards broadening the canon, and the discussion above contrasts Heaney's advocacy of texts that might well be included within the canon of literature in English with the constructions of canons that omit them. John Dryden positions Chaucer as the father of English poetry and omits Henryson from his account of the literary history of Troilus and Criseyde; Harold Bloom's version of the Western Canon is centred on Shakespeare, and takes no account of Old English literature. Heaney's translations of *Beowulf* and *The Testament of Cresseid* are acts of advocacy that contrast with Dryden and Bloom's canon-making in seeking to reinstate these medieval texts within the literary mainstream.

Heaney's work also seeks to take account of the non-English literatures of Britain and Ireland (something explicit in the anthology *The School Bag*), and to acknowledge a canon of Irish literature in Irish that may now be recuperated into an Irish literature in English.[3] This seems the case with the recent translation of 'Pangur Bán': in his comments following the translation, Heaney alludes to versions by Robin Flower and Gerard Murphy, and notes that the poem is one 'that Irish writers like to try their hand at, not in order to outdo the previous versions, but simply to get a more exact and intimate grip on the canonical goods' (p. 5). There's not much

---

[1] Michael O' Neill, 'Contemporary Northern Irish Poets and Romantic Poetry,' in *English Romanticism and the Celtic World,* ed. Gerard Carruthers and Alan Rawes (Cambridge: Cambridge University Press, 2003), 196–209 at 199.

[2] Corcoran, *Poetry of Seamus Heaney*, 219–24.

[3] On which see Seamus Heaney, 'The Poems of the Dispossessed Repossessed,' in *The Government of the Tongue*, 30–35 at 30.

doubt that 'Pangur Bán' forms a part of the Irish literary canon. The poem has often been translated; Heaney himself nominated it for inclusion in the canon-building collection of Irish and Scots Gaelic poetry, *An Leabhar Mòr*; and when we see in Paul Muldoon's 'Hopewell Haiku' sequence that the poet has adopted a wild cat, it's no surprise to find that the cat has been named Pangur Ban, for what else would an Irish poet call a cat?[1] All that said, the poem is probably not much known outside Ireland, and so Heaney's translation also has the force of advocacy. If Heaney's engagement with the Middle Ages involves an invocation of the canon, then, it also involves its reworking; in drawing on the past, Heaney also seeks to rethink it.

Translating the Middle Ages, rethinking the past

This discussion began by suggesting that Seamus Heaney's translations and adaptations of medieval poetry now form a substantial body of work, and while the survey above of Heaney's ongoing dialogue with medieval literature has focused most substantially on four books – *Sweeney Astray*, *Station Island*, *Beowulf*, and *The Testament of Cresseid* – it has extended to brief discussions of *North*, *Field Work*, and *Seeing Things*, with further allusions to medieval material in *Stations*, *The Spirit Level*, *Electric Light*, and *District and Circle*. Three source texts – *Buile Suibhne*, Dante's *Commedia*, and *Beowulf* – have proved of enduring concern, and elicited multiple responses across Heaney's work, but the list of medieval texts that Heaney has drawn upon extends much further, and includes works as diverse as Bede's *Ecclesiastical History*, *The Battle of Maldon*, *Njal's Saga*, and 'Pangur Bán,' amongst others. More recently, there has been a substantial response to the Middle Scots poet Robert Henryson with the translation of *The Testament of Cresseid* and an indication of further translations from Henryson's *Fables* to follow.

As argued throughout the discussion above, Heaney's practice has been to draw upon medieval texts in grappling with contemporary concerns, and his translations of medieval poetry have allowed him to explore issues both personal and political. Heaney identifies or empathises with medieval figures such as Suibhne Geilt, Dante Alighieri, and Cædmon, and uses the *Beowulf* translation to inscribe his own point of origin, Mossbawn in County Derry, into the foundations of English literature. Both *Sweeney Astray* and *Station Island* cover personal and political issues in drawing on medieval texts in part to explore the poet's role in relation to his society at a time of conflict. *Beowulf* and *The Testament of Cresseid* are still concerned

[1] Muldoon, *Poems*, 421, 426, 428.

with the themes of conflict and its consequences, but the focus in these texts has moved away from questions of poetic responsibility and towards the themes of empathy and endurance in times of trouble. Such a difference in focus is explicable in part through a change in political circumstances: where *Sweeney Astray* and *Station Island* are the work of the late 1970s and early 1980s, of what would turn out to be the midpoint of the Northern Ireland conflict, *Beowulf* and *The Testament of Cresseid* are the work of the decade that followed the IRA ceasefire in 1994. Hard-and-fast divisions between these works, however, would be artificial and misleading, for there are visible continuties in evidence; it's noticeable, for instance, that Mandelstam's essay on Dante is prominently cited at the very beginning of Heaney's introduction to the *Beowulf* translation (p. ix). Thematically, the subject of exclusion and exile is prominent in all four texts discussed above, and outcast figures such as Sweeney, Dante, Grendel, and Cresseid are treated with empathy or sympathy. Linguistically, Heaney's commitment to avoiding divisions constructed between Irish and English has been a prominent point of discussion in relation to the *Beowulf* translation, but it applies equally to his earlier work, including the translation of a medieval Irish text in *Sweeney Astray*.

As argued at the beginning of this discussion, then, Heaney's engagement with medieval literature is a coherent one. From the very outset, his work engages with medieval culture as a complex resource for examining the contemporary, producing multiple responses to individual source texts, involving a two-way dialogue between translation practice and original composition, displaying a commitment to vernacularity suggestive of multicultural affinities for medieval texts, creating complex layerings visible within the poetry as medieval texts are given a contemporary voice and brought to bear upon contemporary concerns. The result is a representation of the Middle Ages as a reality of similar complexity to our own, a view at odds with the received opinion of the Middle Ages as premodern and marginal to the concerns of contemporary existence.

This urge to embrace the canon but also rewrite it is part of a broader urge to revisit and rethink the past visible in Heaney's engagement with the medieval and in his work at large. Helen Vendler notes Heaney's ability to revisit and reconsider his own work[1] – visible here in the reworking of *Buile Suibhne* in 'Sweeney Redivivus,' in the reworking of earlier responses to Dante in 'Station Island' and 'The Flight Path,' and in the multiple responses to Germanic material in *North* and *Beowulf* – and if this is a visible element in Heaney's ongoing rethinking of his own work, it is also a visible imperative in his response to medieval writing. In relation to the

---

[1] Vendler, *Seamus Heaney*, 10.

Middle Ages, this urge to revisit and rethink the past is an urge to consider the connections that may be forged between the writers of a variety of medieval texts and a contemporary Irish poet; an acknowledgement that the past is not stable and eternally fixed, but open to reimagining and re-working; an urge to question old certainties, and in doing so, to forge new possibilities from what has previously been given. This need to rethink the past is based on a realization that our understanding of the past plays a crucial determining role in our understanding of the present, and also in our understanding of the future. The epigraph to the *Beowulf* translation, taken from Heaney's poem 'The Settle Bed,' suggests that the medieval poem being translated is an inheritance. If the medieval is an inheritance, in Heaney's view, it is not an inheritance that is given, fixed, and inert, but rather a gift from the past that can be turned to face the future, remade and further remade, 'willable forward / again and again and again.'[1]

---

[1] *Beowulf*, trans. Heaney, p. ix, citing Heaney, *Seeing Things*, 28; Heaney, *Opened Ground*, 345.

Bibliography

Primary texts

WORKS BY SEAMUS HEANEY

HEANEY, Seamus. *Death of a Naturalist* (London: Faber, 1966).
——. *Door Into the Dark* (London: Faber, 1969).
——. *Wintering Out* (London: Faber, 1972).
——. *North* (London: Faber, 1975).
——. *Field Work* (London: Faber, 1979).
——. *Preoccupations: Selected Prose, 1968–1978* (London: Faber, 1980):
    'Mossbawn,' pp. 17–27.
    'Belfast,' pp. 28–37.
    'Feeling Into Words,' pp. 41–60.
    'The Sense of Place,' pp. 131–49.
    'Englands of the Mind,' pp. 150–69.
    'The God in the Tree: Early Irish Nature Poetry,' pp. 181–89.
——. *Sweeney Astray* (Derry: Field Day, 1983; London: Faber, 1984).
——. *Station Island* (London: Faber, 1984).
——. 'An Open Letter.' In *Ireland's Field Day* (London: Hutchinson, 1985), 23–30.
——. 'Envies and Identifications: Dante and the Modern Poet,' *Irish University Review* 15 (1985), 5–19. Repr. in *Dante Readings*, ed. Eric Haywood (Dublin: Irish Academic Press, 1987), 29–46.
——. *The Haw Lantern* (London: Faber, 1987).
——. *The Government of the Tongue: The 1986 T. S. Eliot Memorial Lectures and Other Critical Writings* (London: Faber, 1988):
    'The Murmur of Malvern,' pp. 23–29.
    'The Poems of the Dispossessed Repossessed,' pp. 30–35.
    'The Government of the Tongue,' pp. 91–108.
——. *Seeing Things* (London: Faber, 1991).
——. *The Cure at Troy: A Version of Sophocles' Philoctetes* (New York: Farrar Strauss Giroux, 1991).
——. *The Midnight Verdict* (Oldcastle: Gallery, 1993, repr. 2000).

——. *The Redress of Poetry: Oxford Lectures* (London: Faber, 1995):

'Extending the Alphabet: On Christopher Marlowe's "Hero and Leander",' pp. 17–37.

'Orpheus in Ireland: On Brian Merriman's *The Midnight Court*,' pp. 38–62.

'Frontiers of Writing,' pp. 186–203.

——. *The Spirit Level* (London: Faber, 1996).

——. *Opened Ground: Poems 1966–1996* (London: Faber, 1998):

'Crediting Poetry: The Nobel Lecture, 1995,' pp. 445–67.

——. 'The Drag of the Golden Chain,' *TLS* (12 Nov. 1999).

——. *Electric Light* (London: Faber, 2001).

——. *Finders Keepers: Selected Prose 1971–2001* (London: Faber, 2002):

'Something to Write Home About,' pp. 48–58.

'Earning a Rhyme,' pp. 59–66. First published in *Poetry Ireland Review* (Spring 1989).

'Place and Displacement: Recent Poetry from Northern Ireland,' pp. 112–33.

'Edwin Muir,' pp. 246–56. First published in *Verse* 6/1 (March 1989).

'A Torchlight Procession of One: Hugh MacDiarmid,' pp. 293–311. First published in Heaney, *The Redress of Poetry: Oxford Lectures* (London: Faber, 1995), 103–23.

'Burns's Art Speech,' pp. 347–63. First published in *Robert Burns and Cultural Authority*, ed. Robert Crawford (Edinburgh: Edinburgh University Press, 1997).

'Through-Other Places, Through-Other Times: The Irish Poet and Britain,' pp. 364–82.

'Norman MacCaig,' pp. 399–402.

——. 'The Trance and the Translation,' *The Guardian* (30 Nov. 2002).

——. *The Testament of Cresseid: A Retelling of Robert Henryson's Poem by Seamus Heaney with images by Hughie O'Donoghue* (London: Enitharmon Editions, 2004).

——. *The Burial at Thebes: Sophocles' Antigone* (London: Faber, 2004).

——. 'A Story that Sings down the Centuries,' *The Sunday Times* (21 March 2004).

——. 'Three Poems,' *Salmagundi* 148–49 (Fall 2005 – Winter 2006), 96–99.

——. *District and Circle* (London: Faber, 2006).

HEANEY, Seamus (trans.). *Beowulf* (London: Faber, 1999).

—— (trans.). *Beowulf: A New Verse Translation* (New York: Farrar, Strauss and Giroux, 2000).

—— (trans.). Daniel Donoghue (ed.), *Beowulf: A Verse Translation* (New York and London: Norton, 2002).

—— (trans.). 'Pangur Bán,' *Poetry* 188.1 (April 2006), 3–5.

HEANEY, Seamus, and GIESE, Rachel. *Sweeney's Flight* (London: Faber, 1992).

HEANEY, Seamus, and HUGHES, Ted (eds.). *The School Bag* (London: Faber, 1997).

WORKS BY MEDIEVAL AUTHORS

ALIGHIERI, Dante. *The Divine Comedy of Dante Alighieri*, ed. and trans. John D. Sinclair, rev. edn, 3 vols. (1948; repr. Oxford: Oxford University Press, 1971).

ANDERSON, J. J. (ed.). *Sir Gawain and the Green Knight; Pearl; Cleanness; Patience* (London: Dent, 1996).

ANDREW, Malcolm, and WALDRON, Ronald (eds.). *The Poems of the Pearl Manuscript: Pearl; Cleanness; Patience; Sir Gawain and the Green Knight* (Exeter: University of Exeter Press, 1987).

BEDE. *A History of the English Church and People*, trans. Leo Sherley-Price (Harmondsworth: Penguin, 1955).

BENNETT, J. A. W., and SMITHERS, G. V., with Norman Davis (eds.). *Early Middle English Verse and Prose*, 2nd edn (Oxford: Oxford University Press, 1968).

BERGIN, O. J., BEST, R. I., MEYER, Kuno, and O'KEEFFE, J. G. (eds.). *Anecdota from Irish Manuscripts*, iii (Halle: Max Niemeyer; Dublin: Hodges Figgis, 1910).

CHAUCER, Geoffrey. *The Riverside Chaucer*, ed. Larry D. Benson (Boston: Houghton Mifflin, 1987).

CHRÉTIEN de Troyes. *Arthurian Romances*, trans. D. D. R. Owen (London: Dent, 1993).

DUNBAR, William. *The Poems of William Dunbar*, ed. Priscilla Bawcutt, 2 vols., Association for Scottish Literary Studies 27–28 (Glasgow: Association for Scottish Literary Studies, 1998).

EASTING, Robert (ed.). *St Patrick's Purgatory: Two Versions of Owayne Miles and The Vision of William of Stranton together with the Long Text of the Tractatus de Purgatorio Sancti Patricii*, EETS 298 (Oxford: Oxford University Press, 1991).

GARMONSWAY, G. N., and SIMPSON, Jacqueline (trans.). *Beowulf and its Analogues* (London, 1980).

GEOFFREY of Monmouth. *The History of the Kings of Britain*, trans. Lewis Thorpe (Harmondsworth: Penguin, 1966).

GERALD of Wales. *The History and Topography of Ireland*, trans. John J. O'Meara (Harmondsworth: Penguin, 1982).

GRAY, Douglas (ed.). *Selected Poems of Robert Henryson and William Dunbar* (London: Penguin, 1998).

GUILLAUME de Lorris and JEAN de Meun. *Le Roman de la Rose*, ed. Ernst Langlois, 3 vols. (Paris: Champion, 1914–21).

———. *The Romance of the Rose*, trans. Frances Horgan (Oxford: Oxford University Press, 1994).

HAMER, Richard (ed. and trans.). *A Choice of Anglo-Saxon Verse* (London: Faber, 1970).

HAVELY, N. R. (ed. and trans.). *Chaucer's Boccaccio: Sources of 'Troilus' and the 'Knight's' and 'Franklin's Tales'* (Cambridge: Brewer, 1980).

HENRYSON, Robert. *The Poems of Robert Henryson*, ed. Denton Fox (Oxford: Oxford University Press, 1981).

HUGH of St Victor. *The Didiscalion of Hugh of St Victor: A Medieval Guide to the Arts*, trans. Jerome Taylor (New York: Columbia University Press, 1961).

JONES, Gwyn, and JONES, Thomas (trans.). *The Mabinogion* (London: Dent, 1993).

LANGLAND, William. *The Vision of Piers Plowman*, ed. A. V. C. Schmidt (London: Dent, 1987).

MARIE de France. *Saint Patrick's Purgatory: A Poem by Marie de France*, trans. Michael Curley (Binghamton, NY: Medieval & Renaissance Texts & Studies, 1993).

MAGNUSSON, Magnus, and PÁLSSON, Hermann (trans.). *Njal's Saga* (Harmondsworth: Penguin, 1960).

MINNIS, A. J., and SCOTT, A. B., with David Wallace (eds.). *Medieval Literary Theory and Criticism, c.1100–1375: The Commentary Tradition*, rev. edn (Oxford: Oxford University Press, 1988).

MURPHY, Gerard (ed.). *Early Irish Lyrics: Eighth to Twelfth Century* (Oxford: Oxford University Press, 1956).

Ó CÚIV, Brian. 'The Romance of Mis and Dubh Ruis,' *Celtica* 2/2 (1954), 325–33.

O'DONOGHUE, Bernard. *The Courtly Love Tradition* (Manchester: Manchester University Press, 1982).

O'DONOGHUE, Bernard (trans.). *Sir Gawain and the Green Knight* (London: Penguin, 2006).

O'KEEFFE, J. G. (ed. and trans.). *Buile Suibhne (The Frenzy of Suibhne), being The Adventures of Suibhne Geilt: A Middle-Irish Romance* (London: Irish Texts Society, 1913).

PETRARCH [PETRARCA, Francesco]. *Petrarch's Lyric Poems: The Rime sparse and Other Lyrics*, ed. and trans. Robert M. Durling (Cambridge, MA, and London: Harvard University Press, 1976).

PICARD, Jean-Michel (trans.). *Saint Patrick's Purgatory: A Twelfth Century Tale of a Journey to the Other World*, introd. Yolande de Pontfarcy (Dublin: Four Courts, 1985).

WARNKE, Karl (ed.). *Das Buch vom Espurgatoire S. Patrice der Marie de France und seine Quelle* (Halle: Max Niemeyer, 1938).

WRENN, C. L., and BOLTON, W. F. (eds.). *Beowulf with the Finnesburg Fragment*, 5th edn (Exeter: University of Exeter Press, 1996).

OTHER PRIMARY TEXTS

ABRAMS, M. H., GREENBLATT, Stephen, et al. (eds.). *The Norton Anthology of English Literature*, 7th edn, 2 vols. (New York and London: Norton, 2000).

BOLGER, Dermot. *A Second Life* (Harmondsworth: Penguin, 1994).

BLACK, Ronald I. M. (ed.). *An Tuil: Anthology of 20th Century Scottish Gaelic Verse* (Edinburgh: Polygon, 1999).

BOURKE, Angela, et al. (eds.). *The Field Day Anthology of Irish Writing*, iv–v: *Irish Women's Writing and Traditions* (Cork: Cork University Press in association with Field Day, 2002).

CARSON, Ciaran. *First Language* (Oldcastle: Gallery, 1993).

——. *The Inferno of Dante Alighieri* (London: Granta, 2002).

——. *The Midnight Court* (Oldcastle: Gallery, 2005).

CLARKE, Austin. *Collected Poems*, ed. Liam Miller (Dublin: Dolmen, 1974).

DRYDEN, John. *The Poems and Fables of John Dryden*, ed. James Kinsley (London: Oxford University Press, 1962).

——. *The Works of John Dryden*, xiii: *Plays: All for Love; Oedipus; Troilus and Cressida*, ed. Maximilian E. Novak et al. (Berkeley, Los Angeles, and London: University of California Press, 1984).

DEANE, Seamus, et al. (eds.). *The Field Day Anthology of Irish Writing*, 3 vols. (Derry: Field Day, 1991).

DUHIG, Ian. *The Bradford Count* (Newcastle upon Tyne: Bloodaxe, 1991).

ELIOT, T. S. *Dante* (London: Faber, 1965).

——. *Collected Poems, 1909–1962* (London: Faber, 1974).

FRIEL, Brian. *Translations*. In Friel, *Plays: One* (London: Faber, 1996), 377–451.

GREENE, David, and O'CONNOR, Frank (eds. and trans.). *A Golden Treasury of Irish Poetry* (London: Macmillan, 1967).

GRIFFITHS, Eric, and REYNOLDS, Matthew (eds.). *Dante in English* (London: Penguin, 2005).

HALPERN, Daniel (ed.). *Dante's Inferno: Translations by Twenty Contemporary Poets* (New York: Ecco, 1993).

HEANEY, Marie. *Over Nine Waves* (London: Faber, 1994).

HOFMAN, Michael, and LASDUN, James (eds.). *After Ovid: New Metamorphoses* (London: Faber, 1994).

HILL, Geoffrey. *Mercian Hymns* (London: Deutsch, 1971).

HUGHES, Ted. *Wodwo* (London: Faber, 1967).

JOYCE, James. *A Portrait of the Artist as a Young Man* (London: Cape, 1964).

KAVANAGH, Patrick. *Selected Poems*, ed. Antoinette Quinn (Harmondsworth: Penguin, 1996).

KENNELLY, Brendan. *Euripedes' The Trojan Women: A New Version by Brendan Kennelly* (Newcastle upon Tyne: Bloodaxe, 1993).

KINSELLA, Thomas. *The Tain, translated from the Irish epic Tain Bo Cuailgne* (Dublin: Dolmen, 1969; repr. Oxford: Oxford University Press, 1970).

KINSELLA, Thomas (ed.). *The New Oxford Book of Irish Verse* (Oxford: Oxford University Press, 1986).

LESLIE, Shane. *Saint Patrick's Purgatory: A Record from History and Literature* (London: Burns Oates & Washbourne, 1932).

LONGLEY, Michael. *The Ghost Orchid* (London: Cape, 1995).

MACINTYRE, Tom. *The Harper's Turn* (Oldcastle: Gallery, 1982).

——. *The Word for Yes* (Oldcastle: Gallery, 1991).

MACLEAN, Malcolm, and DORGAN, Theo (eds.). *An Leabhar Mòr: The Great Book of Gaelic* (Edinburgh: Canongate, 2002).

MACGILL-EAIN, Somhairle / MACLEAN, Sorley. *O Choille gu Bearradh / From Wood to Ridge: Collected Poems in Gaelic and in English Translation* (Manchester: Carcanet; Edinburgh: Birlinn, 1999).

MacNeice, Louis. *The Collected Poems of Louis MacNeice*, ed. E. R. Dodds (London: Faber, 1966).

Mahon, Derek. *The Snow Party* (London: Oxford University Press, 1975).

Mandelstam, Osip. 'Conversation about Dante', trans. Clarence Brown and Robert Hughes. In *Osip Mandelstam: Selected Essays*, trans. Sidney Monas (Austin and London: University of Texas Press, 1977), 3–44.

Montague, John. *A Chosen Light* (London: MacGibbon and Kee, 1967).

——. *The Rough Field 1961–1971*, 5th edn (Newcastle upon Tyne: Bloodaxe, 1990).

——. *The Figure in the Cave and Other Essays*, ed. Antoinette Quinn (Syracuse, NY: Syracuse University Press, 1989):
   'A Primal Gaeltacht,' pp. 42–45.
   'A Slow Dance,' pp. 52–53.

Muldoon, Paul. *Poems 1968–1998* (London: Faber, 2001).

——. *Moy Sand and Gravel* (London: Faber, 2002).

Ní Dhomhnaill, Nuala. *Selected Poems: Rogha Dánta* (Dublin: Raven Arts Press, 1991).

O'Brien, Flann. *At Swim-Two-Birds* (London: Longmans Green, 1939; repr. Harmondsworth: Penguin, 1967).

O'Donoghue, Bernard. *The Weakness* (London: Chatto, 1991).

——. *Here Nor There* (London: Chatto, 1999).

O'Searcaigh, Cathal. *Súile Shuibhne* (1983).

——. *Suibhne* (1987).

Ó Tuama, Seán (ed.), and Kinsella, Thomas (trans.). *An Duanaire, 1600–1900: Poems of the Dispossessed* (Portlaoise: Dolmen / Bord na Gaeilge, 1981).

Shapcott, Jo, and Sweeney, Matthew (eds.). *Emergency Kit: Poems for Strange Times* (London: Faber, 1996).

Shakespeare, William. *Hamlet*, ed. Harold Jenkins (London: Methuen, 1982; repr. Surrey: Nelson, 1997).

——. *King Lear*, ed. R. A. Foakes (Surrey: Nelson, 1997).

Spenser, Edmund. *A View of the State of Ireland*, ed. Andrew Hadfield and Willy Maley (Oxford: Blackwell, 1997).

Yeats, W. B. *The Poems*, ed. Daniel Albright (London: Dent, 1994).

Secondary texts

Andrew, Malcolm. 'The Fall of Troy in *Sir Gawain and the Green Knight* and *Troilus and Crisedye*.' In *The European Tragedy of Troilus*, ed. Piero Boitani (Oxford: Oxford University Press, 1989), 75–93.

Andrews, Elmer (ed.). *The Poetry of Seamus Heaney* (Cambridge: Icon, 1998).

Antonelli, Roberto. 'The Birth of Criseyde – An Exemplary Triangle: 'Classical' Troilus and the Question of Love at the Anglo-Norman Court.' In *The European Tragedy of Troilus*, ed. Piero Boitani (Oxford: Oxford University Press, 1989), 21–48.

ARONSTEIN, Susan. 'Cresseid reading Cresseid: Redemption and Translation in Henryson's *Testament*,' *Scottish Literary Journal* 21 (1994), 5–22.

BITEL, Lisa M. *Land of Women: Tales of Sex and Gender from Early Ireland* (Ithaca and London: Cornell University Press, 1996).

BLOOM, Harold. *The Western Canon: The Books and School of the Ages* (New York: Harcourt Brace, 1994).

BOITANI, Piero. 'Antiquity and Beyond: The Death of Troilus.' In *The European Tragedy of Troilus*, ed. Piero Boitani (Oxford: Oxford University Press, 1989), 1–19.

BORGES, Jorge Luis. 'The False Problem of Ugolino.' In Borges, *The Total Library: Non-Fiction, 1922–1986*, ed. Eliot Weinberger, trans. Esther Allen, Suzanne Jill Levine, and Eliot Weinberger (London: Penguin, 2001), 277–79.

BRADSHAW, Brendan, and MORRILL, John (eds.). *The British Problem, c.1534–1707: State Formation in the Atlantic Archipelago* (Basingstoke: Macmillan, 1996).

BRANDES, Randy. 'Seamus Heaney: An Interview,' *Salmagundi* 80 (1988), 4–21.

BRAZEAU, Robert. 'Thomas Kinsella and Seamus Heaney: Translation and Representation,' *New Hibernia Review / Iris Éireannach Nua* 5/2 (Summer / Samhraidh 2001), 82–98.

BREWER, Derek. 'Comedy and Tragedy in *Troilus and Crisedye*.' In *The European Tragedy of Troilus*, ed. Piero Boitani (Oxford: Oxford University Press, 1989), 95–109.

BRINK, Jean. 'Constructing a View of the Present State of Ireland,' *Spenser Studies* 11 (1990), 203–28.

BROWN, Terence. 'The Witnessing Eye and the Speaking Tongue.' In *Seamus Heaney: A Collection of Critical Essays*, ed. Elmer Andrews (New York: St Martin's Press, 1992), 182–92.

BYNUM, Caroline Walker. 'Metamorphosis, or Gerald and the Werewolf,' *Speculum* 73 (1998), 987–1013.

CAMILLE, Michael. *Image on the Edge: The Margins of Medieval Art* (London: Reaktion, 1992, repr. 2000).

CANNY, Nicholas. *Making Ireland British, 1580–1650* (Oxford: Oxford University Press, 2001).

CAREY, John. 'Suibhne Geilt and Tuán Mac Cairill,' *Éigse* 20 (1984), 93–105.

CAREY, John. 'Coghill, Nevill Henry Kendal Aylmer (1899–1980).' In *Oxford Dictionary of National Biography* (Oxford: Oxford University Press, 2004).

CARNEY, James. '"Suibhne Geilt" and "The Children of Lir",' *Éigse* 6 (1950), 83–110.

——. 'Language and Literature to 1169.' In *A New History of Ireland*, i: *Prehistoric and Early Ireland*, ed. Dáibhí Ó Cróinín (Oxford: Oxford University Press, 2005), 451–510.

CARSON, Ciaran. '*Sweeney Astray*: Escaping from Limbo.' In *The Art of Seamus Heaney*, ed. Tony Curtis, 4th edn (Bridgend: Seren, 2001), 141–48.

CHANCE, Jane. *Woman as Hero in Old English Literature* (Syracuse, NY: Syracuse University Press, 1986).

CLUNE, Anne. 'Mythologising Sweeney,' *Irish University Review* 26 (1996), 48–60.

COHEN, Jeffrey Jerome. 'Hybrids, Monsters, Borderlands: The Bodies of Gerald of Wales.' In *The Postcolonial Middle Ages*, ed. Cohen (New York: St Martin's, 2000), 85–104.

COHEN, Jeffrey Jerome (ed.). *The Postcolonial Middle Ages*, (New York: St Martin's, 2000).

CORCORAN, Neil. *After Yeats and Joyce: Reading Modern Irish Literature* (Oxford: Oxford University Press, 1997).

———. *The Poetry of Seamus Heaney: A Critical Study* (London: Faber, 1998).

———. *Poets of Modern Ireland: Text, Context, Intertext* (Cardiff: University of Wales Press, 1999):

    'Strange letters: reading and writing in contemporary Northern Irish poetry,' pp. 77–94.

    'Examples of Heaney,' pp. 95–120.

    'A languorous cutting edge: Muldoon versus Heaney?' pp. 121–36.

CRONIN, Michael. *Translating Ireland: Translation, Languages, Cultures* (Cork: Cork University Press, 1996).

CROTTY, Patrick. 'All I Believe that Happened There was Revision: *Selected Poems 1965–75* and *New Selected Poems 1966–1987*.' In *The Art of Seamus Heaney*, ed. Tony Curtis, 4th edn (Bridgend: Seren, 2001), 193–204.

DAVIES, Norman. *The Isles: A History* (London: Macmillan, 1999).

DAVIES, R. R. *The First English Empire: Power and Identities in the British Isles, 1093–1343* (Oxford: Oxford University Press, 2000).

DONOGHUE, Daniel. 'The Philologer Poet: Seamus Heaney and the Translation of *Beowulf*.' In *Beowulf: A Verse Translation*, trans. Seamus Heaney, ed. Donoghue (New York and London: Norton, 2002), 237–47. First published in *Harvard Review*.

DONOGHUE, Denis. 'Heaney's Sweeney.' In Donoghue, *We Irish: Essays on Irish Literature and Society* (New York: Knopf, 1986), 267–71. First published in *The New Republic* (30 April 1984).

DOOB, Penelope B. R. *Nebuchadnezzar's Children: Conventions of Madness in Middle English Literature* (New Haven and London: Yale University Press, 1974).

DRONKE, Ursula. 'Beowulf and Ragnarok,' *Sagabook* 17 (1969–70), 302–25.

EAGLETON, Terry. 'Hasped and Hooped and Hirpling,' *London Review of Books* (11 Nov. 1999).

EASTHOPE, Antony. 'How Good is Seamus Heaney?' *English* 46 (1997), 21–36.

ECO, Umberto. 'A Portrait of the Artist as a Bachelor.' In Eco and Liberato Santoro-Brienza, *Talking of Joyce*, ed. J. C. Mays (Dublin: UCD Press, 1998).

ELLIS, Steve. *Chaucer at Large: The Poet in the Modern Imagination*, Medieval Cultures 24 (Minneapolis and London: University of Minnesota Press, 2000).

ELLIS, Steven G. *Tudor Ireland: Crown, Community and the Conflict of Cultures, 1470–1603* (London: Longman, 1985).

ELLMANN, Richard. *Ulysses on the Liffey* (London: Faber, 1972).

FEDERICO, Sylvia. *New Troy: Fantasies of Empire in the Late Middle Ages*, Medieval Cultures 36 (Minneapolis and London: University of Minnesota Press, 2003).

FELL, Christine. 'Perceptions of Transience.' In *The Cambridge Companion to Old*

English Literature, ed. M. Godden and M. Lapidge (Cambridge: Cambridge University Press, 1991), 172–89.

FINN, Christine. *Past Poetic: Archaeology in the Poetry of W. B. Yeats and Seamus Heaney* (London: Duckworth, 2004).

FLOWER, Robin. *The Irish Tradition* (Oxford: Oxford University Press, 1947).

FRAME, Robin. *The Political Development of the British Isles, 1100–1400* (Oxford: Oxford University Press, 1990; rev. pbk edn, 1995).

FRANK, Roberta. 'Skaldic Verse and the Date of Beowulf.' In *The Dating of Beowulf*, ed. Colin Chase (Toronto, 1981), 123–39.

FRANTZEN, Allen J. *Desire for Origins: New Language, Old English, and Teaching the Tradition* (New Brunswick, NJ, and London: Rutgers University Press, 1990).

FRAZIER, Adrian. 'Anger and Nostalgia: Seamus Heaney and the Ghost of the Father,' *Eire–Ireland: A Journal of Irish Studies* 36 (Fall–Winter 2001), 7–38.

FUMAGALLI, Maria Cristina. '"Station Island": Seamus Heaney's *Divina Commedia*,' *Irish University Review* 26/1 (1996), 127–42.

——. *The Flight of the Vernacular: Seamus Heaney, Derek Walcott, and the Impress of Dante* (Amsterdam and New York: Rodopi, 2001).

GRAY, Douglas. *Robert Henryson* (Leiden: Brill, 1979).

GREEN, Richard Firth. *A Crisis of Truth: Literature and Law in Ricardian England* (Philadelphia: University of Pennsylvania Press, 1999).

GREENBLATT, Stephen. *Hamlet in Purgatory* (Princeton: Princeton University Press, 2001).

GRUBER, Loren C. '"So." So What? It's a Culture War. That's Hwæt!' *In Geardagum* 23 (2002), 67–84.

HAFFENDEN, John. 'Meeting Seamus Heaney,' *London Magazine* 19/3 (1979), 5–28.

HART, Henry. *Seamus Heaney: Poet of Contrary Progressions* (Syracuse, NY: Syracuse University Press, 1992).

HAWLIN, Stefan. 'Seamus Heaney's "Station Island": The Shaping of a Modern Purgatory,' *English Studies* (1992), 35–50.

HENRY, P. L. *The Early English and Celtic Lyric* (London: Allen & Unwin, 1966).

HOWE, Nicholas. 'Scullionspeak,' *The New Republic* (28 Feb. 2000).

JACKSON, H. J. *Marginalia: Readers Writing in Books* (New Haven and London: Yale University Press, 2001).

JACKSON, Kenneth. 'A Further Note on Suibhne Geilt and Merlin,' *Éigse* 7 (1953), 112–16.

JONES, Chris. *Strange Likeness: The Use of Old English in Twentieth-Century Poetry* (Oxford: Oxford University Press, 2006).

KARKOV, Catherine E. 'Tales of the Ancients: Colonial Werewolves and the Mapping of Postcolonial Ireland.' In *Postcolonial Moves: Medieval Through Modern*, ed. Patricia Clare Ingham and Michelle R. Warren (Basingstoke and New York: Palgrave Macmillan, 2003), 93–109.

KEARNEY, Hugh. *The British Isles: A History of Four Nations* (Cambridge: Cambridge University Press, 1989).

KEARNEY, Richard. *Transitions: Narratives in Modern Irish Culture* (Dublin: Wolfhound, 1988).

KEARNEY, Richard. *Postnationalist Ireland: Politics, Culture, Philosophy* (London and New York: Routledge, 1997).

KANE, George. 'The Liberating Truth.' In Kane, *Chaucer and Langland: Historical and Textual Approaches* (London: Athlone, 1989).

KELLY, H. A. 'Heaney's Sweeney: The Poet as Version-Maker,' *Philological Quarterly* 65 (1986), 293–310.

——. *Chaucerian Tragedy* (Cambridge: Brewer, 1997).

KERMODE, Frank. 'The Modern Beowulf.' In Kermode, *Pleasing Myself: From Beowulf to Philip Roth* (London: Penguin, 2001), 1–12. First published in *The New York Review of Books*.

KERRIGAN, John. 'Ulster Ovids.' In *The Chosen Ground: Essays on the Contemporary Poetry of Northern Ireland*, ed. Neil Corcoran (Bridgend: Seren, 1992), 237–69.

KIBERD, Declan. *Inventing Ireland: The Literature of the Modern Nation* (London: Cape, 1995; repr. Vintage, 1996).

KIERNAN, Kevin S. 'Reading Cædmon's "Hymn" with Someone Else's Glosses.' In *Old English Literature: Critical Essays*, ed. R. M. Liuzza (New Haven and London: Yale University Press, 2002), 103–24. First published in *Representations* 32 (1990), 157–74.

LE GOFF, Jacques. *The Birth of Purgatory*, trans. Arthur Goldhammer (Chicago: University of Chicago Press, 1984).

LERER, Seth. *Chaucer and his Readers: Imagining the Author in Late Medieval England* (Princeton: Princeton University Press, 1993).

——. '"On fagne flor": The Postcolonial *Beowulf*, from Heorot to Heaney.' In *Postcolonial Approaches to the European Middle Ages: Translating Cultures*, ed. Ananya Jahanara Kabir and Deanne Williams (Cambridge: Cambridge University Press, 2005), 77–102.

LONGLEY, Edna. *The Living Stream: Literature and Revisionism in Ireland* (Newcastle upon Tyne: Bloodaxe, 1994).

——. 'The Room where MacNeice wrote "Snow".' In Longley, *The Living Stream: Literature & Revisionism in Ireland* (Newcastle upon Tyne: Bloodaxe, 1994), 252–270. First published in *The Crows Behind the Plough: History and Violence in Anglo-Irish Poetry and Drama*, ed. Geert Lernout (Amsterdam: Rodopi, 1991).

——. 'North: "Inner Emigré" or "Artful Voyeur?' In *The Art of Seamus Heaney*, ed. Tony Curtis, 4th edn (Bridgend: Seren, 2001), 65–95.

——. 'Multi-Culturalism and Northern Ireland: Making Differences Fruitful.' In Longley and Declan Kiberd, *Multi-Culturalism: The View from the Two Irelands* (Cork: Cork University Press, 2001), 1–44.

LYNCH, Michael. *Scotland: A New History* (London: Century, 1991).

McCRACKEN, Kathleen. 'Madness or Inspiration? The Poet and Poetry in Seamus Heaney's *Sweeney Astray*,' *Notes on Modern Irish Literature* 2 (1990), 42–51.

McGOWAN, Joseph. 'Heaney, Cædmon, *Beowulf*,' *New Hibernia Review / Iris Éireannach Nua* 6/2 (Summer / Samhraidh 2002), 25–42.

McGUIRE, Thomas. 'Violence and Vernacular in Seamus Heaney's *Beowulf*,' *New Hibernia Review / Iris Éireannach Nua* 10/1 (Spring / Earrach 2006), 79–99.

MACLEAN, Malcolm. General Introduction to *An Leabhar Mòr: The Great Book of Gaelic*, ed. Maclean and Theo Dorgan (Edinburgh: Canongate, 2002), 1–5.

MCLEOD, Wilson. *Divided Gaels: Gaelic Cultural Identities in Scotland and Ireland, c.1200–c.1650* (Oxford: Oxford University Press, 2004).

MALEY, Willy. '"Kilt by kelt shell kithagain with kinagain": Joyce and Scotland.' In *Semicolonial Joyce*, ed. Derek Attridge and Marjorie Howes (Cambridge: Cambridge University Press, 2000), 201–218.

MANN, Jill. *Feminizing Chaucer* (Cambridge: Brewer, 2002).

MIESZKOWSKI, Gretchen. 'The Reputation of Criseyde, 1155–1500,' *Transactions of the Connecticut Academy of Arts and Sciences* 43 (1971), 73–153.

MINNIS, A. J. *Medieval Theory of Authorship: Scholastic Literary Attitudes in the later Middle Ages*, 2nd edn (Aldershot: Scolar Press, 1988).

MORGAN, Gerald. 'Natural and Rational Love in Medieval Literature,' *Yearbook of English Studies* 7 (1977), 43–52.

MURPHY, Gerard. *Early Irish Metrics* (Dublin: Royal Irish Academy, 1961).

NAGY, J. F. 'The Wisdom of the Geilt,' *Éigse* 19 (1982), 44–60.

Ó CRÓINÍN, Dáibhí. 'Ireland, 400–800.' In *A New History of Ireland*, i: *Prehistoric and Early Ireland*, ed. Dáibhí Ó Cróinín (Oxford: Oxford University Press, 2005), 182–234.

O'DONOGHUE, Bernard. *Seamus Heaney and the Language of Poetry* (Hemel Hempstead: Harvester, 1994).

——. 'Dante's Versatility and Seamus Heaney's Modernism.' In *Dante's Modern Afterlife: Reception and Response from Blake to Heaney*, ed. Nick Havely (London: Macmillan, 1998), 242–57.

——. 'The Master's Voice-Right,' *Irish Times* (9 Oct. 1999).

——. 'Seamus Heaney: *North*.' In *A Companion to Twentieth Century Poetry*, ed. Neil Roberts (Oxford: Blackwell, 2001), 524–35.

——. 'The Pastoral Power Station,' *The Independent* (31 March 2001).

——. 'Cider and Pear-Gall,' *TLS* (18 Feb. 2005).

O'NEILL, Michael. 'Contemporary Northern Irish Poets and Romantic Poetry.' In *English Romanticism and the Celtic World,* ed. Gerard Carruthers and Alan Rawes (Cambridge: Cambridge University Press, 2003), 196–209.

Ó RIAIN, Pádraig. 'A Study of the Irish Legend of the Wild Man,' *Éigse* 14 (1972), 179–206.

ORCHARD, Andy. *Pride and Prodigies: Studies in the Monsters of the 'Beowulf'-Manuscript* (Cambridge: Brewer, 1995).

——. *A Critical Companion to 'Beowulf'* (Cambridge: Brewer, 2003).

ORTON, Peter. 'The Form and Structure of *The Seafarer*.' In *Old English Literature: Critical Essays*, ed. R. M. Liuzza (New Haven and London: Yale University Press, 2002), 353–380. First published in *Studia Neophilologica* 33 (1991), 37–55.

——. 'To be a Pilgrim: The Old English *Seafarer* and its Irish Affinities.' In *Lexis and Texts in Early English: Studies presented to Jane Roberts*, ed. Christian J. Kay and Louise M. Sylvester (Amsterdam and Atlanta: Rodopi, 2001), 213–23.

OVERING, Gillian R. *Language, Sign, and Gender in* Beowulf (Carbondale and Edwardsville: Southern Illinois University Press, 1993).

OWEN-CROCKER, Gale R. *The Four Funerals in 'Beowulf' and the Structure of the Poem* (Manchester and New York: Manchester University Press, 2000).

PARKER, Michael. *Seamus Heaney: The Making of the Poet* (Basingstoke: Macmillan, 1993).

PATCH, Howard R. *The Other World according to Descriptions in Medieval Literature* (1950; repr. New York: Octagon, 1970).

PATTERSON, Lee W. 'Christian and Pagan in *The Testament of Cresseid*,' *Philological Quarterly* 52/4 (1973), 696–714.

PATTERSON, Lee. 'On the Margin: Postmodernism, Ironic History, and Medieval Studies,' *Speculum* 65 (1990), 87–108.

——. *Chaucer and the Subject of History* (London: Routledge, 1991).

PEARSALL, Derek. '"Quha Wait Gif All that Chaucer Wrait was Trew?": Henryson's *Testament of Cresseid*.' In *New Perspectives on Middle English Texts: A Festschrift for R. A. Waldron*, ed. Susan Powell and Jeremy J. Smith (Cambridge: Brewer, 2000), 169–82.

PHILLIPS, Helen. 'Seamus Heaney's *Beowulf*.' In *The Art of Seamus Heaney*, ed. Tony Curtis, 4th edn (Bridgend: Seren, 2001), 265–85.

POCOCK, J. G. A. *The Discovery of Islands: Essays in British History* (Cambridge: Cambridge University Press, 2005):
  'British History: A Plea for a New Subject,' pp. 24–43. First published in *New Zealand Journal of History* 8 (1974), 3–21.
  'The Field Enlarged: An Introduction,' pp. 47–57.
  'The Politics of the New British History,' pp. 289–300.

PUHVEL, Martin. *'Beowulf' and Celtic Tradition* (Waterloo, Ontario: Wilfred Laurier University Press, 1979).

RICKS, Christopher. 'The Mouth, the Meal, and the Book: Review of *Field Work*.' In *Seamus Heaney*, ed. Michael Allen (London: Macmillan, 1997), 95–101. First published in *London Review of Books* (8 Nov. 1979).

RIDDY, Felicity. '"Abject odious": Feminine and Masculine in Henryson's *Testament of Cresseid*.' In *The Long Fifteenth Century: Essays for Douglas Gray*, ed. Helen Cooper and Sally Mapstone (Oxford: Oxford University Press, 1997), 229–48.

ROBINSON, Fred C. *'Beowulf' and the Appositive Style* (Knoxville: The University of Tennessee Press, 1985).

RYAN, Ray. *Ireland and Scotland: Literature and Culture, State and Nation, 1966–2000* (Oxford: Oxford University Press, 2002).

SAUNDERS, Corinne J. *The Forest of Medieval Romance: Avernus, Broceliande, Arden* (Cambridge: Brewer, 1993).

SCOWCROFT, R. Mark. 'The Irish Analogues to *Beowulf*,' *Speculum* 74 (1999), 22–64.

SHATTUCK, Roger. *Proust's Binoculars: A Study of Memory, Time and Recognition in 'A la recherche du temps perdu'* (Princeton: Princeton University Press, 1962; repr. 1983).

SHIPPEY, Tom. 'Beowulf for the Big-Voiced Scullions,' *TLS* (1 Oct. 1999).

SIEWERS, Alfred K. 'Landscapes of Conversion: Guthlac's Mound and Grendel's Mere as Expressions of Anglo-Saxon Nation Building,' *Viator* 34 (2003), 1–39.

SKLUTE, L. John. '*Freoðuwebbe* in Old English Poetry.' In *New Readings on Women in Old English Literature*, ed. H. Damico and A. H. Olsen (Bloomington, IN, 1990), 204–210.

SMITH, Roland M. 'King Lear and the Merlin Tradition,' *Modern Language Quarterly* 7 (1946), 153–74.

STALLWORTHY, Jon. 'The Poet as Archaeologist: W. B. Yeats and Seamus Heaney,' *Review of English Studies* 33 (1982), 158–74.

TAYLOR, Peter. *Brits: The War against the IRA* (London: Bloomsbury, 2001).

TRACY, Robert. 'Into an Irish Free State: Heaney, Sweeney and Clearing Away.' In *Poetry in Contemporary Irish Literature*, ed. Michael Kenneally (Gerrards Cross: Colin Smythe, 1995), 238–62.

TOLKIEN, J. R. R. '*Beowulf*: The Monsters and the Critics.' In *An Anthology of Beowulf Criticism*, ed. Louis E. Nicholson (Indiana: University of Notre Dame Press, 1963), 51–103. First published in *Proceedings of the British Academy* 22 (1937), 245–95.

VENDLER, Helen. *Seamus Heaney* (Cambridge, MA: Harvard University Press, 1998; repr. 2000).

WELCH, Robert (ed.). *The Oxford Companion to Irish Literature* (Oxford: Oxford University Press, 1996).

——. *The Concise Oxford Companion to Irish Literature* (Oxford: Oxford University Press, 2000).

WINDEATT, Barry. *Oxford Guides to Chaucer: Troilus and Criseyde* (Oxford: Oxford University Press, 1992).

REFERENCE WORKS

The Concise Scots Dictionary, ed. Mairi Robinson (Aberdeen: Aberdeen University Press, 1985).

Dictionary of the Older Scottish Tongue from the Twelfth Century to the End of the Seventeenth, ed. Sir William Craigie et al., 12 vols. (Oxford: Oxford University Press, 1937–2002).

Dictionary of the Irish Language based mostly on Old and Middle Irish Materials (Dublin: Royal Irish Academy, 1990). [*DIL*]

Foclóir Gaedhilge agus Béarla: An Irish–English Dictionary, ed. Patrick S. Dinneen (Dublin: Irish Texts Society, 1927).

Foclóir Gaeilge–Béarla, ed. Niall Ó Dónaill (Dublin / Baile Átha Cliath: Oifig an tSoláthair, 1977).

Middle English Dictionary, ed. Hans Kurath et al., 14 vols. (Ann Arbor: University of Michigan Press; Oxford: Oxford University Press, 1952–2001). [*MED*]

Oxford English Dictionary, 2nd edn, ed. J. A. Simpson and E. S. C. Weiner, 20 vols. (Oxford: Oxford University Press, 1989). On-line resource, http://dictionary.oed.com/ [*OED*]

Index

Footnotes containing comment are included in this index; footnotes for reference are not. The titles of writings by Seamus Heaney are indexed separately, not collected under Heaney's name.

Lightning Source UK Ltd.
Milton Keynes UK
07 December 2009

147210UK00001B/16/P